Robert Winnett is the deputy political editor of the *Daily Telegraph*. During his eleven-year career on Fleet Street, which started at the *Sunday Times*, he has been behind some of the country's biggest political scoops, including exposing the cash-for-honours scandal under Tony Blair and Derek Conway's controversial employment of his sons.

He has been shortlisted for three 'scoop of the year' awards at the British Press Awards and has won other prizes for his work, which has included reporting on the global credit crunch and several British general elections.

Gordon Rayner is chief reporter of the *Daily Telegraph*. He began his career at the *Banbury Guardian* before moving to the *Sun* and later the *Daily Mail*, where he helped uncover one of the biggest scandals of Tony Blair's premiership by revealing emails between Cherie Blair and the fraudster Peter Foster which proved No.10 had lied over the 'Cheriegate' affair.

During his fourteen years on national newspapers, Gordon has reported from more than twenty countries and covered many of the biggest stories of recent years, including the death of Princess Diana, the trial of Harold Shipman, the Soham murders, the 7/7 suicide bombings and the ongoing financial crisis.

D0995594

www.rbooks.co.uk

No Expenses Spared

Robert Winnett and Gordon Rayner

Cartoons by Matt

CORGI BOOKS

TRANSWORLD PUBLISHERS
61–63 Uxbridge Road, London W5 5SA
A Random House Group Company
www.rbooks.co.uk

NO EXPENSES SPARED
A CORGI BOOK: 9780552162227

First published in Great Britain
in 2009 by Bantam Press
an imprint of Transworld Publishers
Corgi edition published 2010

Addresses for Random House Group Ltd companies outside the UK
can be found at: www.randomhouse.co.uk
The Random House Group Ltd Reg. No. 954009

The Random House Group Limited supports The Forest Stewardship Council
(FSC), the leading international forest certification organisation. All our titles that
are printed on Greenpeace approved FSC certified paper carry the FSC logo. Our
paper procurement policy can be found at www.rbooks.co.uk/environment

Typeset in 11/15pt Minion by Falcon Oast Graphic Art Ltd.
Printed in the UK by CPI Cox & Wyman, Reading, RG1 8EX.

2 4 6 8 10 9 7 5 3 1

Contents

Acknowledgements

Although it is our names that appear on the cover, this book would not have been possible without the help and support of the team who worked on the investigation into MPs' expenses.

The investigation itself could not have gone ahead had it not been for the courage and conviction of the Barclay family and Murdoch MacLennan, the chief executive of Telegraph Media Group, who backed their staff to the hilt. William Lewis, our editor, put his own neck on the block in deciding to go ahead with one of the riskiest stories in the *Telegraph*'s history; he also gave us limitless amounts of his time to provide his own recollections for this book and constant guidance during the writing process.

We are indebted to all those who worked in the bunker for their help in providing first-hand material and anecdotes for this book. In particular, thanks must go to reporters Holly Watt, Rosa Prince, Christopher Hope, Martin Beckford, Jon Swaine, Nick Allen and Caroline Gammell for their enthusiastic support throughout. Others who played vital roles in the bunker, including Duncan Hooper, Ian Douglas, Richard Oliver, Keith Hoggins, Himesh

Patel and Veronica Hale, also deserve special mention.

News executives Tony Gallagher, Chris Evans and Matthew Bayley gave us vital help in reconstructing some of the key meetings which took place during the investigation, and also cast their expert eyes over the manuscript.

Arthur Wynn Davies, the *Telegraph*'s chief lawyer, has our gratitude for bringing his unrivalled experience and infectious good humour to the expenses project from start to finish.

Thanks also go to Andrew Porter, Andrew Pierce, Benedict Brogan and James Kirkup for their invaluable insights into what was going on in Parliament and in the wider world at the height of the investigation, and for so admirably representing the *Telegraph* by satisfying the countless requests for interviews during May, June and July.

Thank you to Rhidian Wynn Davies for helping us shape this book into its final form; to Matt Pritchett, the *Telegraph*'s peerless cartoonist, for allowing us to reproduce his work; and to Bill Scott-Kerr, Simon Thorogood and everyone at Bantam Press for steering us so expertly through the editing process.

Others at the *Telegraph* who played their part in the hugely complex expenses investigation are too numerous to name individually here, but they know who they are, and they can rest assured we appreciate the efforts of each and every one.

Lastly, our thanks must go to John Wick for his professionalism in handling such delicate material and his help in enabling us to tell the full story of how the leak of the expenses data came about.

Robert Winnett and Gordon Rayner
London, September 2009

Prologue

Thursday, 7 May 2009

'Who'd have thought we'd look
back at the Gurkha row as
the good old days?'

MICHAEL ELLAM HAD been expecting a relatively quiet day when he arrived for work at 8 a.m. sharp – or at least, as quiet a day as was possible for anyone working in the hothouse environment of 10 Downing Street. The Prime Minister's director of communications, a career civil servant who had worked for Gordon Brown ever since he became Chancellor in 1997, had spent the previous fortnight handling a deluge of media enquiries about the government's reluctance to allow Gurkha veterans to settle in the UK, but the furore had finally abated after the Prime Minister had held a private meeting with the Gurkhas' campaign leader, the actress Joanna Lumley.

Ellam had already read the morning's newspapers before he left home, and had been satisfied to see that they were generally positive from the Prime Minister's point of view, giving him credit for finally doing right by the Gurkhas, one of the British Army's most distinguished regiments. Crisis over, he thought to himself. So when he received a text message on his mobile phone from Robert Winnett, the deputy political editor of the *Daily Telegraph*, just after 1 p.m., it certainly didn't set off any alarm bells, even though Winnett's text urged him to call back 'ASAP'. He phoned Winnett back around fifteen minutes later, no doubt expecting to field a straightforward question about one or two loose ends in the Gurkha story.

In fact, Winnett was about to fire the starting gun in what would become the biggest parliamentary scandal in centuries.

'What's up?' Ellam asked.

Trying his best to keep any emotion out of his voice, Winnett replied: 'What it is, I've got some questions about the Prime Minister's personal expenses claims which I need to email to a secure email address, so I just wondered if you could give me the best address to send it to?'

'I'd hope all of the email addresses in Downing Street were secure,' joked Ellam, before suggesting the letter should be sent to his own No. 10 email account so he could draw it to the Prime Minister's attention.

Despite his light-hearted response, Ellam knew from Winnett's mention of 'expenses' that this could spell trouble. Like everyone else working in Westminster, he was aware of a rumour that a copy of a computer disk containing the details of expenses claims made by all 646 Members of Parliament over a four-year period had gone missing several weeks earlier. MPs had spent the past four years fighting demands for the information to be released until, after losing a controversial High Court case, Parliament had agreed to publish the details later in the year. Even so, much of the information in the expenses claims was to be censored (on grounds of 'security', that familiar parliamentary fallback), so that many of the most compromising and embarrassing details of what MPs had been up to would never see the light of day.

Or at least, that had been the plan. But the rumour was that the missing disk contained the full, unexpurgated version of the expenses claims, and MPs were in no doubt about the damage that information could cause if it were made public.

Although Ellam was no doubt confident that the Prime Minister had been scrupulous with his own expenses, the fact that the *Telegraph* was asking questions about Brown's claims – signalling that the paper believed it was on to something – could not be good news.

Did this mean that the *Telegraph* had the disk? Would any other members of the government be getting phone calls from the newspaper? And what exactly was it that the *Telegraph* thought the Prime Minister had done?

Ellam didn't have to wait long to find out. At 1.22 p.m., within a minute of putting the phone down on Ellam, Winnett pressed the 'send' button on his computer.

The email he sent contained a formal, carefully worded letter presenting details of the Prime Minister's expenses claims and inviting him to explain how they fell within the rules. They included the fact that Brown had paid his brother, Andrew, more than £6,000 of taxpayers' money to pass on to a cleaner; that he had switched the designation of his 'second' home from his London house to his house in Scotland; and that he had claimed twice for the same £153 plumber's bill. It was a dry, precise, narrowly drawn communication giving little indication of the fact that

Winnett and a team of nine other reporters had for some time been quietly sitting on the journalistic equivalent of an atomic bomb. For the previous week, they had spent every waking hour in a back room at the *Telegraph*'s head office above Victoria railway station, working in such secrecy that only a handful of people outside the room had any idea what they were up to.

The *Telegraph* did indeed have the computer disk, and the information the reporters discovered on it left them in no doubt that they were working on the story of a lifetime. Even for such a cynical, world-weary breed as national newspaper journalists, the details of what MPs had been claiming on their expenses had been startling. They were genuinely shocked to discover that many of the most senior members of the government, including Cabinet ministers, had been blatantly playing the system for years to squeeze every last penny they could out of the taxpayer.

Parliament had set up a system of expenses and allowances which enabled MPs to claim for the costs of running a second home. On the face of it, this seemed only reasonable: the vast majority of MPs represented constituencies that were not within easy reach of London, meaning they had to stay overnight in the capital during the months that Parliament was sitting. But some ministers had claimed thousands of pounds in expenses to furnish and help pay for one of their properties, before arbitrarily shifting the designation of 'second home' from their London base to their constituency home so they could furnish that property too. Others appeared to have avoided paying capital gains tax by switching the designation when they came to sell their second home so that they could tell the taxman it was, in fact, their main home and exempt from tax. With each passing day the reporters had discovered another scam, until they were faced with a mind-boggling array of ingenious ways in which MPs had managed to milk a publicly funded system which was so inadequately policed by civil servants that it almost seemed to have been designed to be abused.

On another level, the reporters had been amazed at the bizarre, the trivial and the downright baffling items which many MPs had put on their expenses: a 5p carrier bag, a packet of HobNobs, a glittery toilet seat, a jar of Branston Pickle. Some parsimonious MPs submitted such detailed and lengthy expenses claims that it was hard to imagine they had much time left to do anything else. One had even put in a phone bill for a single penny.

*

Thursday, 7 May had been designated as 'go day' for the *Daily Telegraph*'s expenses investigation by the editor, William Lewis, but he was acutely aware that the newspaper was entering uncharted territory in which many obstacles would still have to be overcome before any of the stories could go to press.

Until now, an ambitious newspaper investigation might have culminated in a single government minister being exposed for an apparent abuse of his or her position. The

Telegraph was about to hold no fewer than thirteen members of the Cabinet up to such scrutiny in a single day, with the intention of doing the same again with a new set of ministers or MPs every day for a week or more. And while many newspaper investigations might spend weeks looking into the activities of one person, the *Telegraph*'s reporting team had spent precisely one week checking out dozens of MPs, having obtained the information on 29 April. The pace of the investigation had raised concerns among everyone involved that important material might have been over-looked, or that mistakes might have been made by reporters who were all on a steep learning curve.

By 7 May the reporting team had only looked at a fraction of the material on the disk – but an agreement with the man who had passed the disk on to the newspaper meant publication had to go ahead by the end of that week, if at all: so Lewis knew he had no option but to press ahead. The team would just have to carry on combing through the documents on the disk as they went along.

Lewis had told Winnett and his team to spend that morning preparing email letters to all of the ministers he intended to feature in the next day's paper – but not to send them. Yet.

At this point in the operation the spotlight fell on one of its central figures: Arthur Wynn Davies, the paper's highly experienced chief in-house lawyer. Approaching his sixty-fifth birthday, he might have been expected to be look-ing forward to a relaxing retirement in his native north Wales. But Wynn Davies, rake-thin and hyperactive, a newspaperman first and a lawyer second, was as excited as any of the reporters about what he knew might be journalistic history in the making. After more than thirty years as a barrister in the press world, he still got as much of a buzz from working on a big breaking news story as a trainee reporter would in their first week on the job.

Wynn Davies had endured a sleepless night as he went over and over the possible ways in which the government or Parliament might try to scupper the story. At the very least, he reckoned the authorities would seek a High Court injunction on the grounds that the disk was 'stolen' and publication might threaten the privacy of MPs or break data protection laws. The worst-case scenario was that the police would be called in to investigate how the *Telegraph* came to be in possession of the disk. Key members of staff might even find themselves under arrest. But despite the legal complexities, Wynn Davies was certain in his own mind that the way in which the *Telegraph* had obtained the information and what it was about to do with it were legitimate. He felt strongly that publication of the material was in the public interest and that any attempt to gag the paper could be seen off. To be doubly sure, it was essential that the *Telegraph* be in a position to convince a judge that each of the MPs it was about to expose had been given a decent opportunity to respond to the allegations so that due weight could be given to what they had to say.

At 10.45 a.m. six senior *Daily Telegraph* executives had assembled for one final meeting in the editor's office to decide whether to press ahead.

The letters to the ministers were ready to be sent; once they had gone, there could be no turning back. The *Telegraph* was a traditionally cautious newspaper, conservative with a small 'c'. To take on the entire political class in such an aggressive and direct way was not a decision to be taken lightly. The issue of whether the authorities would try to stop the newspaper in its tracks remained a very real concern, and the dispatch of the letters carried a high risk of triggering legal action – or, worse, an unannounced police raid.

Wynn Davies sat in the middle of the editor's glass-walled office, visible but not audible to everyone in the newsroom outside.

'Can you give me any sort of guarantee that we won't be injuncted?' Lewis asked.

'No, but I'm confident we're on solid ground.'

'What about the chances of the police being called in?'

Wynn Davies said it was highly unlikely the police would get involved, but that, in the event they were, they should be sent to see the paper's executive director (editorial), Richard Ellis, who would politely inform the officers that they would need a warrant to search the building.

Lewis listened intently to what each person had to say, but as much as anything he was looking at their body language, watching for clues as to whether any of them had serious doubts.

No one did. The *Telegraph* had to press on, they all agreed.

Although everyone in the room was calm and

businesslike, pulses were racing as each of them contemplated what was at stake.

Lewis then began 'scenario planning', working out how the paper could get the story out even if the police were called in or the courts tried to injunct. Rhidian Wynn Davies, the *Telegraph*'s consulting editor and Arthur's son, was tasked with finding a secure location off-site for a copy of the disk in case all the copies in the office were seized.

'Don't worry, Rhids,' Lewis reassured him with a smile. 'If you get nicked you'll be in a cell next to me.'

Plans were also laid out for publishing the expenses stories online even if an injunction was granted. A team of reporters and production staff would be scrambled to an off-site location where they could load stories on to the *Telegraph*'s website.

'If we're going to go ahead with this, we have to do it no matter what,' said Lewis.

Meanwhile an in-house cameraman was told to be ready to film the police if they searched the office.

Lewis then called Winnett in. 'We're on,' he said. 'Let's get the letters out.'

As Winnett returned to the back corridor to brief the reporting team, Lewis strolled across to the circular table in the centre of the newsroom known as 'the hub', where executives were gathering for the midday editorial conference.

The expenses story remained so hush-hush that most of the departmental heads were still completely in the dark, and on what was otherwise a desperately quiet news day,

Matthew Bayley, the *Telegraph*'s news editor, went through the motions of preparing a 'dummy' newspaper he knew would almost certainly never see the light of day.

'I'm embarrassed at how bad the news list is today,' Bayley said as he began listing one dull story after another.

'Well, we'll just have to hope something better comes along later, won't we?' said a smirking Lewis as he wound up the conference twenty minutes later.

Lewis had arranged to have lunch that day with Nick Robinson, the BBC's political editor, and Andrew Porter, the *Daily Telegraph*'s political editor, at Santini's, a favourite of the England football manager Fabio Capello. As the three chatted about the state of the nation, Lewis was as tense as he had ever been, waiting for news from the office as Robinson grilled him on whether the *Telegraph* would be giving its unequivocal support to the Conservative Party at the next election.

Back at the office, Winnett was about to send the first, vital email to Michael Ellam. As he did so, five of the reporters sitting around him began making identical phone calls to the staff of twelve other Cabinet ministers – and, for good measure, the former Deputy Prime Minister, John Prescott. The calls were followed up by emails similar to that sent to Ellam, all of which had been written during the course of that morning and approved by Arthur Wynn Davies. Within an hour, fourteen of the most senior politicians in the country had been placed on notice that their expenses claims were about to made public. They included Alistair Darling, the Chancellor; David Miliband, the foreign secretary; Andy Burnham, the culture secretary; Geoff Hoon, the transport secretary; Hazel Blears, the communities secretary; and Paul Murphy, the Welsh secretary. One by one, Whitehall departments discovered that ministers might be in trouble; and one by one they alerted Downing Street, where it soon became obvious to Michael Ellam, and to the Prime Minister, that instead of having a quiet end to the week, they were about to be swamped.

As soon as he had received the email from Winnett, Ellam had called Michael Dugher, Brown's press aide, and asked him to leave his lunch and return to Downing Street that very minute to coordinate the government's response to the *Telegraph*'s allegations. Dugher spoke to each minister involved – or their advisers – and told them they would each have to compose their own response to the *Telegraph*'s questions, though they should all stress that they had not broken any rules and explain the justification for claims where they could.

Meanwhile Joe Irvin, the Prime Minister's political director, headed a small team which was given the unlikely task of sitting down and going through Brown's own expenses.

Less than a mile away, at the *Telegraph*'s offices, tension was mounting by the minute as the investigation team busily wrote up their stories on the individual ministers, constantly checking the clock as they waited for the first response to come in.

Aside from the concerns over whether the Cabinet

ministers – or even the parliamentary authorities – would try to injunct the *Telegraph*, Lewis had a lingering unease about whether the entire disk could turn out to be a fake. The *Sunday Times*, where Lewis had once worked, had been the victim of one of the most elaborate hoaxes in history when it published details in the early 1980s of a document which appeared to be Hitler's newly discovered personal diaries. The 'Hitler diaries' fiasco had passed into infamy and had become a case study for every journalism student on the importance of checking source material. More recently, Piers Morgan had lost his job as editor of the *Daily Mirror* after publishing what turned out to be faked photographs of British soldiers assaulting Iraqi prisoners; and in 1996 the *Sun* had been hugely embarrassed by its publication of stills from a video of the Princess of Wales canoodling with James Hewitt which turned out to have been staged by lookalikes.

It remains every editor's worst fear that they will become the unwitting victim of the next big hoax, and Lewis was determined it wasn't going to be him. It had all seemed too easy, he kept saying to himself. Surely there had to be a catch?

The expenses team's back office, which had become known, rather unimaginatively, as 'the bunker', began to resemble an operations room in a black-and-white war film as executives anxiously walked in and out, asking, 'Any news?' like commanding officers waiting to hear if a top-secret bombing raid had been successful. 'Not yet,' was the repeated refrain.

*

During the endless discussions about who might try to stop the *Telegraph* publishing the expenses story, one minister's name kept cropping up: Jack Straw, the justice secretary.

Straw knew all about injunctions. Newspapers had been prevented from identifying him or members of his family in a 1998 story about his son selling cannabis after the Attorney General obtained an injunction (which was later overturned by a judge). He was also almost uniquely placed to understand the significance of what was happening. He had been home secretary when the government took the controversial decision to introduce the Freedom of Information Act which had led to the expenses data being compiled electronically. And he had been Leader of the House when the Commons decided to attempt to block the release of information about MPs' expenses. He was now the head of the department that oversaw the freedom of information legislation; and, in his additional role as Lord Chancellor, he would also oversee any government attempt to block publication by the *Telegraph*.

Straw was sitting in the back seat of his ministerial car on the way to Whitemoor prison in Cambridgeshire when his travelling companion, his special adviser Mark Davies, pulled his BlackBerry out of his pocket and read him an email which had arrived from the *Telegraph*'s chief reporter, Gordon Rayner, at 1.50 p.m. The email contained five questions about Straw's expenses, the most damaging of which was a query over why he had overclaimed for council tax for four years on his second home in his constituency of Blackburn.

Straw didn't need reminding that he had claimed a 50 per cent council tax discount from his local authority while simultaneously billing the taxpayer for the full, undiscounted total. Straw had pocketed £1,500 over and above what he should have claimed. He had eventually paid back the money, sending a cheque to the parliamentary authorities in July 2008 – only to realize weeks later that he hadn't repaid enough. He sent a second cheque to cover the outstanding balance with a letter which said: 'Sorry – accountancy does not appear to be my strongest suit.' Although Straw had repaid the money, his government department had prosecuted people for similar transgressions, making this a hugely embarrassing disclosure.

So it was somewhat to the surprise of the *Telegraph* team that it was Straw who was first with his response.

At 2.24 p.m., as the reporters in the bunker were wolfing down sandwiches from the local Pret a Manger, a message popped up in the corner of Rayner's screen to say he had an email from Mark Davies.

'Straw's responded,' Rayner tried, less than successfully, to announce to the room through a mouthful of dolphin-friendly tuna.

The reply from Straw's office was remarkably straightforward. 'Suffice to say, Jack takes this very seriously,' it began. 'He applies very high standards to the way he carries out his obligations.' He had made 'errors' in claiming his council tax, it went on, and had also overclaimed around £200 in mortgage interest 'in error'.

There were no threats of action, no threats of police

involvement and no suggestion that the documents were faked.

'Blimey, he's admitted everything,' said Rosa Prince, the *Telegraph*'s political correspondent, as she read the message which Rayner had forwarded to the other reporters, as well as to Wynn Davies.

'Unbelievable,' added Christopher Hope, the paper's Whitehall editor. 'Looks like we're on, then!'

The justice secretary admitting that he had overclaimed public money would normally be one of the biggest scoops of a reporter's career. But everyone in the room knew that this was just the start.

As Lewis got back from lunch, a copy of the Jack Straw email was thrust into his hand by Chris Evans, the *Telegraph*'s head of news.

It was only as he read the words in front of him that Lewis's fears of a hoax finally dissipated, and he felt the tension in his body easing. 'Well, that's it then,' he said to Evans.

At the same time Arthur Wynn Davies rushed into the bunker, smiling and waving a printout of the email above his head.

'We're in business!' he proclaimed.

Freedom of Information?

February 2004

'My MP bought a plasma TV
here. Can I return him?'

CHAPTER 1

Mᴏʀᴇ ᴛʜᴀɴ ꜰɪᴠᴇ ʏᴇᴀʀꜱ before the *Telegraph*'s expenses investigation began, freelance journalist Heather Brooke sat in her makeshift office in the corner of a friend's attic painting studio, picked up the phone and dialled the number for the switchboard at the Houses of Parliament.

'Hello, is it possible to speak to someone who deals with freedom of information requests?' she asked, in her distinctive mid-Atlantic accent.

'What's that?' came the reply.

'There was a law passed four years ago,' the reporter continued. 'It lets members of the public have access to information and I'd like to speak to the person in charge of that.'

'Um, I don't know who that would be,' said the switchboard operator. 'I'll put you through to the public enquiry office.'

Oh joy, thought Brooke. They haven't got a clue.

Parliament had passed its first Freedom of Information Act as long ago as 2000, and its full provisions were due to come into force at the beginning of 2005. Brooke was interested in finding out how MPs were spending public money, and had decided to see whether Parliament, having had four years to prepare for the new Act to come into use, might already be in a position to help. But her enquiries were quickly leading her to the conclusion that Parliament was nowhere near ready for the introduction of the Act. From the way she was bounced between various departments, it seemed that few people had even heard of it.

Brooke had been born and raised in Seattle, though she had dual British–American nationality through her parents, who had moved to the US from their native Liverpool. It was during a previous life as an intern on *The Spokesman–Review*, a small-town daily newspaper in Spokane, Washington State, that Brooke had first developed a taste for exposing the expenses claims of politicians. America's long-established freedom of information laws allowed her to dig through public records in the state capital, Olympia, to find out what local representatives had been spending public money on. Although she found little evidence of malfeasance, Brooke saw the relative honesty of local politicians as proof that transparency was a vital weapon in preventing abuses in public office.

From Spokane, Brooke had moved on to the *Spartanburg Herald–Journal* in South Carolina, but fell out of love with journalism after covering more than three hundred murders, telling friends she felt 'burnt out'. A move to England, where she had been shocked at how difficult it was to get access to information held by officialdom, gave her the idea of writing a guide to using the forthcoming Freedom of Information Act, and she had become an expert in navigating this fiendishly complex piece of legislation, which seemed to some as if it had been designed to confound and frustrate those who tried to use it, rather than to encourage greater openness.

It was against this background that Brooke, by now aged in her mid-thirties, made her first approach to Parliament in February 2004 from her temporary office in Putney, south London, where her documents and ring binders competed for space with easels and painting materials belonging to her artist friend.

Brooke was particularly interested in the issue of MPs' expenses, which had already provided a rich seam of newspaper stories guaranteed to provoke outrage among a British public who had an inherent distrust of politicians and believed they were all on the take. The most controversial element of what the MPs could claim for was something called the additional costs allowance (ACA), which gave them the right to claim up to £23,038 a year (at 2007/8 levels) for maintaining a second home.

Although MPs earn a good living (their basic salary in 2007/8 was £64,766), it was deemed insufficient for them to afford the cost of homes both in their constituencies – where they were expected to spend weekends and Parliament's long periods of recess – and in London, one of the world's most expensive cities. Successive governments had shied away from the idea of giving MPs a large pay rise to enable them to shoulder the expense of two homes, and so an alternative system was devised to allow them to claim the costs of their second home – including the interest on their mortgage – on expenses, in the same way that Joe Public might claim a train fare or a lunch.

Brooke was one of the first journalists to make a direct request to Parliament for details of MPs' expenses. Having got nowhere with her telephone enquiries, she eventually received an email from Judy Wilson, Parliament's data protection officer, who said she would also be handling FoI requests. Brooke called her and asked if she would be able to repeat the exercise she had carried out in America, digging through MPs' expenses receipts to see what they had been spending public money on.

'That's really interesting,' said Wilson, who assured Brooke that Parliament would be publishing details of MPs' expenses in October 2004. Brooke decided there was nothing to do but wait.

When October came, however, Parliament published nothing more than a summary of the total amount which each MP had claimed on their expenses, backdated to 2001 and broken down into travel, office costs and the ACA.

Brooke called again. 'Is this it?' she asked. She was told it was.

Undaunted, Brooke decided to submit a written request for details of MPs' expenses as soon as the Freedom of Information Act came into force in January 2005. She decided to go for broke by putting in a request for the expenses claims of all 646 MPs.

It was no great surprise to Brooke when her request was refused by the House of Commons on the grounds that it would be too expensive to collate and publish such a huge volume of information. But her motto was 'never take no for an answer', and where less combative reporters might have given up, she saw this as merely the opening round in a battle with the Commons authorities which she was quite happy to fight for years, if need be. And so it was to prove.

Brooke tried several different angles of attack, including requests for travel expenses; for the names and salaries of MPs' staff; and for the ACA claims of all MPs. In each case her requests were swatted away by the parliamentary authorities, who seemed to regard her as something of an irritation.

'They pretty much laughed in my face, because it was just so unheard of that a common person would dare to ask for them,' she later said.

Parliament's release of summaries of how much each MP had claimed was not without interest for reporters, however. Armed with even this most basic information, journalists had been able to uncover what appeared to most right-minded people to be blatant abuses of the expenses system, many involving MPs whose constituencies were in Greater London, less than half an hour's commute from Parliament, deciding to treat themselves to a second home in Westminster courtesy of the taxpayer.

One of the most notorious examples involved Alan and Ann Keen, husband and wife Labour MPs who represented next-door constituencies in west London and had a home in Brentford, just 9 miles from Parliament. Despite living closer to work than thousands, if not millions, of Londoners, the Keens had for years been claiming his'n'hers second-home allowances to fund the cost of a swish serviced apartment on the banks of the Thames. The couple were dubbed 'Mr and Mrs Expenses' by one newspaper, and the name stuck.

But journalists sensed that they were barely scratching the surface when it came to MPs' expenses claims, knowing as they did that MPs were allowed to claim for furniture, electrical equipment and food, among other things. To a nation of cynics it seemed impossible that MPs, faced with such temptation, could have done anything other than misbehave.

As Brooke kept on submitting her requests for more information, two other reporters joined the fray. On 4 January 2005 Jon Ungoed-Thomas of the *Sunday Times* asked for the expenses claims of the then Prime Minister, Tony Blair, and the then environment secretary, Margaret Beckett. The following day Ben Leapman, a reporter at the London *Evening Standard* (who would later move to the *Sunday Telegraph*), put in a freedom of information request for the expenses claims of six MPs, including Blair and Alan and Ann Keen.

After hitting a brick wall in their attempts to get even a crumb of information, all three reporters appealed to the Information Commissioner, Richard Thomas, who acted as ombudsman in disputed FoI requests. It was the start of a four-year legal battle in which the FoI requests were constantly batted back and forth between Parliament and various tribunals and courts.

The Commissioner ruled that the expenses details of the fourteen MPs named by the reporters should be made public

– setting a precedent which was greeted with utter horror by many other MPs, who had been merrily putting in highly questionable expenses claims for years on end, certain that the public would never be able to find out what their money was being spent on. In what was seen by many observers as the ultimate act of hypocrisy, David Maclean, the Conservative MP for Penrith, in Cumbria, put forward a Private Member's Bill (a method by which backbench MPs can propose new laws) to exempt Parliament from the Freedom of Information Act.

The move appalled parliamentarians like David Winnick, the Labour MP for Walsall North, who said the amendment would 'make a mockery' of the House of Commons, and be 'disastrous' for the reputation of Parliament. Debates on the issue were dominated by opponents of the Bill, including Norman Baker, a Liberal Democrat MP, who warned that it would encourage a 'culture of secrecy', and the Conservative MP Richard Shepherd, who said that voting to exempt Parliament from transparency laws which it wanted to apply to everyone else would be a 'staggering misjudgement'. Maclean was the only MP who spoke in favour of the amendment; nevertheless, in May 2007 the Bill was passed by 96 votes to 25 on a Friday afternoon (a time of the week when most MPs were on their way back to their constituencies), revealing just how worried MPs were about allowing daylight to shine into one of the darkest corners of public spending.

The *Daily Mail* described the vote as 'a dark day for democracy', the *Guardian* said the result was 'about as far as it is possible to get from openness and accountability', and the *Daily Telegraph* accused Parliament of acting like 'Communist officials in East Germany'. An incandescent Norman Baker claimed the vote was a 'stitch-up' involving the collusion of the parliamentary authorities, pointing out that the two Deputy Speakers who chaired the debates, Sylvia Heal and Sir Michael Lord, allowed two 'closure votes' to stop opponents running down the clock with long speeches to prevent the Bill going forward – the first time in twenty years such votes had been held on a Friday. The clear implication was that the Bill had tacit support from the supposedly impartial Speaker of the House of Commons, Michael Martin, a man who would cast a long shadow over the whole expenses furore for the following two years until it was finally played out with the *Daily Telegraph*'s disclosures in May 2009.

In the event, the amendment Bill never became law because the House of Lords saw the proposed measure for what it was and refused to have anything to do with it. No law can be passed in the UK without the approval of Parliament's upper chamber and, ultimately, the Queen, and while the House of Commons has the power to overrule the Lords, the peers can considerably slow a Bill's progress by rejecting it, which was what they did now. Although David Maclean refused to admit defeat, Gordon Brown made it clear when he took over from Tony Blair as Prime Minister in June 2007 that he did not see the justification in exempting MPs from FoI laws, leaving Maclean with little choice but to withdraw his Bill.

But that was by no means the end of Parliament's fight against transparency. In June 2007 the House of Commons authorities, guided by Michael Martin, appealed against the Information Commissioner's decision that details of fourteen named MPs' expenses should be published. As it happens, the journalists also appealed against the Commissioner's ruling; for although he had decided that the public should be given a breakdown of what the MPs had claimed under several specific categories, he did not recommend the publication of individual receipts, which was what the reporters wanted. The matter would be decided by an information tribunal, an independent panel which settled disputes over FoI requests, but the hearing would not take place until the following year – a convenient delay from the MPs' point of view.

Meanwhile the clamour for the release of information on MPs' expenses claims was amplified by a constant drip of newspaper stories on the subject, which eroded the public's already fragile trust. The most damaging revelation had come in May 2007 in the *Sunday Times*, which reported that Derek Conway, a Conservative backbencher, had used public money to employ his son as a parliamentary assistant even though he was a full-time student at Newcastle University at the time. The disclosure had led to a parliamentary investigation, which in January 2008 ordered Conway to hand back £13,000 of the money which had been paid to his son, and suspended him from the Commons for ten days. Conway was also expelled from the Conservative Party by its leader, David Cameron, leaving him with no choice but to announce his retirement at the next general election. The *Sunday Times* reporters responsible for Conway's downfall happened to be Robert Winnett and Holly Watt, both of whom would go on to play instrumental roles in the 2009 expenses scandal after defecting to the *Daily Telegraph*.

When the information tribunal was convened in February 2008, public anger was notched up to a new level by a series of astonishing admissions from Andrew Walker, the balding, bespectacled and slightly bumptious Commons director of resources. Giving evidence to the packed tribunal in Bedford Square, next to the British Museum in central London, Walker was questioned on the somewhat opaque workings of the parliamentary fees office, the branch of the civil service responsible for scrutinizing MPs' expenses claims.

The barrister representing Heather Brooke asked Walker what his staff did to verify MPs' claims.

'There is checking where there are receipts,' he said. 'Where there are no receipts there is no checking. If it's below £250 then the assumption is that it's going to be reasonable.'

MPs were also entitled to claim up to £400 per month for food, he said, without the need to submit receipts.

Reporters in the room, many of whom were experts in 'creative accounting' when it came to their own expenses claims, collectively raised their eyebrows at the concept of being given such free rein.

Walker was then asked how officials decided how much an MP could claim for individual items of furniture for their second home, such as a sofa or a television.

Backed into a corner, Walker was forced to confirm the existence of the so-called 'John Lewis list', a document which had taken on almost mythical status among journalists, who had been trying to get their hands on it for years. Officially entitled the 'Additional Costs Claims Guide', the list was a jealously guarded pamphlet produced by the parliamentary fees office containing the maximum amounts of money the office could pay out for various household items. All the price limits were set according to the typical prices of such goods at John Lewis, middle England's favourite department store, which the fees office had deemed to be a suitable benchmark for what could be considered a reasonable place for MPs to shop: good quality, but not extravagant.

'May we see this list?' Brooke's barrister asked. No, said Walker. Asked why not, he replied that he feared that if the list were published, and MPs found out the maximum they were allowed to claim for individual items, that would 'become the going rate'. In other words, MPs would claim the absolute maximum amount for everything they could get away with. Walker's concerns were hardly an endorsement of his earlier statement that MPs could be expected to put in 'reasonable' claims.

Almost before Walker had finished giving his evidence, the Press Association filed an FoI request for the release of the John Lewis list, and on 13 March the parliamentary authorities quickly agreed to publish it.

Even the most cynical journalists and campaigners gasped when they read the details of what MPs were allowed to claim for. Among the thirty-eight items specified (though the list was by no means an exhaustive record of everything an MP could buy on expenses) were beds for £1,000, TVs at £750 and bookcases at £500, as well as fridges, washing machines, cookers, coffee machines and, appropriately, shredders (at up to £50). What seemed to enrage the public most of all was the fact that MPs were also allowed to bill the taxpayer for the cost of a new kitchen (up to £10,000) and bathroom (£6,335), making it clear they could renovate and furnish their entire second home using public money.

News websites were bombarded with comments from readers aghast at finding out that MPs were able to claim more on their expenses than many people earned in a year. One message, from a man in Northumberland to the BBC website, summed up the public mood.

'This is utterly disgraceful,' he wrote. 'These people can claim an amount that most people in this country can't even earn. If they need somewhere to live when in London, then the nation should build something along the lines of a Travel Inn and each MP could be allocated a room for the duration of his tenure.'

Others contrasted the MPs' cushy lifestyles with the plight of members of the armed forces, whose dilapidated accommodation had become a major embarrassment for the government that month after soldiers sent photographs of their slum-like barracks to various media organizations.

The tribunal upheld the decision of the Information Commissioner, saying in its judgment that 'The ACA system is so deeply flawed, the shortfall in accountability is so substantial, and the necessity of full disclosure so convincingly established, that only the most pressing privacy needs should in our view be permitted to prevail.'

Faced with this latest defeat, and a growing public backlash, it seemed unlikely to most observers that Parliament would put up any further resistance to the publication of MPs' expenses. Even the Speaker's own legal team advised him against any further appeals, telling him the game was up. But Michael Martin wasn't about to let a trio of journalistic upstarts poke their noses into what he regarded as the sacred world of MPs' finances; so he found a new legal team who were happy to take on the case – and pocket large fees which would, of course, be footed by the taxpayer.

Martin, a former shop steward from Scotland, had already become something of a pantomime villain for the press long before the expenses row. The son of an alcoholic merchant seaman and a cleaner, Martin had been brought up in a Glasgow tenement with four siblings, and worked as a sheet-metal worker before his long climb up the political ladder via the union movement and the local council. His election as Speaker in 2000 (the first Roman Catholic to hold the post since the Reformation in the sixteenth century) caused controversy by breaking with the loose tradition of alternating between Conservative and Labour incumbents (his predecessor, Betty Boothroyd, had also been a Labour MP), and after a series of rows which saw him parting company with three members of his civil service staff, one of whom he had deemed 'too pompous', his detractors began to suggest he wasn't up to the job.

Quentin Letts, the *Daily Mail*'s irreverent parliamentary sketch writer, nicknamed him 'Gorbals Mick' after Glasgow's working-class heartland – a jibe which so infuriated Martin that he tried to have Letts banned from setting foot in the Commons. More damaging was the fact that in 2007 he spent £20,000 of public money employing the media law firm Carter-Ruck to fire off warning letters to newspapers that dared to write negative stories about him, fostering accusations that he had such a high opinion of himself – and, by implication, of the institution of Parliament – that he believed he, and it, should be beyond scrutiny.

That view was only reinforced by Speaker Martin's announcement on 25 March, the day the expenses details were due to be made public, that he would, on behalf of the House of Commons, be lodging an eleventh-hour appeal against the decision of the information tribunal.

On 7 May 2008 Parliament's expensively assembled legal team gathered at London's High Court, a Victorian Gothic cathedral of justice whose users, should they be in any doubt about the solemnity of its business, must pass underneath carvings of Christ, Moses and Solomon as they enter.

Nigel Giffin QC, appearing for the Commons, argued that the publication of receipts would be 'a substantial intrusion' into the lives of MPs. The three judges presiding over the case seemed less than convinced, and it was no surprise when they handed down their written judgment on 16 May that they had found in favour of the three journalists.

In giving their reasons for rejecting Parliament's appeal,

Sir Igor Judge, Lord Justice Latham and Mr Justice Blake stated:

> We have no doubt that the public interest is at stake. We are not here dealing with idle gossip, or public curiosity about what in truth are trivialities. The expenditure of public money through the payment of MPs' salaries and allowances is a matter of direct and reasonable interest to taxpayers. They are obliged to pay their taxes at whatever level and on whatever basis the legislature may decide, in part at least to fund the legislative process. Their interest is reinforced by the absence of a coherent system for the exercise of control over and the lack of a clear understanding of the arrangements which govern the payment of ACA. Although the relevant rules are made by the House itself, questions whether the payments have in fact been made within the rules, and even when made within them, whether the rules are appropriate in contemporary society, have a wide resonance throughout the body politic. In the end they bear on public confidence in the operation of our democratic system at its very pinnacle, the House of Commons itself. The nature of the legitimate public interest engaged by these applications is obvious.

Speaker Martin had lost hands down. His attempts to block the publication of MPs' expenses had cost the taxpayer an estimated £100,000 in legal fees.

Aware that the ruling meant it would be unable to resist any further FoI requests for MPs' expenses, the Commons grudgingly announced it would publish all of the expenses claims and receipts submitted by every MP between April 2004 and March 2008. The publication date was set for October, then put back to December, only for the renewed deadline to come and go without so much as a single slip of paper from Tesco being published.

Were MPs up to something? The answer came when Parliament returned from the Christmas recess, at which point Harriet Harman, the Leader of the House of Commons, suddenly and unexpectedly tabled a motion to exempt MPs' expenses from the Freedom of Information Act. Labour MPs would be subject to a three-line whip on the issue – meaning they were obliged to support the vote or face disciplinary action from the party. There was more than a whiff of panic about the move, heightening the already fevered speculation that MPs, including senior members of the government, had something terrible to hide.

Then, on 21 January 2009, after opposition parties had made it clear they would vote against the government, Gordon Brown backed down, paving the way for the expenses to be published, albeit in a censored form.

A new date was set for the publication of the expenses: 1 July 2009. But long before that date arrived, events were to take a rather different course.

Basra

2008

'To help with the children we've got these marvellous little taxpayers. I don't know how I'd manage without them'

CHAPTER 2

Patrolling the streets of Basra in southern Iraq in 2008, two British soldiers cursed their luck as the midday sun pushed the temperature above 100° Fahrenheit. They were dressed in standard issue desert fatigues, and the weight of their equipment made the conditions almost unbearable. As the sweat ran freely down their faces and backs, one of the two men, Pete, swore under his breath to his mate Gary* about the bulky body armour he was wearing, weighing a spine-crushing 13 kg (28 lb) and restricting his movement so much that he could barely bend down or put his rifle in the correct firing position on his shoulder. Like every other British soldier, he could only look on with envy at the lightweight Kevlar body vests offered to American soldiers, which had slightly less stopping power but were far more flexible and comfortable.

Back at base, Pete grumbled to Gary about the fact that their equipment was always chosen by 'desk jockeys' who seemed to have little concept of how the kit would perform in battlefield conditions. Controversy about British Army body armour had been raging from day one of the Iraq war.

*Both names have been changed to protect the soldiers' anonymity.

Many troops who had come under fire argued that the standard issue Osprey vests put them at greater risk of being killed than if they were wearing no protection. During fire-fights soldiers had, in some cases, chosen to pull out the inch-thick ceramic plates inside their vests and throw them away, finding that the freedom to move and fire their weapons accurately, and the ability to run faster for cover without the extra weight, was more likely to save their lives than waddling along like a tin man, waiting to find out if their vests really were bullet-proof.

Some soldiers didn't have the luxury of choosing; five years after tank commander Sergeant Steve Roberts was shot dead after having had to hand in his body armour because of kit shortages, troops were still having to share, and some were still having to go without. If one patrol came back to base later than scheduled, the next patrol would in some cases have to go out unprotected because they would not be able to take the returning patrol's body armour.

Pete knew from his fellow soldiers that the lightweight Kevlar body vests favoured by US soldiers cost between £500 and £750, depending on the model. He didn't have that sort of money, but he resolved that when he finished his tour and went home, he would scrape enough together to get his own Kevlar vest.

For Gary, the main problem was his boots. British Army issue boots had also proved to be woefully inadequate for the searing heat in Iraq; many soldiers had discovered the soles were literally melting after a day on foot patrol, and even when improved models were introduced, troops often found them impossible to get on with. Gary had decided that when he got home he would buy his own boots, having been recommended American 5.11 Tactical desert boots, with a heat-resistant sole, which he knew he could buy online for around £125. He also wanted a good-quality pair of gloves to protect his hands from burns during weapon firing, and a pair of Oakley wraparound sunglasses with reinforced glass to protect his eyes both from the sun and from spent bullet casings, which had caused eye injuries to other soldiers.

Both Pete and Gary were experienced soldiers, and they could live with the discomfort of their standard equipment in southern Iraq, where the danger was now relatively subdued. However, both men were expecting to be posted to Helmand province in Afghanistan the following year. That was an entirely different war. British soldiers were having 'contacts' with the Taleban on a daily basis, and the fighting was getting more, not less, intense. In 2006 the then defence secretary, John Reid, had said he 'would be perfectly happy' for British troops to complete their mission in Helmand in three years 'without firing one shot'. But by 2008 the Army was firing four million bullets per year in the province during its fiercest engagement in half a century, and before long the number of British soldiers killed in Afghanistan would outstrip the total in Iraq. There would be a very real possibility that having the right kit would mean the difference between life and death. Pete, in particular, was likely to get plenty of chances to test his theory about the greater agility afforded by lightweight body armour being critical in the heat of battle.

Like every other soldier in their regiment, Pete and Gary had lost friends during their service in Iraq. By the time Britain's six-year military mission in the country came to an end the following year, the armed forces would have lost 136 personnel as a result of enemy action. Pete had been to more than one funeral in between previous tours; both he and Gary had become used to losing friends, and they accepted it as part of the job. No war had been fought without soldiers getting killed, and they knew that when they joined up.

But what they didn't accept was being sent to war without the proper tools for the job. Lives were being lost unnecessarily because of the government's failure to supply adequate kit. Dozens had been killed in Iraq and Afghanistan while travelling in Snatch Land-Rovers, vehicles originally designed for use in Northern Ireland and totally unable to protect their occupants from the blast of a roadside bomb. In the months ahead, controversy would also rage about the Army's chronic lack of helicopters.

The military's top brass had become increasingly critical of government policy, complaining that they were being asked to do too much in too many different theatres without the money or resources to do the job properly. Overstretch, they liked to call it. With Britain in the grip of the worst recession for eighty years, though, there wasn't any prospect of defence spending being increased. Pete and Gary were resigned to the fact that if they wanted to have the best equipment for the job, they would just have to earn some extra money so they could go out and buy it themselves.

The Leak

July 2008

CHAPTER 3

WHEN SOLDIERS PETE and Gary returned to the UK, one of their first priorities was to find temporary work during their leave period so they could earn enough cash to buy the body armour, boots and other kit they wanted to have before their next deployment overseas. Although moonlighting is technically forbidden under Ministry of Defence rules, many soldiers do it to top up their modest wages and senior commanders usually turn a blind eye to the practice; so when an opportunity to work for a security firm presented itself, they took it.

Pete and Gary were told to report to The Stationery Office (TSO) in south London, which was gearing up for an important contract. TSO, which had been Her Majesty's Stationery Office until it was privatized in 1996 and later bought by the multinational Williams Lea Group, processes thousands of government reports and official documents every year. The Hutton report into the death of the government weapons inspector Dr David Kelly and the annual budget report were among the documents which had passed through the doors of TSO; so security was paramount.

When the two soldiers turned up for their first day,

however, they were told they would be securing not government reports, but details of MPs' expenses claims. More than one and a half million individual receipts put in by MPs over the previous four years were to be electronically scanned and then 'redacted', meaning the electronic copies would have sensitive information such as bank account numbers blacked out, before the documents were made public the following year. It all sounded pretty straightforward. The main parts of the soldiers' job would involve keeping a register of who went in and out of secure rooms; making sure staff emptied their pockets of phones, cameras and other personal items before they started work; and transporting sensitive documents between government offices and TSO for processing.

Pete and Gary were joined on the job by another two soldiers, family men, who were working so they could afford Christmas presents for their children and to pay for the odd family treat during the summer holidays. Like Pete and Gary, they had also lost comrades in the increasingly bitter Afghan war.

On arriving for their first day's work at TSO, the soldiers were given details of exactly what they would be required to do. A secure document storage company was holding the MPs' receipts at a secret location. From there, they were being transported in batches to a room in a parliamentary office building in Millbank – a short walk from the Houses of Parliament – where officials were collating files for each MP, divided into different folders for each financial year. Every day, a van would be sent by TSO with a private security guard on board to pick up several cardboard boxes, known as lawyer's boxes, to take them to TSO.

The work of processing the MPs' receipts was to be carried out in two rooms at TSO. First, the receipts, the MPs' claim forms and any other relevant material were taken to a room where a small team of Stationery Office staff, together with parliamentary officials working on secondment, fed the documents into photocopier-sized scanners to make electronic copies of them. This room, unsurprisingly, was known as the scanning room. At the end of each day the boxes were returned to the Millbank office and then put back into storage.

That was the easy part. The really painstaking part of the job, which was scheduled to take several months, involved redacting the documents, which was done in a 20-foot-square office known equally unsurprisingly as the redaction room. Around two dozen people had been chosen to carry out the tedious process of redaction. Most of them worked either for TSO or as civil servants in Parliament, with a few agency staff hired to make up the numbers for the job. They included men and women, ranged in age from the twenties to the sixties, and came from a broad range of social and ethnic backgrounds. The soldiers would not only secure the rooms and the documents but also observe the people carrying out the redaction. The soldiers themselves would not be directly involved in the redaction process.

The workers were surprised, to say the least, when they were greeted at the door on their first day by well-built military men who asked them to surrender all mobile phones, pens, cameras and anything else which could be used to copy anything they saw inside. A couple of the staff claimed their human rights were being infringed, but submitted to the restrictions. TSO, well aware of the sensitivity of the data being handled, had gone to extra lengths to protect the MPs' expenses files – but others had not been so careful.

Most government or parliamentary documents are given a security classification – confidential, restricted, secret or top secret. It was Parliament's job, not TSO's, to decide whether to give the documents a protective marking. However, in this case Parliament had not assigned the MPs' expenses files any security marking at all. Why would such sensitive and potentially embarrassing information not carry a protective mark? Was it because the Speaker, Michael Martin, had thought it unnecessary? Was it sheer arrogance on his part, or perhaps a failure to consider the implications of any possible leak? Or was it simply that Speaker Martin decided the material did not warrant any protection because the High Court had already ordered its publication? Whatever the reason, the decision meant that those seeing the documents could freely discuss the contents of what they were reading without falling foul of the Official Secrets Act. It was an oversight which was later to prove crucial for the *Telegraph*'s investigation.

Despite the lack of a security classification, Stationery Office executives were concerned about the situation and had privately consulted the security services about how the material should be treated before the project started. 'Treat it as if it were a secret document,' was the advice from intelligence officers.

Once the redaction team had handed in their personal belongings, they filed into the room to find computers arranged in a square around the walls of the redaction room. A security guard was stationed at all times at a desk in the corner, another just inside the door. One worker commented that it was like entering an exam room. A line manager entered and explained the mammoth task that lay ahead. Each of them would be going through MPs' expenses claims, which would arrive as PDF files from the scanning room next door. Using specialist redaction software, they would blank out certain details, referring to a list (provided by the parliamentary authorities) of twenty-two different types of information which had to be removed. These included bank account numbers, home addresses, and information on suppliers of goods and services. The guide handed out to workers said: 'The overall aim is to remove information which would impact on the privacy, financial interests or security of MPs and third parties.' The information to be censored would be highlighted in light grey so that it could be checked by the MPs before being blacked out at a later stage.

During the first morning the redaction team, accompanied by two line managers and an IT manager, practised on dummy files. They broke for lunch, and when they returned the 'live' files began to be distributed.

For the first day or so, the staff concentrated on getting to grips with the software and the task in hand. But by the second day the workers, having mastered the technical side of the job, began to pay more attention to the material on the screens in front of them. All of them were troubled by what they saw.

It usually began with a quiet sigh or a shake of the head. Some workers folded their arms and sat back in their chairs, staring in disbelief at the screen. Aware that they were being observed by security staff and managers, the workers were reluctant, at first, to voice their opinions, but by the afternoon of the second day they were beginning to nudge colleagues sitting at neighbouring desks.

'Have a look at this!' one would whisper to another.

'That's nothing, look at this one,' was a typical reply.

One of the first claims to attract attention was that of Yvette Cooper, the Labour MP married to schools secretary Ed Balls. The worker looking at her claims was dismayed that Cooper had been able to claim tens of thousands of pounds even though her husband was also an MP, and also claimed expenses. Another worker was incensed to discover that the Cabinet minister Hazel Blears had billed the taxpayer for a Kit-Kat bar she had eaten during a hotel stay.

Many of the staff had just received a modest 1.3 per cent pay rise, and they were appalled to see that their taxes were being spent by MPs on household goods which the workers could never afford for themselves, but which the MPs deemed to be 'essential'.

Gordon Brown's expenses were among the first to be redacted. The staff were particularly vexed to discover that the Prime Minister was claiming back the cost of his Sky TV package, as well as claiming for a burglar alarm, despite having round-the-clock police protection. One member of the parliamentary staff pointed out that Brown had to keep up with current events, hence the Sky TV, but his colleague replied: 'Why can't he just watch BBC News 24 like other people?'

As the managers in the room began to sense that anger was brewing in the room, one of the supervisors decided to intervene before the atmosphere deteriorated any further.

'OK guys,' he said. 'I know some of the stuff you're seeing on your screens isn't good, but we're here to do a job, it's as simple as that, and you have to remain detached from the subject matter. You have to be professional about this and do what you're being paid to do. You can't leave this room and share this information down the pub with your mates over a beer tonight. You're dealing with highly sensitive information, and you're all here because you're cleared to work with information of this sensitivity, so let's keep our opinions to ourselves and get through this.'

Over the following days the workers became less vocal, but every now and then the anger would resurface with a shake of the head, deep breaths or other tell-tale signs. They were frustrated not only by what the MPs had been claiming, but also by the fact that they were actively taking part in concealing these claims from the public, removing evidence of wrongdoing or abuse. Some workers began openly to question why they were having to take out certain details. Their managers simply replied that that was what they were being paid to do.

The security team, who were becoming increasingly aware of the apparent abuses from the conversations between the workers, were also finding the MPs' claims hard to stomach. They were operating a shift system, and when a new shift came in each day, they would be filled in on the day's highlights of who had claimed for what.

'You should see some of the stuff they claim for their second homes,' one of the soldiers said to a colleague as he came on shift one day.

'Second homes? I'd just like a decent first home,' replied the other, referring to the parlous state of service accommodation.

Having caught the end of a conversation about MPs' travel expenses, another member of the security team, also a member of the armed forces, pointed out that he and other servicemen were given just two travel warrants per year for rail journeys, after which they had to pay their own way.

Some of the workers, overhearing the conversation, nodded their heads in agreement as the veterans, who had put their lives on the line every day in Iraq and Afghanistan, contrasted their own living and working conditions with the lavish lifestyle of some of the MPs who had sent them there. The soldiers swapped stories about the unforgiving conditions they had experienced on their tours of duty, sleeping in tents, if they were lucky, though they had often had to sleep in the open when they went on long patrols in the desert.

A line manager quietly asked the security team to keep their personal opinions to themselves. The soldiers apologized, but the manager waved the apology away, making it clear that everyone in the room had their own opinions, but that the job needed to be done without fuss.

As the staff got over the initial shock of seeing what their tax money was being spent on by the MPs, the atmosphere in the room gradually began to settle. However, TSO had decided that because of the laborious nature of the work the staff working in the redaction room should be rotated every few days, and each time this happened six of the workers would be replaced with new faces who weren't familiar with what they were about to see.

One of the first files to be handed to the first batch of new entrants was that of Anthony Steen, a Conservative MP who had claimed for thousands of pounds for maintaining his country estate in Devon, including a bill for a forestry expert to inspect up to five hundred trees in the grounds. The rookie worker reacted in the same way that the other staff had done when they had seen their first expenses files, questioning how Steen could possibly have been allowed to claim for so much gardening work.

Over the coming weeks, the security team began to open up more and more to their civilian colleagues with their thoughts on what was going on.

'The thing is,' explained one soldier, 'we're sent out to Iraq or Afghanistan to do a job. Sometimes we lose people, but that comes with the job, and it's a job that we signed up for. These MPs send us off to Afghanistan, and we've got no problem with that either; as far as we're concerned, we've got an objective to achieve and we're there until we achieve that objective.

'But how come these MPs are getting paid £64,000 and

claiming another £100,000 on expenses when we're having to work in our time off to afford presents for the wife and kids or to buy kit that the MoD doesn't supply? How can they possibly justify getting all this money?'

As well as filling in the civilian workers on the short-comings of Snatch Land-Rovers and ill-fitting body armour, the soldiers also talked about Headley Court, the rehabilitation centre for injured servicemen. A lack of investment in the facilities there means veterans have to use a local public swimming pool, where members of the public have objected to the presence of amputees, saying they might scare the children.

Another complaint voiced by one of the soldiers was that none of the MPs had bothered 'to show their faces at Wootton Bassett to see the bodies home'. Wootton Bassett in Wiltshire had become synonymous with the nation's respect for Britain's armed forces, as large crowds turned out to pay their respects whenever funeral processions passed through the town after bodies had been repatriated to the nearby RAF Lyneham.

'They don't even have the decency to send anyone down,' said the serviceman. Where, he asked, was the Prime Minister when the coffins were being driven through the streets. And where, for that matter, was Tony Blair?

The soldiers were not alone in being unable to stomach the contrast between their own lives and the gilded existence of the public servants whose expenses they were processing. As the weeks went on, the soldiers, parliamentary staff, Stationery Office workers and agency staff became united in their disgust at the MPs' behaviour.

As well as the more outrageous individual claims, the workers in the room were growing increasingly agitated about the amount of money that could seemingly be claimed without receipts. Many MPs were claiming £400 a month for food, but there were no receipts. Others had submitted bills for suspiciously round numbers.

One of the workers noted that the MPs 'must never have to put their hands in their pockets', surmising that they could simply bank their salary and live off their expenses. Another suggested that many of the MPs 'should be charged with embezzlement'.

In mid-October, the first phase of the process came to an end as the redacted files were sent back to Parliament to be reviewed. The workers returned to their regular jobs, taking their opinions with them. Meanwhile the security team closed down the rooms and secured all the data and information held at TSO before they, too, were stood down.

However, within weeks the redaction operation was up and running again. Parliamentary officials had decided that even more material needed to be removed from the files, so at the beginning of December the redaction room sprang back into life.

Some of the soldiers who had been involved in the security team had now been redeployed overseas. There was less work to be done in the redacting room, with fewer staff employed on the project than before. What none of them knew at that point was that someone involved in the original project, strongly influenced by their dismay at the fact that soldiers were having to work in their leave periods to earn money to buy decent equipment, had made up their mind that the public should know what was going on. They had decided to orchestrate a leak of the MPs' expenses files and had contacted a media consultant, giving them a sample of the material.

For weeks nothing at all happened, and as the mole waited in vain, they assumed that the deafening silence meant people in the outside world did not share the same level of anger and disgust as those who had worked on the redaction process.

As Christmas and the New Year came and went, work continued on redacting more MPs' files. New files, which had been mislaid in Parliament, were coming to light all the time, and it was still a Herculean task checking and rechecking those which had already been altered.

Meanwhile, the mole was taking a keen interest in the debate raging in the media over the apparent foot-dragging by Parliament on the public release of the expenses data.

Then, on 8 February 2009, the first bombshell exploded. The *Mail on Sunday* published a story on the home secretary's expenses. The newspaper revealed that Jacqui Smith had claimed more than £116,000 in parliamentary expenses over the years for her 'second home', having given this designation to her large family home in her constituency in Redditch, near Birmingham, where her husband and two young children were permanently based. Meanwhile, Smith told the Commons authorities that her 'main' home was a spare bedroom in her sister's house in London where she lodged during parliamentary sessions.

Two weeks later, the *Mail on Sunday* followed up its report with a similar exposé on the employment minister Tony McNulty – whose 'second' home on the outskirts of London was lived in by his parents.

However, the mole was not pleased. The material which had been passed on to the media consultant was supposed to be a sample, not for use by any newspaper. They thought it was unfair for Smith and McNulty to be singled out and pilloried. This was a scandal which stretched across Parliament, embroiling politicians from all parties, and that was the message which the source of the leak wanted to get across.

The first attempt to release the information had been a bruising experience for the would-be whistleblower. But the mole's resolve was strengthened by having accidentally hung Jacqui Smith out to dry. They needed a different strategy to ensure the information was released as they intended. A series of phone calls led them to the door of a former SAS officer who they felt certain would be the perfect man for the job. His name was John Wick.

The 'Missing Disk'

Saturday, 28 March 2009

'We're scrapping ID cards.
We don't want anyone to
know we're MPs'

CHAPTER 4

IN HIS SHORT TENURE as Prime Minister, Gordon Brown had acquired a reputation as a man who was more comfortable immersed in the complexities of public spending plans than in the role of international statesman. His predecessor, Tony Blair, had loved nothing better than touring the globe, attending glitzy state occasions and talking 'big picture' politics with the likes of George W. Bush. Blair had been a natural showman, but Brown was seen as a dour Scot who preferred his own company. Whereas Blair had a 1,000-watt smile that wowed audiences the world over, critics joked that Brown's attempts at grinning to order were more akin to someone taking part in a gurning contest.

But the forthcoming G20 summit of world leaders, to be held in London at the start of April 2009, would give Brown his big chance to prove that he, too, had the charisma to be the cheerleader at a meeting of the most powerful people on the planet, including the recently elected US President Obama. Brown had led the world the previous year in devising a model for coping with Britain's banking crisis which had been widely praised by other leaders, and he believed that the G20 summit, intended as a chance to thrash out a global solution to what had become a global financial crisis, could turn out to be his finest hour.

To prepare the ground and try to obtain a consensus, Brown had embarked on a whirlwind bridge-building tour taking in France, the US, Brazil and Chile, chartering a British Airways Boeing 747 to carry his entourage and a group of a dozen or so political journalists on the 16,000-mile round trip. Far from being the anticipated triumph, however, the tour was turning out to be little short of a disaster for Brown, whose mood had become blacker with each passing day. In New York Les Hinton, one of Rupert Murdoch's most senior and long-serving executives, had introduced Brown to Wall Street bankers with a joke about how far his popularity had fallen since he became Prime Minister. Brown, needless to say, hadn't seen the funny side. By the Wednesday of that week, Downing Street aides were furious that the main item on the BBC news had been a comment by the Czech prime minister warning that Brown's plans for economic recovery were 'the way to hell'. Then, in Brazil, President Luiz Inacio Lula da Silva had suggested that the financial crisis had been caused by 'white people with blue eyes', and in Strasbourg a right-wing MEP, Daniel Hannan, had become the surprise YouTube hit of the year after making a withering attack on Brown in a speech to the European Parliament.

So worried were Brown's staff about having their heads bitten off by their fingernail-chewing boss that they tried to hide the British daily newspapers from him in a different cabin on the plane in the hope that it would prevent him finding out how badly he was being savaged back home. The press corps were joking that Brown could apply for asylum in Chile when he arrived there for the last stop of the tour.

Among those on the plane was Robert Winnett, who had joined the *Daily Telegraph* in September 2007, having been lured away from the *Sunday Times*, where he had worked for nine years, starting out as a personal finance reporter before moving on to news. Winnett was now aged thirty-two, though many of his colleagues assumed he was older, partly because his slightly thinning brown hair added a few years to his appearance and partly because of an assumption that anyone who had been a fixture in national newspapers for more than ten years had to be at least in their mid-thirties by now.

During his career at the *Sunday Times*, Winnett had established a reputation as a superb 'digger', able to find front-page stories buried in the minutiae of chunky official documents and to join the dots between seemingly un-connected pieces of information to find a scandal hidden behind them. Whereas many political reporters relied on their talent for networking to pick up stories, the quietly spoken Winnett specialized in carrying out investigations behind closed doors, and had done so with considerable success.

Winnett was viewed as unclubbable, but by no means unsociable, and he jumped at the chance of joining some of his colleagues when the final day of the whistlestop tour, Saturday, 28 March, afforded a rare opportunity for a moment's relaxation for those travelling with the workaholic

Prime Minister. With a few hours to kill between Brown's final meeting in Chile and the take-off slot at Santiago, a handful of journalists and No. 10 aides decided to take a detour to a local vineyard on the way to the airport.

The party included Damian McBride, the Prime Minister's key strategic adviser. McBride, who had worked for Gordon Brown for six years, including a spell as his head of communications at the Treasury, was aged just thirty-four, but could have passed for forty-five owing to his girth and florid complexion, brought on by an accumulation of business lunches and after-work drinking sessions in the bars of Westminster. He loved nothing better than to hold court with the political journalists whom he counted as his friends, giving them delicious titbits about life in Downing Street, though without ever betraying his master.

Although he had no reason to suspect it at the time, McBride's career in No. 10 was about to come to an ugly end. In another two weeks he would resign following the disclosure by the *Daily Telegraph* that he had used his Downing Street email account to exchange messages with the Labour blogger Derek Draper, in which they discussed using the internet to spread smears about the personal lives of prominent Conservative MPs. But for now, both he and the reporters on the trip were enjoying the rare chance in a hectic week to down tools, sample life's finer pleasures and look forward to a well-earned day off when they returned home.

Under a cloudless sky, the party was given a brief tour of the grape vines, together with three elderly and rather more sedate American tourists, before heading inside for the all-important wine-tasting session. In truth, few of those present had the stomach for the delicacies on offer, having been up late the night before enjoying an after-hours drink in their hotel bar. Nor could anyone present profess to be a wine buff – particularly not McBride, who was more of an expert on the idiosyncrasies of various European lagers. So it was with a sense of relief that the reporters and political aides were eventually ushered on to a sweeping veranda where they could look forward to the main purpose of their visit – an enormous lunch.

As the party settled down around a large square table, jostling for places under the shade of a faded umbrella, McBride, like everyone else, ordered the staple South American dish of steak, before baffling his hosts by turning down their eager offers of vintage wine and insisting on drinking beer instead.

While waiting for lunch to arrive he fielded regular calls from the Prime Minister's party, anxious that he and the others would miss the 'convoy' back to the airport and the flight back to Britain. Brushing off their concerns, McBride put his phone down on the table in front of him and told his companions that a story was about to break in the following day's *Sunday Express* concerning the parliamentary expenses claims of Jacqui Smith, the home secretary.

The *Sunday Express*, once one of the biggest-selling newspapers in the English-speaking world, had been in decline for decades, becoming so under-resourced that few of those around the table could remember the last time it had broken a story of any great significance. So the fact that the *Sunday Express* had a major exclusive was as unexpected as it was intriguing, and as McBride began speaking, those around him instinctively leaned inwards in expectation.

McBride explained, to the growing amusement of his audience, that the *Sunday Express* had contacted the Home Office earlier that day to ask why the home secretary had put in an expenses claim for the cost of two pay-per-view adult movies which had appeared on a bill sent to her home in Redditch. Before anyone had the chance to ask whether the home secretary herself had watched the films, McBride explained that her husband, Richard Timney, had admitted that he had watched them while his wife had been away. Timney, who was employed by his wife as her parliamentary adviser, had filled in the expenses claims himself on Smith's behalf, and it seemed that the home secretary had known nothing about it until her department got the call from the newspaper.

After speculating about just how bad a day Richard Timney was surely having, the reporters turned their attention to the other obvious question: how the hell had such a good story gone to the *Sunday Express*? And where had that sort of detail come from?

McBride indicated that leaked details of MPs' expenses claims might have been obtained by someone during the process of censoring hundreds of thousands of receipts. It seemed likely that the information had been downloaded electronically by someone with access to the documents, which had all been scanned into a computer in readiness for the day when they would eventually be published online by Parliament. The information would be so easily portable in an electronic format that it was possible the details of all 646 MPs' expenses had been copied, ready to be offered to newspapers.

As lunch finished, the assembled reporters reflected on the knowledge that if one newspaper could get hold of the expenses details of other MPs, or even of all MPs, it would have landed one of the biggest scoops in years.

For the papers that missed out, it would be nothing short of a disaster.

Of course, the *Sunday Express*'s story was not the first newspaper exposé to be based on leaked information from the database of MPs' expenses. On 8 February the *Mail on Sunday* had published its exclusive story about Jacqui Smith's housing arrangements, which had led to calls for her resignation. The home secretary had tried to justify the arrangement in which she had designated her sister's spare bedroom as her 'main' home (while claiming expenses for her family home) by saying she could prove that she spent more nights at her sister's house than she did in the family home, and that the parliamentary authorities had given their approval. Her argument might have worked in a court of law, but in the court of public opinion it was a non-starter. Put simply, how could a large detached house where Smith's family lived possibly be Smith's 'second' home when her only other home was a back bedroom in a relative's house?

On 22 February the *Mail on Sunday* had produced its

second scoop on MPs' expenses, involving Tony McNulty, the employment minister. The paper's political editor, Simon Walters, who had also penned the Jacqui Smith story, discovered that McNulty had nominated as his 'second' home a house in his Harrow constituency in north-west London which was his parents' main home. McNulty's main home was in Westminster, 3 miles from Parliament, where he lived with his wife, the government's chief inspector of schools, Christine Gilbert. McNulty initially tried to justify claiming £60,000 of taxpayers' money for his parents' house by saying he sometimes used it when he was doing constituency work, and protested that his claims were 'all within the rules' – a defence which would become tediously familiar to the public in the months to come.

After he was pressed further by the *Mail on Sunday*, McNulty announced he would stop claiming the second-home allowance. Unlike Smith, he appeared to have understood how ridiculous his expenses claims would seem to the general public, comparing himself to Nazi war criminals who would typically say they were 'only obeying orders'. He said: 'It's not against the rules – though I suppose you might say that is the Nuremberg defence.'

The *Mail on Sunday*'s stories about Smith and McNulty had alerted the public to potentially widespread abuse of the expenses system. Widespread disgust among voters at the way the two ministers appeared to have taken advantage of the taxpayer left other MPs in no doubt of the rough ride they, too, would be in for when Parliament eventually published expenses details later in the year.

But there was an important difference between the *Mail on Sunday*'s stories and the one which was about to appear in the *Sunday Express*. The *Mail on Sunday* had made no direct reference to documents contained in the 'missing disk'; its stories were based on just one key piece of information contained in the files – the addresses which the MPs had nominated as their second homes. It was only when the *Sunday Express* approached Jacqui Smith about the porn films that it became clear that actual documents might be finding their way into journalists' hands.

The story that was published the next day contained the sort of details which could only be obtained by viewing the original documents. The newspaper listed the date when the adult films had been viewed at the home secretary's house, the name of the company – Virgin Media – and the exact amount each film had cost. The following week the same newspaper would publish yet more details of Smith's expenses claims, including a bill for a new kitchen, which included a claim of 88p for a sink plug.

Although few at the Chilean vineyard knew it at the time, the *Sunday Express* had not been the first newspaper to be offered access to information on the computer disk. More than a week earlier, former SAS officer John Wick had approached *The Times* to ask if it would be interested in obtaining the disk, which he had in his possession. He was prepared to let the newspaper see a limited number of documents as a sample to prove its authenticity, he told them; but his offer was turned down flat without *Times* journalists seeing any of the information on the disk.

Reporters had taken legal advice, and had been told that the newspaper should not get involved. It was a decision which would backfire on them badly in the weeks to come, but for now *The Times*'s involvement would remain a strictly guarded secret.

As the prime ministerial party in Chile boarded the 747 to make the fourteen-hour flight home, Gordon Brown was informed of the *Sunday Express*'s story about Jacqui Smith's expenses claims. He reacted by focusing his attention on the mechanics of how pornographic films can be ordered by satellite television, while one of his more worldly-wise aides explained in detail the process of putting in a pin number on a TV's remote controller which enables the user to access X-rated movies. The more pressing issue of how the government might respond to other embarrassing details of ministers' expenses claims being leaked, or how the whole issue might rebound on him, was not yet at the forefront of his mind.

Further back in the aircraft, the reporters were turning their thoughts to how they could get their hands on the disk. That disk, Winnett thought as he looked out of the window across the tarmac, was the holy grail of political reporting.

In keeping with a long-standing tradition on prime ministerial tours, a stewardess served glasses of champagne to the journalists on board while they waited for the pilot to start the engines. Savouring his drink, Winnett settled back into his seat and began contemplating how he might go about trying to find out who had the expenses disk. His conclusion wasn't long in coming.

'Buggered if I know.'

The Cold Call

Sunday, 29 March

*'Can you tell the fees office
I'm designating this as
my main residence?'*

CHAPTER 5

THE PRESS GALLERY of the Houses of Parliament is a work-place unlike any other. Crammed into a warren of back corridors surrounding the upper tier of the Commons chamber, the tiny offices which house scores of national and regional newspaper, television and radio reporters are a messy clash of oak panelling, bricked-up fireplaces, battered wooden desks and grimy computer screens.

The stretch of corridor which houses, among others, the *Daily Telegraph*'s parliamentary office is known as the Burma Road (because of the relentless toil of its inhabitants), and is in a part of the Palace of Westminster which was used as the Commons librarian's house in the days when the parliamentary press corps included a young Charles Dickens.

It was in the *Telegraph*'s office, a room measuring 15 feet by 10 that is home to the newspaper's six-strong political team and situated so close to Big Ben that it vibrates every time the great clock chimes, that Rosa Prince was working alone on the morning when the *Sunday Express* published its exclusive about Jacqui Smith's expenses claim for pornography. One of the most instantly recognizable figures in the press gallery, her corkscrewing blonde hair un-mistakable from a hundred yards away, Prince had spent most of her career at the *Daily Mirror*, first as a news reporter (she had covered the September 11 attacks during a month based in New York) and more recently as part of the tabloid's political team, before joining the *Telegraph* at the end of 2007. Although some political reporters have a habit of working from their newspaper's head office on a Sunday, rather than in a deserted Westminster, Prince preferred the familiarity of her desk overlooking Parliament Square. And it was there that she took a phone call that particular Sunday morning which would change not only her own life, but the lives of everyone who worked in the Houses of Parliament.

On the line was a man with an undiluted New York accent, who asked for the *Telegraph*'s political editor, Andrew Porter.

'He's not here today. Can I help?' asked Prince.

'Well, I've got a computer disk which contains the details of every MP's expenses claims going back four years. Would you be interested?'

You bet your life I'm interested, thought Prince.

'Yes, definitely,' she instinctively replied. Prince had taken a call the night before from Winnett warning her about the imminent *Sunday Express* story on Jacqui Smith's expenses and summarizing what McBride had told him about the possibility of a disk being in circulation. Having read the *Sunday Express* story, Prince was as sure as she could be that the caller was genuine.

'My name is Henry Gewanter and I work for a PR

company,' the voice went on. 'I'm acting on behalf of someone else, and one thing I have to make clear is that they are very keen that details of every MP's expenses are published.'

'Yes, I'm sure that's fine,' said Prince, though in truth she wasn't at all certain it would be, given the sheer scale of what that would involve. 'I'm sure we can come to an arrangement.'

'I have to tell you that the material has been offered to other newspapers,' said Gewanter, 'but they were only interested in one political party. If you were to go ahead with publication, any coverage you give mustn't be partial. We don't want it to be based on any one political party. The source is very keen that it should cover every political party.'

'OK,' replied Prince. 'We need to meet up.'

Gewanter said he would call his contact, who would get in touch with Prince.

Five minutes later, as Prince was still replaying the earlier call in her head, working out what else she needed to do, her phone rang again.

'My name's John Wick,' said the voice on the line. 'You were talking just now to my colleague Henry Gewanter.'

This time the caller was English, well spoken, with a slight hint of a regional accent which Prince couldn't quite place.

'Yes, I was hoping we could meet up,' said Prince. Wick said he did not want to meet at Westminster, in case other journalists were alerted to the fact that Prince was talking to him. Prince racked her brain for a venue where she could be sure she would not bump into any of her colleagues from rival media organizations, then finally suggested the Goring Hotel, a discreet but suitably well-appointed place – a favourite of Baroness Thatcher, indeed – tucked away in a side street near the *Telegraph*'s head office. Wick agreed to meet for lunch the following Wednesday.

Fifteen miles from Westminster, the Prime Minister's plane had just touched down at Heathrow at the end of its overnight flight from Chile. Within minutes of the engines winding down, the Prime Minister's motorcade had pulled up alongside the jet, and moments later Brown and his entourage were on their way back to Downing Street.

The reporters, meanwhile, decamped with their bags on their shoulders and walked the short distance across the tarmac to Heathrow's Royal Suite, the VIP arrivals area which is one of the perks of travelling 'Prime Minister class'. All of them had been given high-level security clearance before the trip, meaning they were spared the usual irritations of lengthy passport checks and customs, and they made a beeline for the taxis waiting outside.

As Winnett sat in the back of a cab heading into London shortly before noon, his BlackBerry vibrated in his pocket to alert him to a new email. It was from Prince, who had decided to contact him following the conversation the previous evening.

'Give me a bell when you get a sec,' it said. 'We've been offered something potentially quite interesting on expenses – hopefully can set up a meeting.'

Prince had deliberately kept the information to a minimum in the email, acutely aware of the potential for any electronic message to end up in the wrong hands. Without stopping to wonder exactly what it was that the *Telegraph* had been offered, Winnett phoned her as the taxi took him east along the M4.

'I've had this call from someone, and it sounds great,' Prince told her colleague excitedly. 'He says he's got a computer disk with the details of all the MPs' expenses on it. It looks like it's the same source as where the Jacqui Smith story came from.'

Winnett could hardly believe what he was hearing. Less than a day after he had first learned about the existence of the disk, hours after he had resigned himself to having little or no chance of acquiring it, it seemed to be about to fall into his lap. If only it was always this easy!

'Sounds brilliant,' said Winnett. 'What's the guy's name?'

'Oh, he's an American with an odd name. Henry Geweder, or Gewader, I've got it written down . . .'

'Not Henry Gewanter?' Winnett instantly recognized the name as one of the financial PRs he had regularly dealt with in his previous incarnation as a personal finance reporter. Gewanter represented several large insurance companies and other personal finance firms, and in years gone by the pair of them had shared long lunches at some of London's top restaurants. Winnett's pulse quickened as he realized that not only had the *Telegraph* been contacted by someone with access to the disk, but that this person, by sheer fluke, also happened to be one of his old contacts, giving him a crucial advantage in building trust between his newspaper and the source.

But how on earth had Gewanter become involved in something like this? He wasn't the sort who made his living by offering leaked documents or exclusive interviews around Fleet Street, as some better-known PR consultants did. In fact, reflected Winnett, Gewanter was about as far removed from the ultra-smooth image of the top PR man as it was possible to be. A former New York cab driver, Gewanter was a wild-eyed chain smoker, in appearance reminiscent of the sort of actors who played CIA agents in 1960s TV shows. In his spare time he collected comic books, fossils and Roman coins. As far as Winnett knew, he had no connections at all to the murky world of Westminster politics. No matter, thought Winnett, as he dug his battered blue contacts book out of his laptop bag and took off the elastic band which was the only thing holding it together. Buried in its dog-eared pages was Gewanter's mobile number, and Winnett wasted no time in dialling it.

'Hi, Henry, it's Robert Winnett.'

'Hey, Robert!' The American seemed relieved to hear from a familiar voice.

After a brief catch-up and the usual exchange of pleasantries, Winnett cut to the chase and said he had been told Gewanter had some information that the *Telegraph* might be interested in. The PR man confirmed he had been approached by someone who had obtained detailed information about MPs' expenses claims which, he said, could amount to the 'story of the century'. Winnett cautioned Gewanter against saying too much over the telephone and the pair agreed to meet the following day.

As the taxi reached Winnett's flat in Docklands, east London, the reporter's mind was racing with the permutations of what the following day might bring. Would Gewanter be ringing other newspapers? Winnett had asked him not to, but there was no guarantee. Did Gewanter really have the sort of information he said he did? Winnett couldn't shake off his doubts about the unlikeliness of Gewanter's involvement.

Even if Gewanter's story checked out, would the *Telegraph* go for it? The possible stumbling blocks were obvious. If the disk was stolen, the newspaper might be reluctant to get involved. Even if it wasn't, how could the paper check that the material was genuine before it committed to anything? Gewanter seemed certain of the authenticity of the information, but hoaxes had happened in the past, and they would no doubt happen again.

No point worrying about all that now, Winnett thought as he unpacked the debris of his hectic week-long tour. It would have to wait until tomorrow. In the meantime, he rang his colleague Andrew Porter to fill him in on the details of his conversation with Gewanter.

The headlines on Monday, 30 March were dominated by news of the home secretary's expenses claim and speculation over whether she could survive in her job. Preparations for the G20 summit merited little attention by comparison. Matthew Bayley was at his desk at eight thirty that morning, contemplating how the newspaper could take the Jacqui Smith story forward, as well as planning how his team would cover the G20 summit later in the week, which was expected to attract potentially violent protests. When Robert Winnett rang in, intending to explain what he would be doing later in the morning, Bayley ambushed him before he had a chance to get his words out with a series of questions about the Jacqui Smith story.

'Where the hell did the Jacqui Smith stuff come from?' he demanded. 'And how did it end up in the *Sunday Express* of all places?'

Reporters become immune to the sort of interrogation which is the speciality of all news editors whenever their paper has missed a story. News editors know they will get a pasting from their superiors, and in an attempt to cover their backs before the inevitable rollocking happens, they will always do their utmost to find an explanation for why a rival paper has got a brilliant exclusive and theirs hasn't.

The most common excuse (which is very often true) is that the other paper has got its story from a 'ring-in' – a reader or tipster making an unsolicited call with details of a story which turns into the next day's splash. Tabloid newspapers, in particular, thrive on such tip-offs, while the staff of other newspapers can only shrug their shoulders and accept that 'you can't do anything about a ring-in'.

On this occasion, though, Winnett had the best possible news for Bayley. Not only did he know where the *Express* story had come from, he was in contact with the source, and he had already arranged a meeting for later that day.

'Really?' replied Bayley. 'Fantastic! Are you sure it's not a set-up?'

Winnett said he knew the person he was meeting and

was confident he was genuine. But Bayley remained slightly nervous.

'Make sure they're not recording the meeting, won't you,' he said. 'You'd better give Chris a call when he gets off the phone.'

Chris Evans was the *Daily Telegraph*'s head of news, whose job involved overseeing the day-to-day news operation but also planning longer-term investigations. Evans, one of several executives who, like Bayley, had joined the *Telegraph* from the *Daily Mail* during a round of changes at the top of the organization, had had a lot of experience of handling major deals for big stories, particularly during his time as news editor of the *Mail*. When Winnett repeated what he had told Bayley, Evans knew that if they played their cards right, and if the offer from Gewanter was genuine, it could turn out to be a defining moment for the *Telegraph*. But, like Winnett and Bayley, Evans had a worm of doubt going through his mind. It all sounded too good to be true. He had enough experience to know that for every world-beating scoop a newspaper pulls off, it will be offered countless other stories which seem just as good but ultimately turn to dust.

Evans told Winnett to give it his best shot, and to keep him up to date with developments. Meanwhile he informed Tony Gallagher, the paper's deputy editor, who also said Winnett should pull out all the stops to get the story. Gallagher, anxious to satisfy himself that there would be no legal obstacle to the newspaper's going ahead with a potential deal, went straight down to Arthur Wynn Davies's tiny glass-walled office at the far end of the newsroom, knocked on the open door and asked the lawyer if, in theory, there would be any legal reason why the newspaper should not take possession of a computer disk containing information about MPs' expenses claims. Could the newspaper be prosecuted for handling stolen goods, for inciting theft, or for a breach of confidence or privacy?

Wynn Davies said he would have to consider the matter. Later he came back with his answer: if the disk itself was the property of the person who was offering it to the newspaper, then no theft had taken place. It would not constitute a breach of the law because there was no such offence as 'stealing' information – certainly not information that was going to be published anyway at some point. Any attempt to prosecute a newspaper for disclosing misuse of public money would also be doomed to fail, as there was an overwhelming public interest defence which would be likely to sway most juries.

The main point the lawyer was keen to establish was that the *Telegraph* had not asked anyone to remove the information or 'procure' the disk. It had not. Wynn Davies also pointed out that the Information Commissioner had already ordered that the data be released, putting the newspaper in a strong position to justify its publication.

So far, so good, thought Gallagher.

At eleven thirty sharp, Winnett stood in the early spring sunshine outside an office on the Embankment and phoned Gewanter on his mobile. Moments later, the American appeared in the street with a friendly smile on his face. It was the first time in more than five years that the two men had seen each other, but it seemed like much less time had elapsed. Gewanter, a slim, slightly hunched figure with wire-rimmed glasses which sat halfway up the bridge of his nose, vividly recalled their last meeting – a rather splendid lunch at the Oxo tower on the other side of the river – as he felt in his pockets for his cigarettes and lighter. Then he took the lead as the two men walked around the corner to Tempio's restaurant in Temple Avenue, a stone's throw from what had once been the *Daily Telegraph*'s head office in Fleet Street. Down in the basement wine bar, Gewanter selected a table in a narrow open-air well between the restaurant and the pavement so he could carry on smoking. There, over a glass of white wine, he repeated his disclosure that his client, John Wick, had obtained details of every MP's expenses claims.

'This stuff is absolutely mind-blowing,' said Gewanter. 'The Jacqui Smith story is just the tip of the iceberg. It's extraordinary material. There are so many different angles to it – this will be the biggest story you ever work on.'

'Sounds great,' said Winnett, though inwardly he remained sceptical. Every reporter who has ever worked on a national newspaper has had at least one similar conversation at some point in their career with someone who claims to have 'the story of a lifetime'. But although Winnett wasn't yet in a position to know it, this would be the one time it turned out to be true.

There was, of course, a catch, and Winnett already knew what it was going to be. The source of the information, Gewanter explained, would need to be compensated for the risky position they had put themselves in. Winnett knew that the *Telegraph* was not in the habit of paying for stories, but he emphasized how keen the newspaper would be to do the story and stressed that it would certainly be happy to give due prominence to all of the political parties, as Gewanter had mentioned in his earlier phone calls.

Gewanter added one more thing – a 'small number' of other newspapers had already been approached, he said.

This was starting to get messy, thought Winnett. The *Sunday Express* had already published one story based on the material on the disk. How much more did the paper know? And if other newspapers had been offered the information, why hadn't they snapped it up? Was there something Gewanter wasn't telling him? The only thing to do was keep the ball in the air, in the hope that his questions would be cleared up at the meeting which Prince had already arranged for Wednesday, where Winnett would meet John Wick, the man who actually had the information.

Winnett left the wine bar excited about the potential of the information, but with lingering doubts about the *Telegraph*'s chances of securing it. After saying goodbye to Gewanter, he made his way to the House of Commons for a prearranged lunch with Oliver Letwin, the Conservatives' head of strategy. Here he discussed with Letwin how the Tories might sort out the public finances if they won the next general election, but really he couldn't wait to get back to the office to update Evans and Gallagher. Both men impressed upon Winnett once again just how important a story this could become for the *Telegraph*. He assured them he was doing his best.

The time had come to tell the editor what was going on. Lewis was intrigued, but hugely sceptical.

'It sounds very interesting,' he said. 'Keep me up to date.' Privately, he thought the chances of the story turning out to be true were almost nil.

In the midst of all the intrigue, Winnett had some pressing domestic matters to attend to: he had arranged to move house that week, from Docklands to Shoreditch. Moving from one furnished flat to another could be done in a series of taxi journeys, and after moving half of his possessions from one address to another after work that Monday, he was ready for an early night.

It wasn't to be. Having watched the ten o'clock news on TV, Winnett flicked over to BBC2 to watch its flagship current affairs programme, *Newsnight*, which often carried agenda-setting stories that would have to be followed up by political reporters the next day. To his utter horror, one of the main items it carried that night was a preview of an article which would appear in the next day's *Times*, one of the *Telegraph*'s biggest rivals, revealing that a 'businessman' was offering newspapers a computer disk containing the details of MPs' expenses. It said the asking price for the disk was £300,000.

Newsnight interviewed Sir Stuart Bell MP, a member of the House of Commons Commission, the body which oversaw the MPs' expenses system. Bell, clearly on the warpath, said the leak was 'a breach of trust' and dropped heavy hints that a police investigation would follow.

'It's probably a breach of the Official Secrets Act,' he said. 'It may be a theft, but we will get to the bottom of it. We have a pretty good idea of not the person, but the source, and that is the subject of a House of Commons investigation.'

The BBC was soon running the story as its main item on its radio and television news bulletins, where it dominated the news agenda throughout the next day. Winnett groaned inwardly as he saw the story slipping away from him. One thing guaranteed to frighten off any whistleblower was a blaze of publicity, and it seemed that before Winnett had even had a chance to get down to business by meeting John Wick, the whole project had been strangled at birth.

The only positive thing about Sir Stuart Bell's television appearance was that it appeared to confirm that the data on the disk were authentic. Had it been a hoax, Sir Stuart would not have been on television at all, because there would have been no story. But now every man and his dog knew of the existence of the disk, so even if Gewanter's source was still prepared to go ahead with a deal, other newspapers were likely to start a bidding war which could spiral out of control.

Well, thought Winnett, we'll just have to see how it all plays out. But he was already thinking about the nightmare scenario of seeing the contents of Gewanter's disk splashed all over the pages of a rival paper.

The story which ran in *The Times* on the Tuesday added little to what *Newsnight* had revealed – but was accompanied by a surprising admission in an article by *The Times*'s political editor, Philip Webster. He disclosed, for the first time, that *The Times* had been 'approached by a businessman who claimed that he was acting in the public interest by offering the details of the expenses claims of all MPs for the past four years. He then asked for £300,000 for his information. At that point we took the matter no further.' Without explaining exactly why *The Times* had decided to turn down the offer, Webster said newspapers 'have a duty to inform' and 'a duty to disclose' but also 'an absolute duty to protect the anonymity of our sources' – the message being that the newspaper would not be handing over the name of the businessman to the Commons authorities.

Weeks later, when the *Telegraph* eventually published the MPs' expenses stories, Peter Preston, a former editor of the *Guardian*, wrote in the *Observer* that Webster's op-ed piece might be regarded by other journalists as 'the most pious suicide note in history'. He wondered 'how any hugely experienced correspondent could get his duty to inform in such a twist'.

In fact, *The Times* would not be the only newspaper which would have to answer awkward questions in the weeks to come about why it had turned down the disk. For the time being, though, the *Times* piece appeared to have scuppered any chance of the uncensored details of MPs' expenses claims appearing – for, as Winnett had feared, Wick took fright when he saw the article.

Gewanter phoned Winnett on the Tuesday morning and told him the meeting planned for the next day would have to be postponed. 'Everything's a bit too hot at the moment,' he said. It was clear that his client had been taken aback by the piece in *The Times*. Although the newspaper had not named either Wick or Gewanter, the very fact that it had revealed that the confidential approach had taken place had dramatically escalated the hunt for the source of the information. Winnett felt Gewanter could hardly be blamed if he wasn't feeling too confident about placing his trust in newspapers right now.

Winnett phoned Evans to tell him the bad news, and the pair agreed that the only thing Winnett could do was to try to keep in touch with Gewanter in the coming weeks in the hope that he might change his mind.

Over the next fortnight, Gewanter sent a number of non-committal text messages, but as Easter approached Winnett left for a week-long holiday feeling that, barring a minor miracle, the scoop had slipped through his fingers.

The Deal

Tuesday, 21 April

'One day, son, all this
will be on expenses'

CHAPTER 6

WINNETT RETURNED to London from his Easter break on 19 April to find that the resignation of Damian McBride over the email smear scandal had become one of the biggest political stories of the year and a major problem for Gordon Brown. The budget was also looming that week, and the bounce in popularity that Brown had experienced after the G20 summit was by now a distant memory. But while every other lobby journalist was preoccupied with finding new angles on the McBride affair, Winnett's mind was elsewhere. He had received a handful of text messages from Gewanter during his holiday. He remained pessimistic about the chances of any deal being resurrected, but when he got home there was another text message from Gewanter, this time asking Winnett to call him. Against the odds, it turned out that Wick was now prepared to meet.

Gewanter suggested getting together in Tempio's wine bar, the same place he and Winnett had met up three weeks before, and on Tuesday, 21 April Winnett was finally introduced to Wick.

He was surprised by the man who was waiting for him

when he arrived. People who approach newspapers to 'blow the whistle' are sometimes rather odd characters. They are often extremely nervous, at the end of their tethers and prone to behaving irrationally. It is not unusual for them to overstate wildly the importance of the information they hold – and their role in the organization or company they represent or work for.

Wick was different. Dressed in his trademark pin-stripe suit, aged in his fifties, his grey hair neatly combed, Wick was the epitome of the traditional *Telegraph* reader. He had caught the train to London from Worthing on the south coast, along with thousands of other commuters. It soon became apparent that he was a supporter of the Conservative Party and had connections at the highest levels. Wick was the former treasurer of the United and Cecil Club, a long-established and rather grand dining club which raises money for the Tories. A member of the Shadow Cabinet is his daughter's godfather.

He also had a distinguished military history. He walked into the wine bar with a slight limp, a reminder of the military service he had seen in the Special Air Service, the Army's elite special forces regiment. Wick had been an officer in the SAS in the 1970s and had led one of the regiment's anti-terrorism teams. Had it not been for his injury, Wick would have been a key figure in the Iranian Embassy siege in 1980, when the SAS famously stormed the building in west London and rescued nineteen hostages who were being held by terrorists. After he left the SAS, Wick became a mercenary, and ended up for a period commanding a Middle Eastern ruler's special forces regiment. Much of his work continued to be funded by the British government at 'arm's length'. By the time he met Winnett, Wick was running a corporate risk management company which – along with other services – specialized in negotiating the release of hostages from some of the world's most dangerous areas. A spate of hostage-taking incidents by Somalian pirates in the Gulf of Aden meant business was brisk at his office in the City of London.

In the days and weeks to come, Winnett would have plenty of reasons to be grateful that he was dealing with someone with Wick's strength of character. It would stand Wick in good stead under the pressures that lay ahead.

Winnett and Wick began their meeting by discussing how David Cameron had overhauled the Conservative Party. They also discussed the *Telegraph*, which had itself been overhauled under Lewis's tenure, to the point where it had been able to build up a successful website and regularly break major news stories for the first time in a decade or more.

Then it was time to address the matter in hand. Wick confirmed that he had obtained a disk containing un-censored details of every MP's expenses claims. The disk had been compiled as part of the preparations for Parliament's release of a censored version of the information later in the year. It had not been stolen, he explained:

'I've spoken to lawyers and I am taking a risk but I believe it to be minimal,' he told Winnett. 'This disk is not stolen, it is simply a copy. I have thought long and hard about this and I firmly believe it is essential the public sees this information. But, if it comes to it, I have seen far worse than the inside of a police cell.'

His frankness and composure impressed Winnett.

Wick set out his terms for any deal with the *Telegraph*. First, despite being a Conservative supporter, he said he wanted the expenses claims of MPs from every party to be covered – this was a scandal encompassing the whole of Parliament. Second, he, along with various other people involved with the disk, would require protection against potential legal action. Finally, he had also advised the ultimate sources of the information that they might suffer financially as a result of the release of the information. Wick had therefore recommended that money be put aside for the sources in a safe location in case this occurred.

Winnett asked further questions about who would receive any money, mindful that the *Telegraph* did not want to be paying criminals. 'These are decent, honourable people who need some insurance in case everything goes very wrong,' Wick said. 'They did not ask for money; they want the information in the public domain. But I have advised them it would be madness not to have any sort of insurance. They are taking a very large risk.'

Wick said that two tabloid newspapers – the *Sun* and the *Sunday Express* – were also interested in the data. However, he said that they wished only to write about certain high-profile politicians – mostly members of the Cabinet – and hence no deal had yet been struck with them.

Wick was highly persuasive, and any lingering doubts

Winnett had about the authenticity of the material were fading quickly.

'We're definitely interested,' he said, adding that he was certain the source's concerns about how the data were presented could be met by the newspaper. But he warned Wick that if the financial elements of the deal were of primary importance, the *Telegraph* would be extremely unlikely to be willing to match the budgets of tabloid newspapers. Winnett told Wick that he and the sources needed to be realistic about what they required as the economy was deep in recession and newspapers were in deeper than most.

Wick said that he fully understood and that he would like the *Telegraph* to have the story if the right deal could be struck.

Then came a surprise: Wick put a leather attaché case on the table, rolled his thumbs over the combination locks, sprang the catches, and took out a CD in an envelope. This, he explained, contained a 'sample' of a handful of MPs' expenses claims to enable Winnett to check the authenticity of the material. The MPs included Jacqui Smith; James Purnell, the work and pensions secretary; and George Osborne, the Shadow Chancellor. He then told Winnett that the *Telegraph* had twenty-four hours to decide whether it wanted to do a deal.

'I'll come back to you,' Winnett promised, though he felt such a tight deadline was optimistic, given the magnitude of what he was dealing with.

Back in the office, Winnett immediately loaded the disk on to his computer. He was struck by the astonishing level of detail contained in the files. Each MP's expenses were broken down into four years: 2004/5, 2005/6, 2006/7 and 2007/8. For each year, there was one file for each MP's claims under the ACA and one file for their office expenses, officially known as the incidental expenses provision (IEP). Because the data were stored in PDF files – in other words, electronic facsimiles of the original documents – Winnett had at his fingertips every single piece of paper submitted by each MP in their expenses claims, from the claim forms they had filled in by hand to individual bills and invoices, right down to itemized supermarket receipts for grocery shopping.

Every time an MP submitted an expenses claim, they were required to fill in a two-page form divided into ten categories: hotel stays; mortgage or rent; food; utilities; council tax or rates; telephone and communications; cleaning; service/maintenance; repairs/insurance/ security; and 'other'. On the second page Members were required to state the address of the second home on which they were making claims, as well as signing and dating a declaration which stated: 'I confirm that I incurred these costs wholly, exclusively and necessarily to enable me to stay overnight away from my only or main home for the purpose of performing my duties as a Member of Parliament.' But even the most cursory glance through the documents showed that MPs had stretched to breaking point – and often beyond – the interpretation of what could be regarded as an expense 'wholly, exclusively and necessarily' incurred to enable them to carry out their duties. Spread out in front of Winnett was a bewildering array of different items which the MPs had been able to buy courtesy of the British taxpayer, usually submitted under the cover-all category of 'other'.

Although some categories of expense claim were already common knowledge, such as mortgage interest, council tax, utility bills and food, the receipts included with the claims showed the full extent to which MPs were able to furnish their homes and subsidize their lifestyles on expenses. As well as Jacqui Smith's infamous claim for pornographic films – which showed up on the very last page of her most recent year's claims – and her claims for a new kitchen, complete with 88p plug, here were claims by James Purnell for items including cutlery (£88), mirrors (£220), a rug (£92.99) and a bouquet of flowers (£34.50). In Smith's case, incidentally, the taxpayer had also footed the bill for someone in her house to watch *Ocean's 13* twice (at £3.75 per viewing) and *Surf's Up* (£3.50).

Winnett was certain the public would be up in arms when they discovered the sort of fripperies their money was being spent on, but this was only one part of the story. Also contained in the files were letters between MPs and the parliamentary office which scrutinized MPs' expenses claims – the Department of Finance and Administration. Winnett thought it sounded like something out of the TV series *Yes, Minister*, but this turned out to be the official name of what was commonly known as the parliamentary fees office. These letters revealed that a degree of cooperation was taking place between the MPs and the authorities, with expenses claims continuing to be met even if there was no immediate evidence or proof of money actually having been spent. All of the letters had a thick pink cross over them, with the word 'deleted' printed across the middle in large red letters. It meant that the public was never intended to see this highly enlightening correspondence, making a mockery of the forthcoming release of the data under the Freedom of Information Act.

Winnett was also able to see which pieces of information on the claim forms and receipts were going to be censored. Grey tinted boxes covered any words or numbers which the parliamentary authorities intended to remove, subject to the approval of the MPs themselves, who would have the final say on what stayed in and what was taken out. Once the MPs gave the go-ahead, these grey boxes would be changed to impermeable black, shielding from prying public eyes anything which was, supposedly, entirely personal, such as bank account numbers, or would pose a security risk if made public. But Winnett suspected – rightly, as it turned out – that this censorship would also be used to cover up anything that might embarrass MPs. Crucially, the grey boxes covered the MPs' addresses, which Winnett knew would be the key to unveiling a whole host of potential scams.

One other thing which immediately struck Winnett was the sheer volume of material. For just these four MPs, there were 6,933 pages of documents. A quick mental calculation gave an average of around 1,700 pages per MP, which would equate to a million pages for the 646 Members of Parliament. Winnett blew out his cheeks and began to wonder whether it would be humanly possible for a team of reporters to go through such a vast amount of data in the limited amount of time which would be available if the project went ahead.

We'll just have to cross that bridge when we come to it, he thought to himself.

Apart from the obvious stories contained in the documents themselves, Winnett knew from the stories on Jacqui Smith and Tony McNulty that if there were bigger scandals behind the expenses claims it would require a fair amount of digging to find them, by checking the claims against public records. The trouble was that Winnett still had his day job to attend to, and with the 2009 budget statement to come the following day, it wasn't exactly a quiet week in Parliament. It was time to ask for help, and Winnett knew just whom to call on.

With impeccable timing, Holly Watt, Winnett's former comrade in arms at the *Sunday Times*, had joined the *Daily Telegraph* just two days earlier, on 20 April. The pair had worked together on the Derek Conway expenses story two years previously, earning a shortlisting for scoop of the year at the 2008 British Press Awards, and the extensive knowledge of the MPs' expenses system that both reporters had gained from that investigation meant that Watt would be the ideal person to help Winnett by going through the files looking for clues that might reveal hidden scandals.

Watt, a Cambridge graduate, had originally set out to become a solicitor, but after spending a year studying for a postgraduate law degree, decided she had made a disastrous choice. Sensing that she might be better suited to journalism, she began sneaking into the office of the *Sunday Times*'s 'Style' section, using a friend's pass to get through the formidable security at News International's Wapping headquarters, and worked there for nothing to gain valuable work experience. Incredible as it may seem, no one ever bothered to ask what she was doing there or how she had got in.

Once her face had become familiar, Watt decided to chance her arm in the newsroom, where the forensic eye for detail she had picked up at law school, coupled with her naturally dogged character, made her a natural for working on investigations. Her *Sunday Times* career almost ended before it began, however, when a manager discovered she had been blagging her way in, rather than applying for work through official channels, and she was banned for more than a month before a deputation of reporters persuaded their superiors to bring her back and give her a contract.

Four years later, having been poached by the *Daily Telegraph*, and before she had even had time to go through any kind of induction training, she found herself immersed in the early stages of the biggest and most complex investigation in the newspaper's history.

Watt suspected that James Purnell had almost certainly avoided paying capital gains tax when he sold his London flat. The Cabinet minister had billed the taxpayer for £395 worth of advice from an accountant which included 'tax advice regarding sale of flat'. Watt's checks of records held at the Land Registry showed that Purnell had bought the

London flat in 2000, then sold it in 2004, after four years encompassing some of the steepest annual price rises of the property boom. She strongly suspected that Purnell's 'tax advice' had enabled him to pay no capital gains tax on the sale. Even though what he had done was perfectly legal, it was clear that the public might not be so forgiving as the taxman.

Winnett reported the findings to Evans and gave him a quick test drive of the disk.

'Wow,' Evans said as he looked through Jacqui Smith's itemized bills for her kitchen. 'The detail on this is amazing. If they're all like this the potential is going to be massive.'

Evans and Winnett were now as sure as they possibly could be that the data were genuine, and Evans urged his colleague to arrange another meeting with Wick as soon as he could.

They also gave editor William Lewis a progress report. Lewis was excited about the potential of the material, but he was careful to maintain a poker face as he listened intently. He didn't want Winnett and Evans to get carried away before the authenticity of the disk had been definitively established, and felt it was important not to give the impression that he had already made up his mind. He still harboured fears that it could all turn out to be a hoax and couldn't shake off the feeling that it all seemed too good to be true.

'Why did other papers turn it down?' he asked. There was no obvious answer. But Lewis knew that if there was a chance the material was genuine, the *Telegraph* had to have it.

'Just get it in, let's have a look at it,' he said. After all, looking at something didn't mean you had to publish it.

By now it was Thursday. Winnett had managed to stretch Wick's original 24-hour deadline, saying they needed more time, but was anxious to wrap up an agreement by the end of the week. He called Gewanter, but what the PR man told him was enough to make his blood run cold.

'We can't see you until next week,' said Gewanter. 'The thing is, we've also been talking to the *Sun*, and we've given them until the end of Friday to decide whether they want to go ahead with a deal.'

It was the worst possible news. Just when Winnett had finally allowed himself to believe that he might be about to pull off the scoop of his career with a story of consuming public interest, he was being told that he was second in the queue behind a newspaper which was not only a stablemate of his old employer the *Sunday Times*, but could also draw on Rupert Murdoch's vast financial resources if it chose to. Winnett felt his mouth starting to dry out as he tried desperately to think of a way to persuade Gewanter not to do a deal with the *Sun*. He repeated his previous assurances about the *Telegraph* covering the story in a thorough, responsible and impartial way, and questioned whether the *Sun* would be as committed to the idea of covering every single MP. Ultimately, though, there was nothing to do but wait.

Winnett broke the news to Evans, Gallagher and Lewis, who took the latest twist in their stride. Gewanter had made it clear from the outset that the *Telegraph* was not the first newspaper he had approached, and the *Sunday Express* stories were proof of that. It was no great surprise that another paper was still in the game.

On the other side of London, senior executives at the *Sun* were involved in intense discussions over whether to publish the MPs' expenses disk. As Winnett suspected, the *Sun* wanted to cherry-pick the expenses claims of the most high-profile MPs, and leave the vast majority untouched. Wick was holding firm: it had to be all or nothing.

By Friday night, no deal had been reached with the *Sun* – though Winnett didn't know it at the time. He spent an anxious weekend covering the Conservative Party's spring conference in Cheltenham, rubbing shoulders with reporters from rival newspapers, most of whom were blissfully unaware of what was going on behind their backs. On Sunday he had lunch with a friend from the *Sun*'s political team, privately wondering whether it would be he whose name would be all over the 'scoop of the decade' while Winnett was left to reflect on what might have been.

In fact, the Tory spring conference was the last political story Winnett would cover before MPs' expenses took over the next four months of his life.

Before setting off for Cheltenham, Winnett had arranged with Gewanter that if the deal with the *Sun* had not been signed, they would meet at the *Telegraph*'s head office in Victoria at nine thirty on the following Monday morning, 27 April. As Winnett made his way to the office that morning, there was no guarantee that anyone was going to show up. There had been no word from Gewanter over the weekend, and he knew from previous experience that no news often means bad news. But at ten past nine, as he emerged from the revolving doors at the entrance to the office, Winnett discovered Gewanter already waiting for him in reception.

'Hey, Robert,' Gewanter said cheerily as he held out his hand. 'John's just on his way.'

Leaving Gewanter in the reception area to wait for Wick, Winnett hurried up the lengthy escalator which leads to the editorial department and found Evans at his desk. After making sure they both knew exactly what the *Telegraph* could and could not offer, they invited Wick and Gewanter upstairs and took them to an office normally used by the *Sunday Telegraph*, whose staff have Mondays off.

Gewanter explained that although he had not entirely closed the door on the *Sun*, he and Wick were ready to discuss a deal.

Evans stressed the unique position that the *Telegraph* was in as the only remaining daily broadsheet newspaper. Not only would the newspaper's broadsheet format lend itself to coverage which might run into dozens of individual stories per day, but the *Telegraph* also had a huge internet operation which was tailor-made for publishing large amounts of data.

'I can promise you the *Sun* will mess you around,' he added. 'They'll say they're interested but then they'll come back to you and say they only want to do a few MPs. If you go with us, we'll do all of them.'

Wick gave the impression that he would prefer to see the

investigation in the *Telegraph* than in a tabloid, feeling that the gravitas of the *Daily Telegraph* would underscore the seriousness of the material concerned.

Later that morning, Evans and Winnett reported to Lewis with news of their meeting. The editor wanted to know if Wick had been able to reveal anything about what else was on the master disk, in terms of possible stories about other MPs.

'He doesn't know for sure,' said Winnett. 'No one knows, because no one's looked through the whole disk, but we need to get the disk first and worry about that later.'

Lewis's response was simple: 'Go for it.'

By lunchtime on Tuesday, after details of the deal had been thrashed out with senior executives, including Gallagher, Winnett was ready to put the *Telegraph*'s proposed offer to Wick and Gewanter.

The paper would offer the pair £10,000, to cover their time and expenses, for an exclusive opportunity to study the full contents of the disk for ten days. If the *Telegraph* decided to push ahead with publication, it would pay a further £100,000, to be disbursed in three tranches.

'I think we've got a deal,' said Gewanter when the offer was put to him. Wick had been insistent all along that money was not the reason the information had been leaked by the ultimate source, and in the weeks to come he was as good as his word: he would later turn down sums of up to £500,000 from other newspapers desperate for the information.

Winnett sank into his chair, scarcely able to believe that

after so many twists and turns the *Telegraph* was finally going to take delivery of the sacred disk.

With fine details still to be ironed out, Arthur Wynn Davies worked through the night on Tuesday drawing up a contract, including the necessary legal indemnity for Wick. A copy of the contract was emailed to Wick on Wednesday, 29 April.

At 5 p.m. that day Wick was back in the *Telegraph* office. After signing a contract guaranteeing the exclusivity of the material, Wick took a brown envelope out of his briefcase, opened the flap, tilted it on to the desk and . . . nothing.

After a slightly awkward pause, he shook the envelope, while Winnett helpfully suggested to Wick that he could simply put his hand inside and pull out the contents.

'I'm not touching it,' replied Wick, as he shook the envelope more vigorously.

Finally a small red disk drive, no bigger than a cigarette case, slipped out on to the desk. The hard work was about to begin.

The Plan

Wednesday, 29 April

'If you put a copy of the
Telegraph in the window it keeps
the politicians away'

CHAPTER 7

ALTHOUGH IT WAS towards the end of normal office hours by the time Wick handed over the prized disk, the clock was already ticking.

One of the conditions of the deal that Wick had insisted upon was that the *Telegraph* had just ten days to analyse the data and begin publishing it. If the newspaper did not go ahead with publication by the tenth day, the deal would lapse and Wick would have the right to approach other media organizations.

Evans and Winnett knew that the scale of the task ahead was nothing short of Herculean. The million or so pages of documents contained on the disk had to be read individually (they could not be automatically searched by any computer program because much of the information was hand-written) and there was, of course, no guide book to point out where the stories could be found.

While the public would no doubt want to know what the most high-profile politicians had been up to, it was just as likely that the biggest scandals might involve anonymous backbench MPs. So every single document would have to be read, analysed, checked against public records (such as Land

Registry property deeds or electoral rolls) and cross-referenced with other MPs to check whether, for example, several MPs were illegally claiming rent for the same address.

In normal circumstances, a newspaper that wanted to investigate possible expenses fraud by an MP might expect a reporter to take several weeks to gather the necessary evidence. The *Telegraph* faced the prospect of carrying out more than sixty such investigations each day if it was going to check every MP's expenses file before the publication date.

And the problems didn't end there. There remained a very real threat that the *Telegraph's* offices could be raided by the police, and the disk seized, if the parliamentary authorities got wind of what was going on. Despite Arthur Wynn Davies's confidence that the newspaper had not broken any laws, and that the disk did not constitute stolen property, it was an argument that might have to be settled in a court of law if Parliament chose to dispute it, with the disk as Exhibit A.

To make matters even more complicated, two other newspapers – the *Sunday Express* and the *Sun* – had also seen part of the database. If word leaked out that the *Telegraph* had secured the rights to the disk, it was a near-certainty that one or both of the newspapers would print 'spoiler' stories about MPs whose files they had looked at, beating the *Telegraph* to the punch.

Two things were clear: the *Daily Telegraph* would have to put together a team of reporters capable of pulling off what might be the most ambitious newspaper investigation in history; and they would have to work in total secrecy to ensure no other newspapers – or the police – knew what was going on.

A newspaper office is never the best place to try to keep a secret, given that its staff spend their entire working lives ferreting out gossip, and journalism is such an incestuous industry that even the most closely guarded secrets become common knowledge across London in a matter of minutes if more than a handful of people know what's going on. So Evans and Winnett, sitting down that evening to discuss how to prevent news of the investigation leaking from the building, decided on a brilliantly simple strategy: they would lie through their teeth. Apart from the handful of people directly involved in the investigation, everyone else who had cause to ask what the team was up to would be sold a cover story. As long as everyone on the team stuck to the script, it just might work.

Clearly the investigation team would need to work in a separate room, away from prying eyes, and after a couple of quick phone calls Evans secured the use of a room in a back corridor which was normally used for staff training. It was called, appropriately enough, Training Room 4.

'If we're going to be using a training room we might as well tell everyone we're involved in a training exercise,' Evans suggested. Winnett agreed, though both realized luck would play a big part in keeping such a huge project under wraps.

The idea that several reporters might suddenly be pulled away from their normal duties to take part in a training exercise was by no means implausible. The *Telegraph* was introducing a series of radical changes to the way reporters were required to work, not least a move towards self-publishing on the internet, meaning a reporter would write a story and publish it online with little input from anyone else. Reporters were in the process of being shown how to do this, and so any awkward questions about why a team of reporters had been asked to drop everything for a training exercise could be fobbed off with excuses about 'orders from on high'.

The next job was to choose a team of reporters who could get the job done.

Holly Watt was an obvious choice, having already begun looking at the sample disk. She was acutely aware that the *Telegraph* could be sitting on Britain's equivalent of Watergate, having recently spent a four-month sabbatical working at the *Washington Post*, the newspaper that carried out the political investigation against which all others are measured.

Winnett felt the team needed another parliamentary reporter to help steer the investigation through the political minefield ahead, and Rosa Prince, who had taken the crucial first phone call from Gewanter and who could be relied upon to pursue a story with ruthless vigour, was next on the team sheet.

Christopher Hope, the Whitehall editor, would also be brought on board. A veteran of political sleaze stories, he had recently helped expose the existence of the emails that led to the resignation of Damian McBride. Having worked on the *Telegraph* for six years, Hope was also the longest-serving *Telegraph* reporter on the team. In the long days which lay ahead, it would be his boyish enthusiasm that would often help keep spirits up as energy levels flagged.

Gordon Rayner, the *Daily Telegraph*'s chief reporter, had already been told about the newspaper's pursuit of the disk by Evans, who was keen to make sure he was not about to take any annual leave. A veteran of the *Sun* and the *Daily Mail*, Rayner had often been called upon to organize teams of reporters covering different elements of major news stories, and would be ideally suited to helping oversee the expenses investigation in what would be a high-pressure environment. At thirty-eight, he was the oldest of the reporters chosen to work on the story.

The youngest would be Jon Swaine, a 24-year-old former *Telegraph* graduate trainee regarded as a rising star at the paper because of his thoroughness and professionalism. This was his opportunity to prove that he could cut it at the highest level of journalism – an opportunity he would grab with both hands in the weeks to come.

The final member of the reporting team would be Martin Beckford, the newspaper's social and religious affairs correspondent. He had repeatedly proved his ability to dig out front-page stories buried inside weighty official documents, making him a natural choice for the work to come. Beckford would have some of the most memorable exchanges with MPs.

Once the seven-strong reporting team had been decided upon, Evans and Matthew Bayley began telling those reporters who did not know about the disk that they would be required for an important, and urgent, training session the next day at 8 a.m. Bayley struggled to keep a straight face as the reporters tried to hide their annoyance at having to disrupt their plans – and come in early – for yet more training. He couldn't wait to break the real news to them.

Christopher Hope was dashing for a 7 p.m. train home to Norfolk when he received an email on his BlackBerry asking him to call Bayley. As he boarded the carriage, he rang the news editor, who said: 'Sorry for the short notice, but could you get in early tomorrow morning for a training session?'

'How early?'

'Eight o'clock.'

Bugger, thought Hope. It would mean getting up at five thirty to catch an early enough train to be back in London on time.

'OK,' he replied, cursing his luck. Bloody training sessions!

Jon Swaine, who had been working an early shift that day, was at the Barbican Theatre being thoroughly confused by a play which, he discovered when the performance began, was in French. He picked up the email message from Bayley during the interval, replied that he would be there, and thought no more of it.

Beckford, meanwhile, unwittingly almost talked his way out of being involved in the biggest story of his career.

'What are you up to tomorrow?' Evans asked him.

'I'm going to Oxford University for a conference on the social impact of couples who have kids without getting married,' Beckford replied. He had been looking forward to a pleasant day out of town and a leisurely lunch at St Hugh's College.

'Well, I'd like you to come into the office instead, for a training session on self-publishing. You'll need to be here at eight. Can you do it?'

'That's going to be difficult, because it'll mean getting up at five,' said Beckford, exaggerating slightly. 'Does it have to be that early?'

'Well, yes. Can you make it?'

'OK.'

As Evans walked off, Beckford turned to a colleague and moaned: 'I'm going to miss out on a great story tomorrow because I've got to come in for a bloody training session at eight. I don't see why it's got to be so early. It's ridiculous.'

Meanwhile, other arrangements had to be made to ensure the smooth running of the paper in the absence of so many reporters. In Parliament, Andrew Porter, the *Telegraph*'s political editor, and James Kirkup, its political correspondent, both already in on the secret, were asked to hold the fort and deflect any questions from other lobby correspondents as to the whereabouts of Winnett and Prince. Porter was also earmarked as one of the front men of the investigation, and would later represent the *Telegraph* in countless television and radio interviews while the rest of the team carried on digging behind closed doors.

Evans and Winnett also had to find a way of copying the disk so that each member of the team would have their own copy when the investigation began the following day.

'Do you have any idea how to copy one of these things?' Evans asked.

'Er, no – do you?'

The pair trotted up to the second floor of the building, looking for the head of the IT department. He was on holiday, it turned out, so Evans asked for his deputy, Toby Wright.

'I'm going to tell you something you mustn't repeat to anyone in any circumstances,' Evans told the mystified Wright. 'Have you heard the story doing the rounds about a disk being offered to newspapers which contains all the details of MPs' expenses?'

'Oh yeah,' he replied.

'Well, this is it.'

Evans and Winnett, who had not yet loaded up the disk, feared that it might be encrypted or password-protected in some way. To their immense relief, when Wright connected it to his computer, they saw that a couple of mouse clicks was all it took to start delving into the MPs' claims.

Evans then explained to a startled-looking Wright that the disk needed to be copied before first thing the next day.

'But I've got to leave in five minutes to pick my kids up,' said Wright.

Evans smiled. 'You might have to make other arrangements.'

Wright agreed to stay late, making two copies of the disk before showing Winnett and Holly Watt how to make more copies, each of which took an hour to complete because of the sheer volume of material.

In the meantime, Evans had to recruit two final members of the team.

Lewis had already decided that the expenses story would

be perfect for the newspaper not only in print but also online; indeed, it was viewed at that stage as being more ideally suited to the website than the print version, as the receipts of every MP could be published online to enable members of the public to search for their local MP's expenses. To this end Ian Douglas, the newspaper's digital production editor, and Duncan Hooper, digital news editor, were attached to the investigation with the task of preparing the expenses claims for online publication in their entirety. They would begin by putting the expenses of every member of the Cabinet online on the day the first newspaper stories were published, with every MP's expenses to be published ten days to two weeks after that.

Or at least, that was the plan . . .

The Bunker

Thursday, 30 April

'Vote for me . . . I think I
have a house somewhere
round here'

CHAPTER 8

As the slightly dishevelled-looking reporters filed into the cheerless, windowless surroundings of Training Room 4 at 8 a.m. the next day, some were already a bit suspicious. National newspaper journalists traditionally start work at 10 a.m., a throwback to the days before 24-hour news channels and the internet, and a much-coveted perk of the job. But as the room filled up, Evans and Bayley chatted normally with the reporters about the stories they had written for that day's paper, ranging from Beckford's coverage of the latest twist in the horrific Baby P child abuse story to Swaine's piece about the furore caused when the winner of a Cornish pasty baking competition had turned out to be from Devon.

Not only did several of the reporters have no idea what they were going to be doing, they were also in the dark about who they would be doing it with, and as each new face entered the room they were met with a light-hearted cheer from their colleagues, like school playground footballers just picked to play on the same side.

Christopher Hope was last in, having had the longest journey to work after his punishingly early start in Norfolk.

Evans asked him to close the room's heavy glass door before sitting on a desk in the centre of the room as his team wheeled their office chairs into an untidy semicircle, notebooks at the ready.

'Thank you all for coming in so early,' he said, giving a toothy grin and self-consciously pushing his glasses up on his nose. 'As I'm sure you've all guessed, you're not here for a training session. You'll all have read stories in recent weeks about a disk with the details of MPs' expenses claims on it. Well, we've got it.'

'I bloody knew it was going to be something like this!' interjected Hope, simultaneously breaking the tension and signalling the instant switch from anticipation to excitement.

'I'm sorry we had to keep you in the dark,' continued Evans, 'but there are only a handful of people outside this room who know about this, and it has to stay that way. As far as everyone else is concerned, we're involved in a training session. I'm afraid you'll have to lie to your colleagues, though I'm sure you can all manage that, but as long as we all stick to the same cover story we should be OK.'

Several of the reporters exchanged doubtful glances at the idea that other journalists on the paper would swallow the story that any kind of training session could require so many senior members of the staff at such short notice, but in the absence of any better ideas it would have to do.

Evans explained that the disk had been the source of the Jacqui Smith and Tony McNulty stories, but that no other paper had been given access to the entire database.

'There are something like a million and a half documents which we're going to have to look at,' he went on, 'and we have to decide by this time next week whether we're going to run with this, so we're going to have to work through the weekend and do a lot of late nights. But if we do decide to go with it, the potential is absolutely enormous.'

As he spoke, the reporters were all doing the mental arithmetic. One and a half million documents, ten people. One hundred and fifty thousand documents each. In a week. How on earth was that going to be even vaguely possible?

Anticipating the obvious questions, Evans said: 'We'll have to divide it up, find a system we can work to and get through as much of this as we can. There's bound to be stuff we'll miss, but don't worry about that because from the limited amount of stuff Rob's looked at so far, there are going to be plenty of brilliant stories in there.'

Each reporter was then handed their own copy of the disk containing the full expenses files. All the work was to be handled on standalone laptop computers so that none of the sensitive information was put on to the *Telegraph*'s main systems until absolutely necessary, to reduce the chance of any leak.

Training Room 4 was not exactly set up for the needs of a reporting team working on a complex investigation. The bland office, 30 feet square, had sets of tables arranged in five clusters in the configuration of a number five on a die. Although each table had its own computer, there were few phones, only one printer and no fax machine. The only other furniture in the room consisted of a small wardrobe, a

four-drawer metal filing cabinet and a flipchart. It did, however, have one crucial advantage: with two walls made of
frosted glass and two walls lined with white-painted metal, it
offered the team total privacy. Tucked away in a corner of the
office, it was out of sight of most people in the building: few
people even walked past it. In the days to come, Training
Room 4 would become known to all who worked in it as 'the
bunker' – a somewhat obvious and inevitable nickname, but
none the less appropriate given the bunker mentality which
developed within it.

The investigation also quickly acquired a nickname. The
portable hard drives on to which the files had been copied
had the trade name Firestorm, a word which came up on
screen every time the disks were loaded.

'It's Operation Firestorm then,' Winnett said sardonic-
ally to no one in particular as he cranked up his computer.
The name stuck, and although it wasn't repeated outside the
room, it subsequently took on a certain resonance, with several politicians and even the Information Commissioner
later referring to the expenses scandal as a 'firestorm'.

Before the disks were loaded, the team decided on a way
of carving up the information between them. Winnett and
Prince would start looking through the Cabinet's expenses,
Rayner and Hope would do the Shadow Cabinet, and
Beckford, Swaine and Hooper were to start looking at the
Liberal Democrats and then backbenchers, one starting
at A, one starting at M and one working backwards
from Z. As each MP's file was examined, the reporter in
question would tick off the name on a master list, adding

their own initials, to keep track of who had done which MP.

Watt was given the task of compiling a spreadsheet of every address for which the MPs had claimed the second-home allowance, so that any anomalies, such as several MPs claiming for the same address, would show up. It was a thankless task, but Watt had the benefit of being the only reporter to glance through every MP's expenses, meaning she was able to comb out the most promising stories and keep a list of which MPs should be prioritized.

Ian Douglas, meanwhile, concentrated on preparing the Cabinet's expenses documents for publication online, working out a system of blacking out genuinely sensitive personal information, such as bank account numbers, while leaving in much of the other data which Parliament wanted to censor.

The atmosphere crackled with anticipation as the reporters got their first sight of what was on the disks, and within a matter of minutes the room was buzzing as members of the team began making discoveries. Despite knowing that they were looking for potential abuses of the expenses system, they still reacted with disbelief at what the MPs had been spending public money on, from the outlandish to the downright trivial.

'This guy's bought a plasma television,' called out Swaine.

'Alan Duncan's claimed hundreds of pounds for having his ride-on lawnmower serviced,' chuckled Hope.

'Oliver Letwin's put in a bill for a pipe to be replaced under his tennis court,' said Rayner.

Each passing minute was punctuated by expressions of

disbelief as reporters found ever more astonishing claims.

'Oh my God . . .'

'You're not going to believe what this guy's claimed for . . .'

'I've got a better one than that . . .'

Within two hours the team had made its first major breakthrough, and it involved none other than the Prime Minister himself.

Rosa Prince had assumed that the job of going through the Cabinet's expenses would be boring and fruitless. Surely ministers in such prominent public roles would be scrupulous in ensuring that every claim for even a penny was above board and beyond reproach, she thought.

Not a bit of it. As she scrolled through Gordon Brown's expenses claims, the rest of the room heard an involuntary gasp as she noticed that the Prime Minister had paid thousands of pounds for cleaning services to a certain Andrew Brown. Prince knew that Brown had a brother called Andrew, who ran the communications department of the French energy firm EDF. Was the PM arranging for public money to be paid to his own brother? For cleaning his flat?

'Looks like Gordon Brown's paying a load of money to his brother,' said Prince, looking across at Winnett.

'What!?'

The rest of the team crowded around Prince's computer to see the evidence for themselves. Could it be a coincidence? they asked each other. Brown was one of the five most common surnames in the country, after all. Maybe it was another Andrew Brown who just happened to have a cleaning company. Even if it was his brother, why would the Prime Minister be paying him for cleaning services? It all looked very odd.

Within a matter of minutes the team had established, by checking publicly available online electoral rolls and Companies House records, that the Andrew Brown whose name and address appeared on the receipts was indeed the Prime Minister's brother. Clearly the Prime Minister had some explaining to do.

As Prince continued her search, Brown's expenses claims threw up other potentially damaging material. The Prime Minister had originally designated as his second home a flat in London where he lived with his wife Sarah. But in September 2006, within a fortnight of discovering that Tony Blair would be stepping down as Prime Minister (and hence that he would be moving into Downing Street as his successor), Brown had switched the designation of his second home to his constituency in Scotland. The implication seemed clear: that Brown had changed his designated second home so that he could carry on claiming thousands of pounds from the taxpayer even after he moved into a grace and favour flat in Downing Street.

There was plenty more besides. Brown had submitted two claims for the same £153 plumber's bill, and had been paid twice. At the very least, it amounted to a deeply embarrassing oversight for the then Chancellor of the Exchequer. The canny Scot had also had an Ikea kitchen installed at a cost of £9,000, spreading the payments over two financial years, which meant that he stayed within the limit for each year's total claim. There had also been a dispute with the fees office over a £105 children's window blind. Officials, on first seeing a receipt which said simply 'Noah's animals', had apparently assumed it was for a toy, and rejected it. Sarah Brown had written to the fees office on paper headed 'Gordon and Sarah Brown' saying: 'The Peter Jones receipt for window blinds for London accommodation needs to be reimbursed.' The fees office promptly paid up.

The Prime Minister, a self-professed sports fan, had even put in £36 monthly claims for the cost of his Sky TV package. How would the public feel about stumping up for Gordon Brown to watch live football on telly? Would voters be happy when they found out they had bought a £265 vacuum cleaner for the then Chancellor, who was at the time paid £144,520 a year? Or that they had paid for Rentokil to get rid of mice at his Fife home, at a cost of £352? The list went on and on.

No one on the investigation team had expected to find many major stories in the Cabinet's expenses, but it turned out that almost every member of the Cabinet appeared to have played the system in one way or another.

Prince looked through Chancellor Alistair Darling's claims and found that he too had switched the designation of his second home between London and his Edinburgh constituency, enabling him to claim £2,500 in stamp duty and legal fees when he bought a flat in London, and more than £4,000 to furnish and carpet it. Winnett discovered that Hazel Blears, the communities secretary, had claimed for three different properties in the space of a year, and during one house move had stayed at a £211 per night hotel whose publicity material stated that 'Heaven will be a let-down after this.' Margaret Beckett, the housing and planning minister, tried to claim £600 for hanging baskets and pot plants, while David Miliband, the foreign secretary, had spent so much money on his house and garden in his South Shields constituency that his own gardener had queried whether all the work was really necessary.

By mid-afternoon on that first day it was clear that the *Telegraph* would have a wealth of stories on the Cabinet alone, never mind the other 620 or so MPs who might have been up to no good.

It had also become obvious that as well as being outraged by the apparent abuses which the team was uncovering, the public would also be fascinated by many of the smaller claims. The Conservative MP Cheryl Gillan, for example, had submitted a supermarket receipt which included £4.47 for two tins of Cesar luxury dog food and a packet of Iams Senior chicken dry meal. Much to the amusement of the bunker team, Phil Woolas, the immigration minister, had claimed back the cost of nappies (£2.99), tampons (£1.19), panty liners (£1.48) and a ladies' blouse (£15). The expenses claims provided a fascinating window on MPs' lives, and the reporters found there was an irresistible vicarious pleasure in picturing powerful ministers musing over which brand of chocolate biscuits to buy (Jaffa Cakes proved to be a favourite) or knowing what flavour crisps certain members of the Cabinet preferred.

It quickly became apparent that the MPs' expenses would also feed the British public's insatiable appetite for toilet humour. The fact that Gordon Brown had claimed back the cost of having his loo unblocked provoked bellows of laughter in the bunker's classroom atmosphere (as well as speculation about who was the culprit), while the fact that the heavyweight former Deputy Prime Minister, John Prescott, had claimed for two loo seats in quick succession would provide a rich vein of *Carry On*-style gags for cartoonists and headline writers when it was revealed to the world. (After several weeks of deliberation, Prescott would eventually announce that he had not broken any loo seats, but had found that the first one didn't fit his loo because he had bought an imperial size instead of metric.) However, even Prescott was overshadowed by Tory MP Peter Luff, who managed to claim for three toilet seats in four years.

There was also a pattern emerging of several different scams which many MPs used to play the system. Winnett and Rayner compiled a list of the most popular, so that reporters could jot down examples of each one as they came across them.

'Loads of them seem to be flipping their second home designation between one place and another so they can do up more than one house,' observed Hope.

Rayner jotted down the word 'flipping' at the top of the list, little knowing at the time that it would soon pass into the national lexicon as a virtual dictionary definition of MPs' dodgy behaviour.

After a few minutes' discussion, the list looked like this:

1 Flipping. MP nominates one property as second home, charges the taxpayer for refurbishment, then flips designation to another property so they can do up that one too.
2 Property ladder. MP renovates property at taxpayers' expense, sells it for a profit, buys another property, does it up, sells it, etc.
3 Council tax. MP claims back full rate of council tax on second home, paid by taxpayer, then claims discounted rate on their other house by telling council this is really their second home.
4 March madness. Members who have not claimed the maximum permissible amount in a financial year go on last-minute spending spree in March to 'use up' the rest of the money available to them before April deadline.
5 Last-minute repairs. Splashing out thousands on renovations just before stepping down from Parliament so they can maximize profits when they sell a house they no longer need.
6 Capital gains tax avoidance. MP tells the taxman their second home is their 'main' home at the time they sell it, so they can avoid paying tax on the profit from the sale.
7 Claiming for 'wrong' address ('doing a Jacqui Smith'). MP nominates their family home as their 'second' home, so taxpayer foots large bills there, while claiming a cheap bedsit, paid for by themselves, is their 'main' home.
8 Long-distance shoppers. MP buys large household goods, then has them delivered to main home, while telling fees office they have bought them for their second home.

9 Maxing out. MP claims £249 for anything they don't have receipts for, meaning they don't have to prove they ever spent the money, as no receipts needed for claims under £250.

10 Binge eaters. MP claims maximum £400 per month food allowance every month of the year – even when Parliament isn't sitting.

'Right, I'll just print off a copy for everyone and then we can keep tally of who's done which scam,' said Rayner, as he sat down and typed up the list.

Five minutes later Rayner suddenly went pale. 'Oh shit.'

'What's up?'

'I've just pressed print, and it hasn't sent it to the printer in here. It might have gone bloody anywhere!'

The team were not impressed. Secrecy was vital to the success of the investigation, and Rayner might have just gone and cocked the whole thing up with a single click of a computer mouse.

'What's the number of the printer it's sent it to?' said Hope. Rayner passed on the number, and Hope rang the *Telegraph*'s building services department to find out the location of the printer.

'They say they don't know where it is.'

'Bollocks.' Feeling physically sick, Rayner grabbed Jon Swaine and headed out into the *Telegraph*'s vast open-plan office to begin a frantic search of every printer they could find. It was almost certainly futile, but it was better than doing nothing.

After an agonizing two minutes, Rayner's mobile rang. 'We've tracked it down,' said Hope.

'Oh, thank God. Where?'

'Rosa was logged into that computer so it's gone to the printer in the parliamentary office. Katriona [the *Telegraph*'s parliamentary secretary] has got it and we've told her to destroy it.'

A red-faced Rayner returned to the bunker feeling he'd let the side down horribly.

'Er, I'll get the teas in, shall I?' he sheepishly suggested.

Beckford, meanwhile, was thanking his lucky stars that Evans had persuaded him not to go to Oxford that day. 'Thanks for twisting my arm yesterday,' he told the news chief, out of earshot of the other reporters.

'That's OK,' said Evans. 'I've asked someone else to write up something on that conference, by the way.' (It made six paragraphs in the next day's paper, leaving Beckford even more grateful he hadn't chosen to go to Oxford instead of joining the expenses team.)

By the end of day one, the bunker team had already got enough material to write explosive stories about several members of the Cabinet. But if they thought a week was a tight deadline for turning around the MPs' expenses files, they were in for a shock when they came in the next morning.

Mark Skipworth, executive editor, strode purposefully into the bunker with an A4 notebook under his arm. He had been discussing the previous day's discoveries with Lewis, Evans and Bayley, and now announced to the room: 'I don't want to alarm you, but it may be we decide to go with the Gordon Brown stuff for tomorrow's paper.'

'Tomorrow!' several voices gasped in unison. Then came a chorus of protests by reporters who felt it was madness to rush into print with a story that was still at such an embryonic stage.

The instinct of every reporter is to get stories into the paper at the first possible opportunity, rather than run the risk of being scooped by another newspaper while the story is being held back. Everyone involved in the expenses story was jumpy about the fact that other newspapers had seen some of the data, knowing that any kind of leak could alert those other papers and give them the chance to run the story first. The ticking bombs which the team had uncovered about Brown and other Cabinet ministers only served to ratchet up the tension, as Wick had told Winnett that Brown was one of those whose expenses had been seen by the *Sun*. But the investigation team felt there was a huge risk of getting key elements of the story wrong if they didn't have time to check the facts properly, and that the whole project could run out of control as a result.

After a nervous morning, the decision was taken by lunchtime on Friday that the *Telegraph* would hold its nerve and keep digging through the files. Cue relief all round.

As the team worked through the May bank holiday weekend, the *Sunday Times* devoted three pages to an investigation into Baroness Uddin's second-home allowance claims. The Labour peer had allegedly bought a small flat in Maidstone and designated it as her 'main' home while claiming £100,000 for overnight stays in London, even though the newspaper claimed her actual main home was in the capital and she never visited the flat in Kent. The story dominated the television and radio news for the next two days, and provided a timely reminder of the public appetite for stories about parliamentary expenses.

'Bloody hell,' said Winnett as he scanned the *Sunday Times* at his desk in the bunker. 'This is just one politician that hardly anyone's ever heard of. We've got dozens of better-known people implicated. Wait until people find out what we've been up to!'

Other newspapers, anticipating the forthcoming 'official' release of MPs' expenses, ran stories about what they would supposedly reveal. One report said several MPs were 'on suicide watch' because they knew their expenses claims had been so heinous. Another said at least three MPs were bracing themselves for the release of hotel receipts which would show they had been having adulterous affairs. A Sunday paper reported that one MP had installed a sauna in his home and claimed it on expenses. And one senior member of the Shadow Cabinet, unaware that the *Telegraph* had obtained the disk, quietly told a *Telegraph* journalist that the main scandal was going to be MPs who lived together and submitted claims for the same property. This led to the bunker team being asked on a daily basis by Evans and Bayley whether they had winkled out the unnamed MPs at the centre of these salacious stories.

'Found any of the shaggers yet?'

'Have we worked out who's on suicide watch?'

'Has the sauna turned up?'

In the event, no evidence was found to suggest any of these stories were true.

By the time the investigation was a few days old, questions were starting to be asked about the absent reporters.

'How long is this bloody training going to go on for?' demanded one staff member, whose patience was wearing thin after almost a week of having to cover for colleagues.

In Parliament, lobby correspondents were starting to wonder where Winnett and Prince had suddenly disappeared to. James Kirkup, who knew the truth about the 'training' cover story, batted away an increasing number of questions.

'Is Rosa around?'

'No, day off. Rob too.'

Then:

'Rosa back yet?'

'No. Still off.'

'Still? Lazy so and so.'

'Yeah. Tell me about it.'

And:

'Haven't seen Rob for ages. Where is he?'

'Up at Victoria. Some training course. Blogging, I think.'

'God, you lot are mad for the internet, aren't you?'

At the outset of the investigation, fewer than ten *Daily Telegraph* staff outside the bunker team knew the truth about what was going on. One features executive emailed Rayner to ask if he could write a piece for the Saturday review section on 'Gordon Brown's worst week', following a plot by some Labour MPs to defect to the Lib Dems and mounting speculation of a leadership challenge.

'I think Brown's week is about to get an awful lot worse,' he said to the other reporters, as he emailed the executive to say he would be unavailable.

Another executive, wandering past the bunker on bank holiday Monday, was shocked to see the room full of activity.

'God, they really shouldn't make you come in for training on a bank holiday,' he said, shaking his head. 'Surely it can't be that important?'

'Not much we can do about it,' shrugged Watt, as others feigned disgruntlement.

Even a trip to the canteen for a cuppa became a hazardous task as members of the bunker team were confronted by increasingly suspicious colleagues.

'So you're doing this training then, are you? What's really going on in there?'

'Oh, wouldn't want to bore you with the details. Can hardly stay awake.'

Meanwhile, Training Room 4 was becoming more of a cesspit than a bunker. The strict secrecy surrounding the investigation meant that cleaners were not allowed anywhere near the place, and as the days wore on the blue speckled carpet tiles started to disappear beneath the takeaway pizza boxes, paper coffee cups, chewing-gum wrappers and plastic bottles which had spilled out of the unemptied bins.

'It's starting to smell like my old student digs in here,' observed Jon Swaine as the smell of leftover Chinese food, delivered to the office as the team worked into the night, lingered heavily one morning.

The team also had to protect the information on the disks as if their lives depended on it; if so much as a single document containing MPs' personal details was seen by someone outside the building, not only would the *Telegraph*'s investigation become common knowledge, but Parliament would be able to turn the tables by accusing the *Telegraph* of compromising security. Instead of reporting the story, the *Telegraph* would become the story.

So a strict set of protocols were observed from the very beginning. Winnett put the master disk on its own in one safe (the location of which was not known even to the other reporters), where it remained untouched, while the working copies were kept in a second safe, where he returned them every night. In the bunker itself, any material which was printed out for reference had to be destroyed at the end of each evening in an old, dustbin-sized shredder which made the whole floor vibrate every time it thrummed into action. One reason for destroying the documents was the fear of a burglary, but it would also be vital to the credibility of the investigation, once it became public, to be able to demonstrate to the outside world that all genuinely sensitive personal data, such as addresses and bank details, were being handled under maximum security conditions. To ensure no electronic leaks of information, the team also imposed a ban on making any references to the investigation in emails. Even so, the fear that the outside world would discover what the *Telegraph* was up to hung in the air every minute of the day.

By now the team had settled into something of a routine, starting at 8 a.m. and working through until 10 p.m., with meals eaten at a desk while staring at the seemingly endless stream of expenses documents. Eyebags and spots became increasingly *de rigueur*, sunlight and fresh air were distant memories, and the third-hottest May on record was something the team could only read about in the papers. During one conversation about the amount of time MPs seemed to spend pursuing their hobbies, Beckford dryly noted: 'My only hobby at the moment is sleeping.' More than anyone else, Beckford had every right to feel exhausted. He had become a father for the first time on 2 April, less than a month before the investigation began, and would have been sleep-deprived even without the punishing hours demanded by Operation Firestorm.

One of the few moments of relaxation came on the evening of Wednesday, 6 May, when the team downed tools to watch the Chelsea v. Barcelona Champions' League semifinal on a computer screen in the bunker. Winnett, a lifelong Chelsea fan, wished he hadn't bothered, as a last-minute Barcelona equalizer knocked Chelsea out of the competition on away goals. 'Hope it's not an omen,' he mumbled, looking crestfallen.

As John Wick's ten-day deadline approached, Chris Evans decided the investigation needed all the resources he could throw at it, and the bunker team gained a new member in the shape of Nick Allen, one of the *Telegraph*'s most thorough and dependable news reporters. Allen, who had joined the *Telegraph* two years earlier from the US news agency Bloomberg, had previously been chief reporter at the Press Association, the UK's national news agency, where he had covered military operations in Iraq and Afghanistan, as well as natural disasters and high-profile Old Bailey trials. He was at his desk in the *Telegraph*'s newsroom being briefed by a member of the news desk to write a story about swine flu when Evans approached. 'This man has to go to the training room immediately,' Evans interjected, in what seemed to Allen a strangely urgent way. Allen, who had just come back from a holiday, had heard about other reporters disappearing from the face of the earth after being selected to work on a 'special project' and feared he was in for a mind-numbing experience learning about new computer software.

'Been sent to the training room?' asked deputy news editor Neville Dean as Allen passed him.

'Yes. Don't know if that's a good thing or a bad thing,' replied Allen.

'Oh, it's very, very good,' whispered Dean, the only member of the eight-strong news desk other than Bayley who knew about the expenses project.

As Allen entered the bunker, he was greeted by silence and nervous glances.

'What's going on, then?' he asked.

Hope was first to speak. Turning to Evans, he asked: 'Can we tell him?' Evans nodded, and Hope, who, like his colleagues, had been burdened by the urge to tell someone about the expenses story, blurted out in relief: 'We've got the disk! The disk with the MPs' expenses. We've got it!'

Allen looked slightly stunned. Then his face broke into a huge smile. 'Fantastic!'

Evans explained the need for watertight security, giving Allen a particularly thorny problem. His girlfriend was a reporter on another national newspaper, and he didn't want to present her with divided loyalties by telling her about the expenses investigation. He decided straight away he would have to lie to her, leading to a series of uncomfortable phone calls.

'Why are you at the office so late, what are you doing?'

'Um, internet training, like I told you.'

'At this time? You're lying. Why are you lying? Are you in the pub?'

'Er, got to go now, training's starting again. Bye.'

One of Allen's first tasks was to plough through the expenses claims of the Tory grandee David Heathcoat-Amory, who had submitted handwritten invoices from his gardener which included regular deliveries of horse manure. After more than two hours of combing through the bills, Allen came up with a grand total: the taxpayer had bought 550 sacks of horse manure at a total cost of £388.80.

'So he's literally dumped a load of shit on the taxpayer,' Allen noted. It seemed like the perfect description for the way the MPs had behaved.

Even with the extra muscle which Allen provided, it was clear that the team would only be able to look at a fraction of the MPs' expenses files by the time the ten-day deadline expired, because it was taking up to half a day to look through each MP's claims. This meant that if the *Telegraph* did go ahead with publication, the reporters would have to divide into two teams, with one team writing stories for publication and the other team carrying on with the task of looking through more MPs.

Problems were also becoming apparent in another area – the planned online publication by the *Telegraph* of the original expenses documents. The intention had been to put all of the Cabinet's expenses receipts online on the day the first stories were published in the newspaper, to enable the public to see for themselves what ministers had done. To make this work, however, Ian Douglas and Duncan Hooper were having to go through individual pages drawing black boxes over bank account details and other private inform-ation, a process which was taking an inordinately long time. Also, the reporters were uneasy about the idea of putting the information online where rival newspapers could see it, fear-ing that if anything had been missed, other papers would be able to scoop the *Telegraph*. There was also the danger of a bank account number or home address slipping through the net, and Arthur Wynn Davies felt the risk was too high: if the *Telegraph* accidentally published the sort of information which could have been used by identity fraudsters, the fall-out would be hugely damaging to the paper's integrity, as well as leading to costly legal action.

In the end, the *Telegraph* decided to publish only some of the documents online as the investigation progressed, with the intention of ultimately publishing extensive details on every MP. The website was also to be used to release key memos and other information which helped reinforce the impact of the scoops in the newspaper, and to break some stories online during the day.

Winnett began compiling a list of the stories which had been uncovered for each of the MPs the team had looked at, ranking the Members into high, medium and low priority. Watt, meanwhile, was keeping detailed notes on MPs whose claims appeared suspicious in some way but would require further investigation, while Rayner kept a file marked 'A to Z' in which the more bizarre items claimed on expenses could be listed alphabetically.

Throughout the week, the reporters shouted out their favourite expenses claims for the A to Z, each trying to outdo the others by finding ever more ludicrous claims.

'I for Ikea carrier bag,' said Swaine, after noticing one MP had claimed 5p for such an item.

'G for Ginger Crinkle biscuits,' Hope chortled, as he looked through the Labour MP Austin Mitchell's file.

With Zanussi ovens, quiche dishes and yucca plants among the items claimed by MPs, even the most awkward letters were covered – except X.

'Don't suppose anyone's claimed for a xylophone?' Rayner asked.

'No, but we could do X-rated moves for Jacqui Smith's porn claim,' replied Beckford. The list was complete.

The bunker team was by now convinced that they were working on one of the biggest stories they would ever be involved with. But it was still by no means certain that any of the material would see the light of day. Although Winnett had given the news executives regular updates on how the investigation was progressing, nothing had been set in stone, and the editor wanted to keep his options open for as long as possible.

William Lewis was about to make the biggest decision of his life.

Decision Time

Wednesday, 6 May

'And is your daddy an MP?'

CHAPTER 9

OVER THE COURSE of the bank holiday weekend, the investigation team had uncovered so much evidence of apparent abuse that the journalistic merit in running the story was beyond question. Everyone involved in the project, however, was acutely aware of the enormity of the decision which would have to be taken before a single word could appear in print.

William Lewis had been convinced from the beginning that the newspaper should go ahead with publication, provided the documents turned out to be genuine and that there was a clear public interest in exposing the expenses claims. But there was still a huge potential for the whole thing to end in disaster. Aside from the tiny percentage chance that the documents were in some way faked, there remained the question of how they had come into the *Daily Telegraph*'s possession. Arthur Wynn Davies had been steadfast in his belief that the disk itself did not constitute stolen property, and that the *Telegraph* would have an overwhelming public interest defence if Parliament tried to get the police involved. However authoritative his opinion, though, it *was* only an opinion, and there remained the very real possibility that the *Telegraph* could find itself at the centre of a criminal investigation over how it got the material. Instead of producing a world-beating scoop, the paper could become mired in a hugely damaging court case which would tarnish its reputation and end Lewis's career. There was even an outside chance that Lewis could go to prison.

Then there was the possibility that Parliament would seek an emergency injunction to prevent the *Telegraph*'s presses rolling.

Lewis knew that the decision on whether or not to publish would define not only his tenure as editor, but also the entire ethos of the newspaper he had set about hauling into the twenty-first century in what had already been a difficult and at times painful process.

A former business journalist who had earned a reputation for breaking agenda-setting scoops during spells at the *Mail on Sunday*, the *Financial Times* and the *Sunday Times*, Lewis had become the youngest editor in the *Daily Telegraph*'s 150-year history when he was given the job in 2006 at the age of just thirty-seven. It was an appointment in keeping with the modernization of the paper, and its sister the *Sunday Telegraph*, that had been under way almost from the day the company had been bought by Sir David and Sir Frederick Barclay two years earlier. This modernization process was led by the next generation of the family – Aidan Barclay (the chairman of what would become Telegraph Media Group) and Howard Barclay. Both were passionate about placing the customer at the heart of everything the new *Telegraph* would do and were determined to transform the brand.

The *Telegraph* had had a long-standing reputation as a place that resembled a gentlemen's club. Journalists would often leave the office for long lunches, while editors would sometimes disappear to the opera or theatre long before the paper was finished and had little day-to-day involvement in the news pages. Although much of the writing was excellent and the newspaper had a loyal following, the *Daily Telegraph* was not considered a major player when it came to breaking agenda-setting news stories.

By the time Lewis took the helm, the *Telegraph* had already gone through several major changes. Lewis himself had led the organization's move from Canary Wharf in the east London docklands area to an office building above Victoria railway station just months before his promotion to editor. The centrepiece of the new headquarters was a vast, open-plan newsroom which had previously been a busy trading floor when the building was occupied by the investment bank Salomon Brothers. As big as a football pitch, with a 50-foot-high ceiling, the ultra-modern newsroom was a statement of intent. At its centre was a large circular table, 'the hub', where all editorial conferences took place. From there, long rows of desks radiated out like spokes, each one used by a different department, in a design which would be copied by, among others, the BBC and, ironically, Gordon Brown, who arranged one of the Downing Street offices in a similar, albeit much smaller, hub-and-spoke design.

The move in premises had enabled Lewis to start modernizing the editorial operation, merging many of the *Daily Telegraph*'s departments with those of the *Sunday*

Telegraph to create a seven-day staff rota, as well as relaunching the *Telegraph* website with the intention of making it the most read newspaper website in the country, and adding an online television service to which reporters would contribute.

Inevitably, there had also been changes in personnel. As part of this, senior news executives – including Gallagher, Evans and Bayley – were recruited from the *Daily Mail* to overhaul the news operation. Lewis was also keen to re-balance the newspaper's political stance, reaching out to the Labour government – which had previously been largely ignored by the staunchly Conservative old 'Torygraph' – in an attempt to give readers a more rounded view of what was happening in Westminster.

Rival newspapers delighted in criticizing the *Telegraph*'s new approach, suggesting that the 'new regime' had taken modernization too far, but many neutral observers had praised the newspaper for its sharper, more on-the-ball editorial content and its consistent ability to respond quickly to breaking news stories ahead of its rivals. All that was lacking was an agenda-setting scoop to make the country truly sit up and take notice of the new-look *Telegraph*.

So the expenses investigation seemed to have come along at exactly the right time. But even if all went according to plan, would the readers approve of the *Telegraph* taking on the entire parliamentary establishment, including the Conservatives, by using leaked information which the *Telegraph* might be accused of stealing?

On the morning of Tuesday, 5 May, Lewis, returning to the office after the bank holiday, called in Winnett to get a run-down of what had been discovered over the weekend. The editor had recently been sent a half-sized polo mallet by the promoters of a tournament and he had taken to waving it around the office as a prop whenever he was discussing the expenses story. As Winnett detailed the latest revelations, Lewis prodded the air with the mallet, saying: 'Great, great – keep pushing, great stuff.' Winnett found himself thinking: If I get one of these stories wrong, that mallet will end up in the back of my skull!

Lewis then called in Philip Johnston, one of the assistant editors of the *Daily Telegraph* and among the most respected voices in the newsroom. 'Phil J' had worked for the newspaper since the 1980s, as a parliamentary correspondent and later as home affairs editor, before becoming a comment and leader writer. Lewis regularly sought Johnston's advice on political issues, and it was he who would later draft the leader article explaining the *Telegraph*'s decision to publish for the editor's approval.

As Winnett began to explain some of the scams that had been uncovered, Johnston looked stunned. 'This is incredible,' he said. 'I worked for years in Westminster and I had no idea this was going on. The readers will be furious.'

Lewis was pleased that Johnston shared his take on the story and its importance. Johnston was later to become one of the strongest advocates for the investigation – and his initial reaction had perfectly predicted how the public would respond to the story.

During the course of that Tuesday and Wednesday, Lewis had a series of similar conversations with other executives about the potential fallout – discussions from which the team working away in the bunker was largely insulated.

'This will be either the biggest thing we ever do or the last thing we ever do,' Lewis told consulting editor Rhidian Wynn Davies in a private moment.

Winnett, meanwhile, was asked by lawyer Arthur Wynn Davies to accompany him to a meeting with a leading QC who had been consulted from an early stage about the potential risks of an injunction and was retained to be on standby to resist any attempt to gag the newspaper. Winnett struggled to keep up with Wynn Davies's frantic walking pace as the two men made their way to Victoria Underground station and on to Middle Temple, part of the cloistered sanctuary behind Fleet Street where barristers have their chambers.

Once inside the QC's cramped, oak-panelled office, Winnett gave the barrister an overview of the Jack Straw council tax story, Gordon Brown's expenses claims and the widespread evidence of 'flipping', to provide a flavour of the sort of material that might be published. The QC, who appeared genuinely excited to be involved, advised the pair against suggesting Parliament was involved in a cover-up (as the censored documents were still subject to change by MPs) but suggested that it was unlikely Parliament would seek an injunction. Nevertheless, nothing was being left to chance and the QC even began preparing witness statements from Winnett.

'Good luck,' he said as Winnett and Wynn Davies left his office.

There remained a separate risk that the *Telegraph* could face a criminal investigation. In the worst-case scenario, the police could raid the offices and arrest journalists and executives involved in the project. Although this was highly unlikely, the legal advice was to plan for every eventuality.

Winnett suggested calling in Steven Barker, one of London's top criminal solicitors and an old friend. Barker provided advice on what to do if detectives arrived at the *Telegraph* headquarters: in short, staff should not impede the police but did not have to help them if they carried out a search.

He added: 'There's a possibility that they will arrest you. They would be on pretty weak grounds to do so, but this is very political and they may want to scare you. If they do arrest you, they'll do it at dawn at your house. If that happens, don't say anything, just call me.'

Winnett repeated the advice to every reporter working on the story, each of whom was provided with a card giving Barker's home and mobile numbers, and another with the details of one of his colleagues, in case they were arrested at home. Barker also arranged for more than ten solicitors to be on standby to represent each of those working from the bunker should there be a coordinated series of arrests after publication. The news that reporters' homes could become the scene of dawn raids did not meet with an enthusiastic welcome from the bunker team's partners when they went home that night.

At midday on Wednesday, 6 May, having briefed Murdoch MacLennan, the chief executive of Telegraph

Media Group, Lewis decided it was time to break the good news to the troops. 'The investigation is going ahead,' he said.

Within the hour, the bunker was transformed from a journalistic research laboratory to a self-contained newsroom capable of putting together a fully fledged newspaper. The reporters were joined by page designers, production journalists and picture researchers who would be putting the stories on to newspaper pages once they were written. Gallagher spoke to the circulation department and warned them to prepare to increase the paper's print run. Evans and Winnett began to plan how the mass of information which had been identified by the team could be distilled into specific articles, not just on the first day of publication, but throughout the following week or so.

At first, the plan had been to break the expenses story in the Saturday edition of the paper, the biggest-selling issue of the week. But did it really make sense to publish the *Telegraph*'s biggest exclusive at the weekend? Far better, it seemed, to print the first stories on a weekday, when the general public is more tuned in to news and current affairs, in the hope that the story would dominate television and radio broadcasts, raise public awareness and make the Saturday paper a 'must read'.

Lewis was keen to begin the campaign with a blockbuster 'shock and awe' edition detailing the expenses claims of the Cabinet. The sheer number of MPs the *Telegraph* would have to get through meant it was not going to be possible to spread the Cabinet out over several days. In addition, the knowledge that other newspapers had seen the expenses claims of Cabinet members when they were offered the disk meant they had to be done in one go, otherwise there remained a risk of rivals getting in on the act. Other MPs whose expenses had been seen by at least one other paper included Keith Vaz, chairman of the Home Affairs Select Committee; John Prescott, the former Deputy Prime Minister; and Michael Martin, the Speaker. All would have to be covered as a priority.

It was decided that the Cabinet should be covered on day one, with the most notable junior ministers to follow the next day. They were the people in power; their expenses were the natural place to start. The *Sunday Telegraph* would then highlight the huge claims made by Sinn Fein MPs and also focus on the first potentially fraudulent claims. The Shadow Cabinet would feature on Monday, followed by the huge gardening claims made by Conservative grandees on Tuesday. Wednesday, Thursday, Friday and the following Saturday would detail the depth of the scandal on the back benches. Winnett, Watt, Prince, Rayner and Beckford would write the articles for the first day, with Swaine, Hope and Allen getting a head start on stories for day two.

After a week of studying endless documents, the investigation team could finally turn to writing their first stories. As the reporters went home that night, they were in no doubt that their entire careers were likely to be defined by the events of the following day.

'Go Day'

Thursday, 7 May

'Buy me a hair shirt and
put it on expenses'

CHAPTER 10

WINNETT, IN COMMON with several of the other reporters, had trouble sleeping after going home on Wednesday night, excited and nervous about what lay ahead. Waking at 4.30 a.m., he decided that if he was up, he might as well be in the office, and arrived in the bunker shortly after dawn, hoping it wouldn't be long before he had company. A quick look at the newspapers showed that, to his relief, there were no major stories which could risk either delaying or distracting attention from the expenses scandal.

By 8 a.m. the entire team had assembled in the bunker. As they arrived, each broke into a smile and made a throwaway comment to relieve the tension as they acknowledged the sheer weight of responsibility on their shoulders.

'Big day!'

'Today's the day then!'

'Another quiet day in the office!'

Each knew that they held a precious opportunity to share in a slice of history. But a parallel thought was equally prevalent: don't, whatever you do, screw up.

As the reporters waited for their computers to start up,

the atmosphere in the room was surprisingly calm. Most of the stories about the Cabinet members who were to feature in the next day's paper had been written the night before, meaning there should be no frantic rush to meet deadlines. Instead, there was a sense that fate was about to take over from journalistic endeavour.

Fourteen MPs in total were scheduled to lead the charge of the *Telegraph*'s expenses exposé: the Prime Minister, Gordon Brown; the Chancellor, Alistair Darling; Geoff Hoon, the transport secretary; David Miliband, the foreign secretary; Jack Straw, the justice secretary; Hazel Blears, the communities secretary; Lord Mandelson, the business secretary; Margaret Beckett, the housing minister; Paul Murphy, the Welsh secretary; Andy Burnham, the culture secretary; Douglas Alexander, the international development secretary; Caroline Flint, the Europe minister; Shaun Woodward, the Northern Ireland secretary; and John Prescott, the former Deputy Prime Minister.

These individuals had been selected for three main reasons: they were in power; they had all made questionable claims; and they had been on a list of twenty MPs whose expenses had been seen by the *Sun*, meaning the *Telegraph* had to get them out of the way before the *Sun* had a chance to catch up. Other members of the Cabinet who did not appear on the list had, on the whole, made apparently 'clean' expenses claims.

Before the *Daily Telegraph* could even contemplate writing stories about any of them, however, each one would have to be 'fronted up' – in other words, the allegations would have to be formally put to them to give them a chance to respond. These were no ordinary front-ups, however. On a normal story, a reporter might bang on someone's door or ring them up to say they were going to appear in the next day's paper after they had been caught breaking the law/ misbehaving/committing adultery. Even in the case of MPs, a phone call would usually suffice.

But the *Daily Telegraph* was about to accuse the Prime Minister and half the Cabinet of misusing public money. The stakes could hardly have been higher; so special measures were called for. Each reporter was told to prepare a formal letter, based on a template approved by Arthur Wynn Davies. It would begin by setting out the fact that the *Telegraph* was investigating MPs' expenses, and then give an assurance that no address or any other details which could compromise security would be revealed; only then would the specific allegations be set out.

So instead of writing stories, the reporters spent the morning writing letters, each of which contained some of the most damaging allegations put to a serving minister in recent times. But writing the letters also served as a useful exercise to concentrate the mind: as the reporters typed them out, they went back through the expenses documents, checking and re-checking their facts, making sure every figure was correct and nothing had been overlooked. Each member of the team was acutely aware that the Labour Party media machine – constructed by Tony Blair's master of spin, Alastair Campbell – was geared up to look for even the tiniest factual inaccuracies in articles which criticized its

MPs, then use that inaccuracy ruthlessly to undermine the entire basis of the story. Any mistake in any story in the following day's coverage could therefore prove fatal to the entire investigation. Not only would Labour seize on such a mistake, but rival media organizations, stung by the fact that they had lost out on the story, might be only too willing to run 'denial' stories to put the *Telegraph* back in its box.

Wynn Davies had stressed that now, more than ever, the *Telegraph* had a duty to stick to the age-old journalistic code of 'fair, balanced and accurate' reporting, meaning that any stories written about the MPs would have to include their responses. If the MPs challenged the accuracy of any of the allegations, executives and lawyers would have to decide whether to expunge them from the stories altogether. The lawyer had also insisted that he should read each letter before it was emailed to its recipient.

As the reporters waited for him to approve the letters towards the end of the morning, Gordon Brown was celebrating some particularly good news. The Crown Prosecution Service announced that it would not be pressing charges against three former Labour Party treasurers following the so-called 'donorgate' scandal of 2007. The three men had brokered a total of £600,000 in donations to the Labour Party from a property developer called David Abrahams via a number of proxies; this had caused a furore at the time, but prosecutors said that after considering the evidence they had decided there had been no breach of electoral law. The Labour Party had responded by putting out a statement making it clear that it should be 'beyond reproach', adding that it had reformed its procedures to ensure 'transparency and accountability'. To those watching from the bunker, it was a delicious irony.

The donorgate affair had been the closest Brown had come to being tarnished by 'sleaze' during his premiership, and by now the Prime Minister was, no doubt, beginning to think that he might get through his entire stay in Downing Street without being dragged into any similar scandals. He was able to enjoy the moment for no more than a couple of hours before the email from Robert Winnett, setting out the fact that the *Daily Telegraph* was intending to run a story about the Prime Minister's expenses claims, signalled that Brown and his government were about to be hit by a tidal wave of public fury.

Having received Winnett's email, Michael Ellam broke the news to the Prime Minister at 2 p.m. Brown was deeply troubled by what he was told. He was under no illusions about the potential damage the allegations could cause, and immediately cleared his diary for the rest of the day to deal with the unfolding crisis.

Brown's advisers were also upset that the *Telegraph* had hit them with what one described as 'a bolt from the blue'. Brown had been at pains to cultivate a good working relationship with the newspaper during his time in office, and wanted to know why the *Telegraph* had not given him any warning before hitting him with the allegations. But that question would have to wait; calls were beginning to come in from almost every Whitehall department to say that other Cabinet members had received similar letters from the *Daily Telegraph*.

'It was like being on the deck of a ship and seeing a tor-
pedo coming which you knew you couldn't stop,' said one
source close to the events inside No. 10. Within the space of
an hour, Brown learned that Alistair Darling, Geoff Hoon
and Hazel Blears had kitted out more than one house at
taxpayers' expense after 'flipping' their second-home
designations, with possible issues over capital gains tax in
relation to Hoon and Blears. Lord Mandelson had claimed
thousands of pounds for repairs to his house after announcing his decision to step down as an MP; Jack Straw had
overclaimed on his council tax; John Prescott had claimed
for three mock Tudor beams to be fitted to the front of his
house (the self-professed bulimic had also claimed the
maximum £4,800 annual food allowance). The list went on
and on.

As Brown retreated to his private office in an anteroom
off 10 Downing Street's open-plan 'war room' where his
chief advisers had their desks, Joe Irvin, his political director,
was told to gather a small team together to comb through
Brown's own expenses in order to respond to the *Telegraph*'s
questions and look out for any other potential problems
buried in the receipts. With the former lobbyist running
Downing Street's response behind the scenes, Brown spent
the entire afternoon in his office, with various advisers going
in and out to brief him on the latest developments from
government departments. As he sat at his extra-large
computer screen, he began drafting his own response to the
Telegraph's questions, with input from Dugher, Ellam, Irvin,
and his permanent secretary Jeremy Heywood. Sir Gus

O'Donnell, the head of the civil service, was also following developments, liaising with a senior Cabinet Office official who was checking that ministers had not broken any government rules.

Back at the *Telegraph*, the investigation team was not expecting a response from any of the ministers much before 5 p.m., the deadline which the letters had given for their replies. But Jack Straw was about to spend the afternoon speaking to inmates at Whitemoor prison in Cambridgeshire, a maximum security gaol which was home to the M25 'road rage' killer Kenneth Noye and the rapist and murderer Michael Sams, among others. Straw, like every other visitor, would have to surrender his mobile phone when he entered the prison, and by the time he came out it would be early evening. An email he had received from Gordon Rayner made it clear that the *Telegraph* had chapter and verse on a council tax overclaim he had made on his constituency home in Blackburn, which he had eventually repaid to the parliamentary authorities. He had also overclaimed for his mortgage and had claimed for a new kitchen after writing to the parliamentary fees office saying that: 'My daughter complains – correctly – that it is less well equipped than her student house in Manchester.'

To his credit, Straw decided to deal with the matter promptly, and at 2.24 p.m., just thirty-four minutes after he had sent the allegations, Rayner had Straw's response, sent by his special adviser, Mark Davies. Quoting 'a spokesman for Jack Straw', it said:

Jack takes this very seriously . . . Any costs claimed in relation to his home in his Blackburn constituency and time spent in Blackburn have been made entirely in accordance with the rules set by the Commons authorities. On the claims relating to mortgage interest payments an error arose because the amount of interest declined rapidly towards the end of the mortgage. This error was identified by the Commons authorities on information provided by Mr Straw and then repaid. It was also Mr Straw himself who spotted errors in the claims for council tax and alerted the authorities. He repaid the difference.

The reporters had been so confident that the ministers would take hours to reply that they had all dispersed to the various sandwich bars in Victoria station to grab their lunches as soon as they had sent off the letters. Most had only got back to the bunker a matter of minutes before Straw's email landed, and their desks were covered in sandwiches, soup cartons and crisp bags as Rayner alerted them to the crucial development.

Straw's response was incredibly straightforward – dull, even. But to the bunker team it was a thing of beauty. Straw might have denied any wrongdoing, but he had not contested the substance of any of the allegations. At a stroke, he had removed most of the possible obstacles which could have prevented publication of the expenses investigation. For a start, the documents were clearly genuine, as Straw confirmed he had overclaimed for council tax and mortgage payments. The *Telegraph* had not been hoaxed. Also, in his role as Lord Chancellor, Straw would be the minister who would oversee any government attempt to block publication, either through an injunction or by calling in the police. His letter contained no such threat. In the space of a few seconds, the mood in the bunker changed from nervous anticipation to relief and celebration.

'Fantastic,' said an emotionally drained Winnett.

'Unbelievable,' said Hope. 'Looks like we're on, then!'

'Yep. Better start writing!'

As the reporters digested the news, Arthur Wynn Davies rushed into the bunker looking more excited than anyone. 'We're in business!' he announced, a smile as wide as the river Taff on his face. 'There's no way any of them can deny it now.' With a slightly melodramatic flourish, Wynn Davies said he had been so nervous waiting for the first, make-or-break response that he could only compare the tension with the Cuban missile crisis of 1962, when he and the rest of the world waited to discover whether America and Russia would start a nuclear war.

There would be more waiting to come, however. After Jack Straw had given the investigation team such a quick start, it would be more than two hours before the next minister replied. In the meantime, another vital member of the *Telegraph*'s staff would have to be briefed on the expenses story – the newspaper's legendary cartoonist, Matt Pritchett.

One of the highlights of the editor's day at the *Telegraph* is his daily meeting with Matt, when the editor must choose between several drawings which the prolific satirist produces each day. William Lewis had already had his 2.45 p.m.

meeting with Matt that day, at which he had chosen a cartoon about the national DNA database, featuring a man who was being told that by wearing socks with his sandals he had committed a sufficiently serious crime to have his DNA retained by police. At around 4 p.m., Tony Gallagher pulled Matt to one side and told him: 'There's another story that might be on the front page tomorrow. We've got details of MPs' expenses, and they've been claiming for some pretty outrageous things. Could you put something together?' With no more details to go on, Matt produced the first of what would become dozens of cartoons on MPs' expenses. It showed an MP in his office telling his secretary: 'Buy me a hair shirt and put it on expenses.'

As the bunker team speculated on the reasons for the delay in getting more replies from the Cabinet, Gordon Brown was holding a crisis meeting in his private office. Dugher had asked every Whitehall department to send him copies of the letters they had received from the *Daily Telegraph* and had laid out the letters, and the ministers' intended responses, on a coffee table in the corner of the office. Brown wanted to know how bad it was, and was particularly concerned with judging how his own expenses claims stood up to scrutiny compared with those of other Cabinet members. Already Brown was displaying a strong instinct for self-preservation, sensing that the story could be seized upon by his rivals and used as a weapon to stab him in the back.

Brown had no idea what his ministers had been claiming, and according to one who saw him that afternoon 'looked really shocked' when he found out. In particular, he was concerned about Blears, who had avoided paying £13,000 in capital gains tax when she 'flipped' her second home at around the time she sold it; Straw, whose council tax aberration was likely to become headline news because of his position as justice secretary; and Mandelson, who had been brought back into government in a huge gamble by Brown after having been twice forced to resign from ministerial posts in the past, once because of questions over his personal mortgage arrangements. But above all, Brown was preoccupied with his own claims and was angry that his personal integrity was being challenged.

Over in Victoria, the vast majority of the *Telegraph*'s staff were still totally unaware of the historic scoop the newspaper had waiting in the wings. Even at the midday news conference, most of the executives planning that day's newspaper had no idea of what was going on in the bunker. Instead, they planned a paper which was going to lead on the latest twist in the Gurkha residency row and include stories about why *Chariots of Fire* was Gordon Brown's 'most inspirational' film and how Sikh police officers were calling for bullet-proof turbans. The exercise was not intended to be entirely redundant, though. William Lewis had decided to use a tried and tested Fleet Street trick to throw rivals off the scent by 'spoofing' the first edition of the newspaper. The plan was to print a limited run of around 25,000 copies containing nothing of the expenses story: these would be picked up by rival newspapers, which would assume that the *Telegraph* had no major stories worth following up.

National newspapers print several different editions each night, enabling them to update the news as it develops during the evening, and one of the most important tasks of a night news editor is checking the stories which every other paper has in its first edition, then putting his reporters to work on their own version of the story so that by the time the final edition is printed it will contain 'spoiler' versions of other papers' exclusives. But by spoofing the first edition editors deny rival publications the chance to catch up, because by the time they see the big story splashed all over the second edition, it's too late to do anything about it.

In this case, a spoof would also buy the newspaper time if the government was thinking of applying for an injunction: if ministers saw the spoof first edition, they would assume the *Telegraph* had held off from printing the stories referred to in the formal letters to ministers, and not bother going for an injunction.

By 5 p.m., however, Lewis had received news of a worrying development. Word had reached him that the *Sun* – and possibly one other newspaper – had been alerted to the *Telegraph*'s expenses exclusive. Although he couldn't prove it, Lewis suspected that Downing Street had tipped off 'friendly' Labour-supporting newspapers in the hope that they could spin the story to them in a more positive way and at the same time burst the *Telegraph*'s bubble. Politics, after all, is a dirty business.

Lewis called Winnett into his office. 'We're going for first,' he announced, informing him of the latest turn of events. Winnett was alarmed, but not entirely surprised. In the bunker, the reporters had repeatedly commented that it would take a minor miracle to keep the lid on the story for more than a week.

Winnett had expected to have several hours to fine-tune the front-page story he had already started writing, but now he was going to have to get a shift on, particularly in view of the number of eyes which would need to see his and the other reporters' stories before they were officially signed off by editors, production journalists and lawyers.

By the time Winnett returned to the bunker, responses from the various departments had started to flow in at a steady rate. Some ministers, like John Prescott, Alistair Darling and Hazel Blears, had sent only the briefest responses, variations on the 'it was all within the rules' theme. Others, however, went to extraordinary lengths to justify every detail of their claims. Margaret Beckett, who had claimed £1,480.84 for a new larder fridge, freezer, dishwasher, dryer and washing machine just a few days before the end of the financial year, phoned Gordon Rayner and spent more than ten minutes explaining why she had gone on the spending spree.

'My tumble dryer started to have hiccups,' she explained. 'Our other white goods were showing signs of wear and tear and we tend to replace things in a batch because it's the best use of our time. It's part of the pattern of life that that sometimes goods go wrong and if so it's a good thing to do it all at once.' Claims she had made for hanging baskets and pot plants 'should not have been claimed', she conceded.

The multi-millionaire Northern Ireland secretary, Shaun Woodward, had received more than £100,000 to help him pay the mortgage interest on a £1.35 million flat that was one of at least seven properties he owned. He did not dispute this, but an aide took issue with the fact that the *Telegraph* had also suggested in a letter to Woodward that he had made an expenses claim for a Muller Crunch Corner yoghurt (38p) and a pizza from Asda (£1.06). The pizza and yoghurt in question had been consumed by a member of his staff, the aide said, not the minister himself.

It all seemed slightly surreal. Ministers and secretaries of state who would often take all day to respond to reporters' questions about even the most serious departmental matters were suddenly falling over themselves to provide excuses for why they had made expenses claims for a hanging basket, a yoghurt or a pizza.

Lord Mandelson, that master of media manipulation, tried an entirely different tactic – claiming that because he was about to get on a plane, he could not possibly answer the *Telegraph*'s questions and so the newspaper would have to wait until the following day, at the very least, before publishing anything. It was a nice try, but the *Telegraph* refused to be browbeaten. Unsurprisingly, Lord Mandelson found that he did, in fact, have time to send a brief answer, as it turned out his time-consuming flight was only going as far as Scotland.

The good news was that no matter how hard the ministers tried to wriggle off the hook in respect of minor details, none disputed that they had made the claims in the first place; nor was there the slightest hint of legal action. For the investigation team, it was full steam ahead.

With the first edition deadline creeping ever closer, Winnett sat down at his computer and began to write the front-page story – the 'splash' – for day one of what would be branded as The Expenses Files. Involuntarily narrowing his eyes, red-rimmed with fatigue after staring at his computer screen for more than twelve hours each day for over a week, he searched for the words that would be, to quote the late publisher of the *Washington Post* Philip Graham, the first draft of history.

The obvious way into the story was Gordon Brown, and so Winnett wrote his first paragraph – the intro – beginning: 'Gordon Brown used taxpayers' money to pay his brother more than £6,000 for cleaning services . . .'

But it was now 7.15 p.m. and there had been an ominous silence from the Prime Minister. Did this mean he was considering legal action? Would his lawyers pounce at the last minute and seek an injunction? Rayner had tried, and failed, to contact Brown's brother Andrew to get his version of why the Prime Minister had paid him for 'cleaning services'.

Winnett's nerves were starting to fray around the edges, and he decided to text the man who was dealing with Brown's expenses, Michael Dugher. Dugher, a straight-talking Yorkshireman, was one of those who had been present in the Chilean vineyard when the first hints of the looming scandal were discussed. Now, he wanted to know, how bad was the *Telegraph*'s coverage going to be for the Prime Minister? Not wanting to give too much away,

Winnett told him it was scheduled to be the focus of the front-page story but that a lot hinged on Brown's explanation for the bizarre arrangement. Dugher told him the answer would soon follow.

At 7.28 p.m. an email arrived from the 'Prime Minister's political office'. Winnett guessed it had been written by Brown himself because it was typed out in large, bold letters, as all of his correspondence has to be because of his partial blindness, the result of a terrible rugby accident he suffered as a teenager. To Winnett's immense relief, it contained no nasty surprises. The Prime Minister had paid the money to his brother because they shared a cleaner, Brown said. It was what the investigation team had suspected, though it still didn't explain why Brown had not simply paid the cleaner directly, as he had done with other cleaners.

The response also contained a classic piece of spin. Referring to a £153 plumber's bill which Brown had claimed for – and been reimbursed for – twice, it said that 'when this inadvertent error was discovered, the amount was immediately repaid'. What it failed to mention was that the error was only 'discovered' when it was pointed out by the *Telegraph*'s letter, and it had only been repaid that very afternoon, as Downing Street was later forced to admit.

Like his ministers, Brown had denied any wrongdoing, but didn't dispute any of the claims. As far as the investigation team was concerned, he was 'bang to rights'; but William Lewis wanted to satisfy himself that the *Telegraph* was not going overboard in its examination of the Prime Minister's expenses claims. Lewis believed that Brown, as

Prime Minister, should be beyond reproach in the matter of his expenses and that the arrangement with his brother was, at the very least, questionable. Brown had also made much of his 'moral compass', and yet the previous summer he had not even bothered to vote on wide-ranging reforms to stamp out some of the worst abuses of the expenses system. Nevertheless, Lewis decided that, on balance, the story should concentrate on the breadth of the scandal rather than any one individual; and so, after a quick rewrite, the story revealed that 'More than half the Cabinet are facing allegations over their use of parliamentary expenses after details of their claims were obtained by the *Daily Telegraph*.'

The story would appear under the headline: 'The truth about the Cabinet's expenses' with pictures of Gordon and Andrew Brown, and one of the cleaning receipts, to illustrate it. The headline was factual, but understated, in keeping with the tone of the entire coverage of the scandal. Lewis felt strongly that the facts spoke for themselves and did not need to be in any way hyped up.

Now it was time to whet the British public's appetite to ensure maximum impact – and maximum circulation – when the paper hit the streets the next day.

Shortly after 8 p.m. Fiona Macdonald, the *Telegraph*'s formidable public relations executive, called the three main news broadcasters to tell them the newspaper had a major story which she felt sure they would want to cover in that evening's ten o'clock news bulletins. If they came to the *Telegraph* HQ they would be briefed on the story, and would also be able to interview a senior member of staff on camera. The BBC's political editor, Nick Robinson, knew that such calls were rare and immediately set off for Victoria. Tom Bradby, his opposite number at ITN, also dropped everything, but Sky News's Jon Craig, standing in for political editor Adam Boulton, was less enthusiastic. 'I hope it won't take long,' he said. 'I'm very busy at the moment, so it had better be good.' Macdonald assured him that he wouldn't regret turning up.

Waiting for them in a conference room were Macdonald, Andrew Porter and Benedict Brogan, the paper's new chief political commentator, who had come over from the *Daily Mail* only two weeks earlier.

'We're launching a major investigation into MPs' expenses,' announced Brogan. 'Tonight and in the coming days we're going to be laying out exactly what MPs have been spending public money on.'

The three broadcasters made notes but said nothing. Hmm, thought Brogan. They seem distinctly underwhelmed by this.

'We're going to tell you about the expenses claims made by Gordon Brown, Jack Straw and Paul Murphy,' he went on; then Winnett was asked to join the briefing to fill in the broadcasters with specific details.

They seemed to have their doubts about whether the story was quite as big as the *Telegraph* claimed. Nick Robinson was particularly interested to learn how the *Telegraph* had acquired the information and whether money had changed hands.

'How much of this is stuff that we already know?' asked one.

'Is it that big a deal to pay money to your brother to pay a cleaner?' asked another.

Then came questions about the rumours they had heard.

'Has someone claimed for a sauna?'

'Found any shagging?'

'You'll have to wait and see,' replied Winnett enigmatically, not wanting to give away the fact that the vast majority of the expenses claims hadn't even been looked at.

Brogan, Winnett and Porter emphasized that the story was about the overwhelming extent to which MPs had been playing the system. Slowly the broadcasters began to nod their heads, but it still seemed uncertain whether or not they were going to go for it. Then, as Robinson left the meeting, he took out his mobile phone and rang his news desk. 'We're going to have to change the running order,' he told them. Bradby and Craig relayed similar messages to their editors.

Winnett left Brogan to record on-camera interviews with the television crews, to be used later in the night, as he prepared to make one last phone call of the day.

John Wick had been told earlier in the week that, barring any last-minute hitches, the *Telegraph* was planning to publish on either Friday or Saturday. At 9.45 p.m., a quarter of an hour after the presses had started rolling, Winnett phoned Wick to tell him: 'It's definitely tomorrow. Watch the television news at ten o'clock, and keep your head down!'

Wick replied: 'Sounds great. Can't wait to see it.'

In the bunker, the team gathered around a computer screen to watch the TV news. The broadcasters' reaction to the story would be critical. Although the investigation team knew they had uncovered a massive scandal, the impact of the story would be severely dented if the hugely influential TV political editors played down its significance. The *Telegraph*, after all, was by tradition a Conservative-leaning newspaper, and the expenses claims being highlighted were those of the Labour Cabinet. Would Robinson, Bradby and Craig try to portray the story as a politically motivated smear campaign?

The answer was emphatic. All three channels led their news bulletins on the expenses story, to a resounding cheer from the bunker team, who at last felt that they could relax, if only until the next day. The BBC devoted almost ten minutes of the programme to the story, and Nick Robinson's verdict was unequivocal. It was, he said, a 'disaster' for the government.

Robinson's report was greeted with dismay in Downing Street. Gordon Brown's advisers had gathered in the 'war room' to watch the coverage, hoping the story would be dismissed as a storm in a teacup. Instead, it was being presented by all three broadcasters as a calamity for the government.

Their best hope now lay with Harriet Harman, the Deputy Prime Minister and Leader of the House, who had been chosen to lead the government's fightback. During a high-level conference call involving Ellam, Dugher, Irvin, deputy chief of staff Gavin Kelly, director of political strategy David Muir and policy adviser Justin Forsyth, it had been decided that Harman, who as an inner London MP did not qualify for the second homes allowance and was therefore largely untainted by the scandal, should go in to bat.

Harman ran through the different facets of the story at home before driving herself to Millbank Studios, a short walk from Parliament, where each of the major broadcasters had its own studio facilities. She was met there by Nicola Burdett, Brown's broadcasting adviser, who gave her a final pep talk.

First up would be *Newsnight*, where Harman had hoped to be able to manage some significant damage limitation. Instead she was confronted by an incredulous Gavin Esler, one of the flagship show's main anchors, who repeatedly harangued her about the *Telegraph*'s expenses revelations. Harman fought a losing battle as she tried to insist that the claims of her colleagues were 'all within the rules'.

'But one of your colleagues claimed 5p for a carrier bag,' said Esler, with a look of genuine disgust on his face. 'It just looks cheap. Don't you accept that?'

Harman quickly found she had been given the job of defending the indefensible, and with the *Telegraph*'s Benedict Brogan as *Newsnight*'s studio guest, Esler had the advantage of knowing more about what was in the next day's paper than Harman did.

Brogan and Porter, together with the *Telegraph*'s highly experienced assistant editor Andrew Pierce, would be the public faces of the expenses investigation over the coming weeks, meeting an almost endless number of requests for interviews from dawn to dusk. Over the coming days, the three of them would give a total of 146 interviews to television and radio stations as far afield as New Zealand, Lithuania, Norway, Russia, France, Dubai, the US and South Africa, as well as to every major broadcaster in the UK. As well as leaving the bunker team free to get on with the job in hand, they would play a vital role in making sure the story received the maximum possible airtime, and defending the *Telegraph* against the many accusations that rivals and MPs would throw at it.

Porter, Brogan and Pierce, along with everyone else at the *Telegraph*, were about to find out just how much pressure the newspaper would have to withstand if it was to carry on with the expenses investigation.

Backlash

Friday, 8 May

'My MP has a better washing
machine than your MP'

CHAPTER 11

A S BROADCASTERS CLEARED their schedules to report every aspect of the *Daily Telegraph*'s expenses revelations when the paper hit the streets on Friday morning, Gordon Brown's closest advisers were bracing themselves for one of the most challenging days of their professional lives.

The Prime Minister had erupted in fury after seeing the *Telegraph*'s front-page disclosure about his cleaning arrangements, and was said to have stayed up much of the night agonizing over the article and reading every word of the coverage on the *Telegraph*'s website. His mood got even worse when he tuned in to Radio Four's *Today* programme at 6 a.m. to find that one of the BBC's most respected daily news shows was following the *Telegraph*'s lead by questioning the validity of his expenses claims. Brown was beside himself over the fact that the BBC was not holding the *Telegraph*'s story at arm's length, and spoke to Michael Dugher before dawn to express his outrage that the BBC thought the story about the payments to his brother to be a major news story.

Brown had a copy of the cleaning contract, showing that the money had gone to the cleaner, and he wanted to release it straight away to shut the story down. Dugher arranged for a copy of the contract to be sent electronically to the BBC; it arrived at 6.35 a.m., but it wasn't enough to stop the BBC and every other news organization giving the expenses story wall-to-wall coverage for the rest of the day.

In Downing Street, the man who had been at the centre of the world only a month earlier, at the G20 summit, had been reduced to fretting about cleaning contracts, plumber's bills and Ikea kitchens. Instead of trying to solve the global financial crisis, he found his integrity threatened by a crisis over his personal finances.

Brown's anger was stoked up even further shortly after dawn that Friday, when he learned that a reporter from the London *Evening Standard* newspaper had entered the private staircase of Andrew Brown's block of flats and videoed an exchange between himself and the Prime Minister's brother – which consisted of him shouting questions at Andrew Brown through the front door over the cleaning arrangement. It was an unedifying moment for the Brown family, who have jealously guarded their privacy throughout the Prime Minister's political career.

So by the time Brown's key strategists dialled into Downing Street for a conference call, the Prime Minister was positively incandescent over what he saw as an unjustified attack on his personal integrity. His advisers couldn't help thinking that, even for a man who was famous for his rages, this was possibly the blackest mood they had even known him to sink into. 'He was absolutely livid,' one adviser later said.

Michael Ellam, senior Brown aide Sue Nye and James

Bowler, Brown's private secretary, were among those involved in discussions that morning. Item one on the agenda was how Downing Street could hit back at the *Telegraph*. Brown's advisers all agreed that the *Telegraph* had treated the Prime Minister unfairly and they decided to release a copy of the cleaning contract to all media organizations in an attempt to prove that he had done nothing wrong. Dugher, meanwhile, was given the task of extracting an apology from the *Telegraph* for its coverage. According to those who spoke to the Prime Minister that morning, his focus was on clearing his own name and that of his brother. There was little discussion about the wider political scandal which was starting to run out of control as broadcasters and websites greedily gobbled up every detail of the *Telegraph*'s expenses stories.

Although Brown had cleared his diary on Thursday afternoon to deal with the crisis, he would not cancel a long-standing engagement on Friday to attend a memorial service in Bradford for the murdered policewoman Sharon Beshenivsky. Onlookers were shocked at his appearance as he boarded the train to Bradford. His eyes were red-rimmed with exhaustion and had dark shadows under them, clear signs of the sleepless night he had chosen to endure. Instead of catching up on some sleep during the journey, however, the Prime Minister sat at a table with a copy of the *Daily Telegraph*, scribbling copious notes across the pages where he thought the government could hit back, and underlining what he perceived to be mistakes.

Brown's narrow-minded reaction to the story troubled

some of his ministers and many backbench MPs, who felt he was failing to get a grip on the situation and to show leadership. They would be proved right in the coming days, when David Cameron's swift and ruthless response to the behaviour of his own MPs saw his popularity rise with the public, even though the Tories had behaved just as badly as their Labour counterparts.

Nevertheless, both Downing Street and the parliamentary authorities would exert immense pressure on the *Daily Telegraph* that Friday in the hope that the newspaper would lose its nerve. Winnett got his first sense of how the day might unfold when he was called into the editor's office shortly before 9 a.m. William Lewis wanted to discuss the following day's coverage, and Winnett went through a list of other senior government ministers who had made questionable expenses claims and whose stories, he had agreed with Chris Evans and Matthew Bayley, should appear on day two. Lewis, however, was acutely aware of the need for the *Telegraph* to avoid accusations of party political bias in its coverage, in order to maintain the maximum credibility for the investigation. Several Labour ministers had been in contact with senior reporters and executives at the *Telegraph* to suggest it would be unfair to focus solely on Labour.

'Presumably you're doing the Tories tomorrow, then?' was the general tenor of their calls. 'Do you realize the sort of things they've been up to?'

So now Lewis asked: 'Should we go for some Tories tomorrow?'

Winnett strongly believed the paper should stick to the original plan of focusing on Labour for the first two days. As the party in government, Labour had had the opportunity to change the system and yet they had squandered, and probably even blocked, previous chances of reform. Also, the *Telegraph* had at least two days of coverage on the Conservatives planned for the following week. That morning's lead story had clearly stated that the newspaper would be covering politicians from all parties in the coming days and there was no need, Winnett argued, to be bounced into covering the Tories early just because Labour were making a lot of noise.

Lewis agreed, but as Winnett got up to leave the office the editor's mobile phone rang. It was Gordon Brown calling. Lewis has never disclosed what was said in the conversation, but as Winnett shut the door behind him he could hear the beginning of what was clearly a rather heated discussion.

'That's me crossed off the Prime Minister's Christmas card list, then,' he said to himself.

At The Stationery Office, workers were still carrying out the process of redaction which had begun the previous summer. Few of them knew that one or more of their number had decided to orchestrate a leak, but after their initial surprise at seeing the *Telegraph*'s expenses stories, the mood was one of quiet celebration.

At a British Army base overseas, two of the soldiers who had been on the security team in the TSO redaction room almost a year before popped into the base's internet room to catch up on the news back home. They had no idea about the furore back in Britain until they logged on to the *Telegraph*'s website.

'Look at this!' one of the two men said, beckoning over his comrade.

'Bugger me,' replied the second soldier. 'How the bloody hell have they got hold of that?'

On a professional level, the soldiers were disappointed that the data they had been hired to protect had leaked out. But on a personal level, both men felt a certain wry satisfaction at seeing the MPs held up to public scrutiny.

'Well, the shit's really going to hit the fan now,' said the soldier sitting at the computer screen.

As senior executives at TSO gathered on the Friday morning, they were far from relaxed at what they were reading in the *Telegraph*. An investigation into the leak of the information was immediately ordered.

In the bunker, the reporters would spend most of that day blissfully unaware of the strain that the newspaper's management was having to bear – which was just as well, as the reporters could ill afford any distractions as they embarked on another mammoth effort to produce just as many stories for the second day's coverage.

Each had a spring in their step after coming in to work with evidence of the scale of the story all around them. Not only was the expenses story dominating the television and radio news almost to the exclusion of everything else, but there were clearly more people than usual reading the *Telegraph* on trains and buses, and other newspapers had scrambled to get the story into their second editions.

Among the audience, too, were the vast majority of the bunker team's colleagues at the *Telegraph*, who had known nothing about the story until it started breaking on the television news the night before, and who were thrilled to discover that their newspaper was suddenly the talk of the nation. Jeff Randall, the *Telegraph* columnist and Sky News presenter, summed up the mood in an email to Winnett. 'BRILLIANT,' he wrote. 'I mean seriously, outstandingly, effin' brilliant. Love it.'

Praise for the *Telegraph*'s story was not universal, however. The left-leaning *Guardian* ran a lengthy article accusing the *Telegraph* of resorting to 'chequebook journalism'.

Porter, Brogan and Pierce were almost omnipresent on the airwaves (Porter texted Lewis to say: 'Story huge. Will have done six broadcasts by 8.30am') while Harriet Harman remained Labour's sole representative on early morning television. Instead of defending her colleagues, Harman attacked the expenses system itself and began talking of the need for reform and investigating those who had broken the rules.

'I know people will be very angry and concerned about this, but I do want to reassure people that we have recognized there's a problem and we've already taken action on this,' she said on GMTV.

She was then asked whether ministers had been caught 'fiddling' their expenses, and answered: 'I think you've got to be quite careful about saying "fiddling". I don't think that because Gordon Brown, the Prime Minister, shared a cleaner for his flat with his brother, that that is fiddling. I don't think anyone's suggesting that Gordon Brown was pocketing that £6,000, nor are they suggesting that his brother was pocketing that £6,000.' Harman was clearly being dragged into territory she would rather have avoided at all costs.

For the investigation team, the reaction was a huge relief. Although they had been confident the story was huge, they also realized that after more than a week in the bunker they had become detached from the outside world and hence lacked objectivity. The response to the story amounted to vindication for all those working on it.

Over in Parliament, the reaction was rather different. James Kirkup, the only *Telegraph* reporter in Westminster while Porter conducted interviews and Winnett and Prince stayed in the bunker, found himself the focus of hostile reaction from MPs. Some simply pretended not to see him. Others looked daggers at him, and one minister made a V-sign. Another minister, however, was rather less condemnatory. 'It's bloody brilliant, your paper,' he bellowed, slapping Kirkup on the back. 'I never realized half the things we could claim until now. I'm going to order a bloody great telly for my flat!'

Kirkup also had to deal with the frenetic questions from rival reporters, who all wanted to know the same things. How did you get the disk? How much more is there to come? What's in tomorrow's paper?

Eventually, Kirkup closed the office door, after pinning on it a note which read:

Telegraph Expenses Story: Answers to frequently asked questions.

1   I'm not telling you.
2   I'm not telling you.
3   I'm not telling you.
4   I'm not telling you.
5   I'm not telling you.

If MPs were suspicious of journalists, however, they were perhaps even more suspicious of each other. In Parliament's tea rooms, usually the setting for lively gossip-swapping, members could barely bring themselves to speak in the days to come. The Labour MP Brian Iddon described how

> A dark cloud descended on the place . . . we wandered round in a state of shock and horror at what some of our colleagues had been doing. I couldn't believe it myself. A sort of feeling of distrust came over the place, you couldn't look people in the eye because you wondered what was coming next, whether they were going to be the subject of another story.

Back at the *Telegraph* HQ, there was a unique challenge ahead. A typical newspaper exclusive involves one big revelation which can be spread over two or three days. If the story is important enough, it develops a life of its own as other newspapers and journalists find their own angles and chase up their own leads. This was entirely different: having printed what might on any other day be career-ending disclosures about the expenses claims of fourteen of the country's most senior politicians (a unique achievement in itself), the *Telegraph* was moving on to a whole new set of MPs, with little time for reflection. Indeed, half the team of reporters had already begun preparing articles for Saturday's newspaper on the previous day while the coverage of the Cabinet's expenses was being put together.

Phil Hope, a health minister, had spent more than £40,000 on furniture for a modest two-bedroomed flat in south London. How was this possible? Evans wanted a floor-plan of the flat to work out if that amount of furniture could even fit into the property. Barbara Follett, the tourism minister who is married to the multi-millionaire novelist Ken Follett, had claimed more than £25,000 for 'private security patrols' outside the couple's London townhouse. She had told the parliamentary fees office that she did not feel safe in central London. How could a Labour tourism minister say such a thing while attempting to sell the country to potential visitors from abroad? Phil Woolas, the gaffe-prone immigration minister, had submitted receipts for tampons, women's tights and even 'ladies' shoes'. Martin Beckford, writing the story, was looking forward to hearing his explanation of how such items were within rules which stipulated that only items for an MP's 'personal use' were claimable. Vera Baird, the solicitor general, had even tried to claim for Christmas tree decorations.

'This is getting totally out of control. Do these people have no shame?' said Beckford as he prepared the letter for Woolas.

The *Telegraph* also had to deal quickly with a number of other senior MPs whose expenses claims had been seen by other newspapers: Michael Martin, the Speaker, and the former minister Keith Vaz. Michael Martin had rather grandly hired liveried chauffeurs to transport him around various locations in Glasgow, including a job centre. Vaz had unusual property arrangements. Despite representing a constituency in Leicester, where he had a constituency home, his 'main' home was a large detached property on the outskirts of London – and his 'second' home was a flat in Westminster. He regularly switched his second-home designation between two properties, enabling him to claim expenses towards both of them. During one financial year he bought twenty-two cushions, most of them silk, at taxpayers' expense. Once again, letters were prepared and sent to the MPs and ministers in question.

By lunchtime, however, debate was raging within the building about whether the investigation was following the right path. Lewis's concerns about continuing to restrict the coverage to Labour had not gone away. He felt there was a need to include at least one Conservative MP in the following day's paper to show readers that this was not a one-party scandal. The bunker team wanted to keep the most high-profile Tories under wraps for a headline-grabbing edition the following Monday; so Greg Barker, the shadow climate change minister, was chosen as a compromise candidate. Barker, who had previously attracted controversy after leaving his wife for a male interior designer, had moved between expensive homes in Chelsea, west London, claiming for extensive renovation work on the properties at taxpayers' expense before making a handsome profit of more than £320,000 on the deal.

Meanwhile Mark Skipworth, who was in charge of the Saturday edition of the paper, wanted to know which backbench MPs had committed the worst abuses. One name stood out from those who had been looked at so far – Margaret Moran, the Labour MP for Luton South.

Moran, who was so obscure that the parliamentary reporters barely even recognized the name, had made a series of extraordinary claims which had been picked up by Holly Watt as she compiled the database of MPs' second homes. A detailed analysis of these claims showed that she had flipped her second-home designation between three different addresses, in London, Luton and Southampton, spending more than £80,000 of public money in total on repairs, renovations and mortgage interest payments. Most extraordinary of all was the claim she had made for the property in Southampton, more than 100 miles away from her constituency. Within a month of designating the property as her second home, Moran had claimed more than £22,000 in taxpayer-funded expenses to treat dry rot at the house, which turned out to be jointly owned by her partner.

Moran would, therefore, be the first backbench MP to feature in the investigation. Rosa Prince duly phoned her to ask for the appropriate email address to send her a letter about her expenses. Before she could get the words out, Moran started screaming at the top of her voice.

'Wait! How can you have seen my expenses when I haven't even seen them?' she shrieked.

Prince replied: 'I have some questions which I need to put to you. What's the best email address to get a confidential letter to you?'

'No! I have some questions for you! How did you get my expenses?!'

'If you just give me your email address, the letter will explain it.'

Moran, who hung up before giving her full email address, was clearly gearing up for a fight, as the events of the next few days would prove.

She wasn't the only one preparing to take on the *Telegraph*. Shortly before 3 p.m., the Press Association wire service issued a news alert to all newspapers and broadcasters. It said simply: 'The Commons authorities have asked the police to investigate the leaking of MPs' expenses details, a spokesman for the House said today.' The bunker team's previous jokes about prison cells and handcuffs started to seem rather hollow as the prospect of a criminal investigation moved a step closer. Did this mean the bunker team were about to have their collars felt? Malcolm Jack, the Clerk of the House of Commons, had contacted Scotland Yard to say he believed there were 'reasonable grounds to believe a criminal offence may have been committed'. The Yard said it was 'considering the request'.

Head of news Chris Evans was unconvinced. 'There's no way the police are going to want to get involved in this,' he said. He was aware that Sir Paul Stephenson, the

Metropolitan Police Commissioner, had given the *Telegraph* an interview to mark his first 100 days in office, to be published the following day, in which he spoke of the need for the Met to concentrate on 'serious crime' and avoid being 'dragged into party political games'.

And there were further developments to come. Just over an hour after the Commons authorities contacted Scotland Yard, Sky News began reporting that 'police sources' had said that they were also considering investigating MPs who had made questionable expenses claims. One MP highlighted by the 'police sources' for possible investigation was Tony McNulty.

As Evans had predicted, police involvement had suddenly become very political and the stakes were growing higher. Scotland Yard appeared to be warning the Commons that if they were put under pressure to investigate the leak they might also start probing MPs.

Some MPs were deeply unhappy that the response of the Commons to the expenses scandal was to attack the *Telegraph*, and detected the hand of the Speaker, Michael Martin, behind the decision. Kate Hoey, the former sports minister, telephoned *Telegraph* political commentator Benedict Brogan to register her support for the newspaper's exposé. In an unusual move, she agreed to be quoted criticizing the Commons' decision to call in the police. She said: 'It is a complete waste of public money. All this is doing is trying to cover up what should have been transparent from the beginning, which is what MPs do with taxpayers' money. The public will not be impressed.' Norman Baker, a Liberal

Democrat who has campaigned for greater disclosure of MPs' expenses, said, 'Calling in the police is a distraction,' while Shami Chakrabarti, the director of the civil rights organization Liberty, said she hoped there would be 'no question of coming after a national newspaper for exposing such a matter of public interest'.

One man who was becoming increasingly worried about police involvement was whistleblower John Wick. That morning he had caught a train to work from his home in Worthing to London, reading the *Telegraph* and *The Times* on the journey. As he did so, he became increasingly convinced that he would be arrested as he passed through the ticket barriers in London. Although his fears proved unfounded, he was alarmed when he heard during the afternoon that Parliament had contacted the police.

Wick decided not to leave anything to chance. Drawing on his SAS training, he called his partner, Tania, and asked her to make her way to Victoria station with a bag of his clothes and other essentials. Wick explained that she was not to acknowledge him in any way when she saw him at the station, in case either of them was being watched, and that he would draw her into a crowd where she should surreptitiously hand over the bag. Tania followed his instructions to the letter and Wick hired a car before driving to Dorset, where he lay low for forty-eight hours. He would later catch a flight from Gatwick Airport to Spain to maintain a safe distance from the unfolding events. (He realized just how big the story had become when he noticed a thriving black market in copies of the *Sunday Telegraph* at the airport newsagent, where people were paying 'touts' more than the cover price for the newspaper after the shops had run out!)

While the debate about police involvement in the story began to rage, in Downing Street attention was still focused on extracting an apology for the Prime Minister from the *Daily Telegraph*. At 5.34 p.m. John Woodcock, another of the Prime Minister's main advisers, emailed senior *Telegraph* executives with a 'proposed clarification' for the following day's newspaper. The email said:

> The PM would like you to agree to print the following statement:
>
> CLARIFICATION
>
> THE *DAILY TELEGRAPH* WISHES TO MAKE IT CLEAR THAT THE £6,000 CLAIMED OVER TWO YEARS BY MR BROWN FOR A CLEANER WAS FOR PAYMENTS MADE TO A PROFESSIONAL CLEANER WHO MAINTAINED HIS FLAT. A FULL CONTRACT SHOWING THIS HAS BEEN SEEN BY THE *DAILY TELEGRAPH*.
>
> THE *DAILY TELEGRAPH* WAS WRONG TO STATE THAT MR BROWN 'USED HIS PARLIAMENTARY ALLOWANCES TO BOOST HIS EXPENSES CLAIMS BY SWITCHING HIS DESIGNATED SECOND HOME SHORTLY BEFORE HE MOVED INTO DOWNING STREET'.
>
> THE *DAILY TELEGRAPH* IS ALSO WRONG TO HAVE CLAIMED THAT MR BROWN 'APPEARS TO HAVE PAID FOR LITTLE OF HIS OWN LIVING COSTS SINCE MOVING INTO NUMBER 10'.

Referring to an article which reprised the fact that Mr Brown had bought his private London flat from the collapsed empire of Robert Maxwell, the late newspaper tycoon, it added:

ANY SUGGESTION THAT HIS FLAT WAS PURCHASED OTHER THAN ON THE OPEN MARKET AFTER BEING WIDELY ADVERTISED IS COMPLETELY UNTRUE.

The *Daily Telegraph* declined to print the clarification but did reflect part of the Prime Minister's response in another article. The newspaper also made it clear that it intended to press on with the publication of revelations about a whole new set of government ministers in the following day's edition. Downing Street aides, predictably enough, were furious. Instead of being able to shift the angle of the story in the other newspapers to one which questioned the *Telegraph*'s motives and the accuracy of its reports, Downing Street found itself having to cope with an avalanche of new allegations, without time to pause for breath. By the following day, no one would be interested in the Prime Minister's rebuttals of the *Telegraph*'s stories, because they would be immersed in this brand new series of disclosures about what other MPs had been up to. Brown became convinced he was the victim of a 'political plot' and that the story had been leaked by a Conservative supporter who was only interested in damaging the Labour Party. (In the coming weeks, the Prime Minister's office would conduct private polling which found that Labour ministers were disproportionately 'hit' by expenses revelations compared to their Conservative counterparts.)

Rosa Prince got a taste of the reaction inside Downing Street when she phoned No. 10. She was told in no uncertain terms that the *Telegraph* would not be receiving much assistance 'for a while'.

'It's nothing personal,' insisted one adviser.

Despite being in the thick of a growing media storm and possible police investigation, those in the bunker had to continue working to get out the following day's paper.

The Saturday edition of the *Telegraph* on 9 May was to carry eleven pages of new revelations over MPs' expenses. At about 6 p.m. on Friday the MPs who were about to be exposed began to respond to the newspaper's earlier enquiries. Ben Bradshaw, then a junior health minister, accused the *Telegraph* of homophobia for questioning whether it was appropriate that the taxpayer now covered the full mortgage interest on a property he owned with his civil partner (the couple had previously split the cost when Bradshaw was claiming for another house in Exeter). Follett, Vaz and virtually every other MP and minister contacted that day defended their behaviour on the basis that they had acted within the rules. Blaming the system was becoming the name of the game. Margaret Moran was one of the few MPs simply not to respond.

One of the most bizarre responses came from Phil Woolas. The Labour MP for Oldham East and Saddleworth is not known for his tact, and had exasperated colleagues in the past with his bluntness and outspoken comments. He had once said that the population of the country could be capped, only to be quickly rebuked by the home secretary. Earlier that week he had been outmanoeuvred by Joanna Lumley when the Gurkha campaigner, having had a meeting with the immigration minister, said in front of television cameras that the minister had, in effect, agreed to all her demands. Woolas, standing beside her at the time, had looked more and more queasy as he watched the actress forcing him into a corner. Now, on the evening of Friday, 8 May, Woolas went to war with the *Telegraph* over whether the taxpayer had paid for tampons he had purchased.

In a series of phone calls to Martin Beckford, he insisted that the reporter had got it wrong. 'There are family items for which I did not claim,' he said. 'The amount of expenses claimed and received was less than the receipt submitted.'

He then began to telephone bemused journalists from other newspapers to inform them he was about to be 'incorrectly outed' as an MP who had bought women's clothing and tampons. The *Telegraph* had got it wrong, he told them.

Beckford held his ground. He double-checked every receipt and compared them to Woolas's claim forms. Beckford was able to prove that Woolas had claimed the full amount for the receipts which included tampons, meaning they had been paid for by the taxpayer.

The irony was that the rules allowed MPs to claim up to £400 per month for groceries without producing receipts. Woolas had voluntarily provided the receipts – a decision which was now causing him acute embarrassment.

They showed that in one weekly shop he spent £1.48 on panty liners, £1.19 on tampons, £2.99 on nappies and £15 on a ladies' blouse. Another trip included claims for £5.96 on disposable bibs, £23 on women's shoes, £1.99 for a child's comic, £1.60 and £1.55 on more comics, £2.88 on baby wipes and £5 on a ladies' jumper.

Inexplicably, one bill from Tesco showed he had received a 10 per cent staff discount.

Head of news Chris Evans was satisfied that despite the minister's vociferous denials, Beckford had got it right. The headline for the article on page nine was written. It read: 'Minister claimed for women's clothing and panty liners'.

Woolas was incensed. After the paper was published, he embarked on a series of television interviews outside his house in which he said the *Telegraph*'s claims were 'absolutely disgusting'. He said: 'It is untrue that I claimed these things. It misunderstands the system. The receipts are there, but I never asked for or got money for these items. To suggest otherwise is disgusting.'

However, he later appeared to concede, when confronted with evidence, that the *Telegraph* had indeed been correct and that he may have made a mistake. 'I am being hung out to dry for being honest,' he said.

By 9 p.m. that Friday, one of the most extraordinary days in the *Telegraph*'s history was coming to a close. The next day's front-page headline read: 'The ministers and the money'. Bradshaw, Hope, Follett and Woolas were all pictured.

For the second night in succession, the investigation

team decamped to the Harvard Bar in the Thistle Hotel next door to the office to unwind and see how their stories were being reported on the television news. Unfortunate hotel guests trying to enjoy a quiet drink had the misfortune of finding themselves surrounded by more than twenty journalists who commandeered the large flat-screen television in the corner of the bar and turned up the volume before flicking between channels to check the coverage on BBC and ITV.

As Robinson on BBC1 and Bradby on ITV both once more led the news with the *Telegraph*'s latest revelations, the journalists sounded more like pub regulars watching a football match as they cheered and jeered every twist and turn of the coverage. Within minutes of the broadcast ending, Winnett received a text message from one of the country's most senior police officers, congratulating him on the scoop.

'No chance we'll be investigated now,' Winnett thought as he smiled to himself, making his way over to a corner of the bar where William Lewis, Mark Skipworth and Rhidian Wynn Davies were sharing a bottle of white wine. All three were concerned about the possibility that if the *Telegraph* kept up its relentless pursuit of MPs for too long, the public might decide they had had enough of the story and accuse the paper of overkill. Judging when this tipping point would come – and ending the investigation before the public had reached saturation point – would be vital to the long-term impact of the campaign.

While his reporters revelled in being involved in the greatest scoop of their careers, Lewis's mind had already raced ahead to the end-game. 'What's the plan, then?' he asked the others.

The challenge for the editor, having pressed the button on the investigation, would be judging when to bring it to a conclusion – 'exiting stage left, with the applause still ringing in our ears'. In theory, the sheer volume of expenses data at the team's disposal meant the investigation could roll on for months while remaining unequivocally in the public interest. But how long would the revelations remain interesting to the public? A week? Ten days? A fortnight?

'We need an exit strategy,' announced Lewis.

The Tories Get their Turn

Sunday, 10 May

'I went into politics to make my
living room a better place'

CHAPTER 12

THE DECISION TO KEEP the investigation focused on the government for a second day in succession had provoked apoplectic fury among many Labour MPs, but the *Telegraph* had made it clear from the word go that every party would have its turn, and the investigation team had decided that focusing on the Tories on Monday, 11 May, at the start of a new working week, would give the story fresh impetus.

In the meantime, the *Sunday Telegraph* would unveil what appeared to be the most serious abuse of the expenses system so far unearthed. Ian MacGregor, the *Sunday Telegraph*'s editor, had been kept abreast of the daily paper's expenses investigation from the beginning so that the coverage could span seven days a week. He had quietly assembled his own team who would soon be scouring some of the files for their own stories under the guidance of Ben Leapman, one of the journalists behind the original freedom of information requests.

The scandal uncovered by the *Sunday Telegraph* involved the second-home claims made by the five MPs representing Sinn Fein, the Irish nationalist party widely referred to as 'the political wing of the IRA'. It was commonly known among journalists that the five Sinn Fein MPs, including former IRA members Gerry Adams and Martin McGuinness, claimed close to the maximum second-home allowance despite refusing to take up their seats in Westminster. In total, the five MPs had claimed almost £500,000 over the course of seven years. The data on the Firestorm disk took the story much further. Receipts submitted by the five MPs showed that, between them, they had rented three London properties from the same family. Investigations by *Sunday Telegraph* reporters Andrew Alderson and David Barrett found that the properties had been rented at rates well above the market norm. Adams and McGuinness had jointly claimed expenses of £3,600 per month to rent a shared two-bedroomed flat in north London, where a local estate agent said a fair market rent would be £1,400. The three other MPs together claimed £5,400 per month for a property which the estate agent said was worth more like £1,800 per month. Neighbours living near the properties did not recognize the MPs from pictures shown to them.

The *Sunday Telegraph* story prompted calls for a parliamentary inquiry into the Sinn Fein MPs' claims, and further strengthened the *Telegraph*'s case that publication of the expenses claims had been overwhelmingly in the public interest. Without the addresses which were included on the disk (but which would have been censored when the documents were released to the public) there would have been no way of knowing about the shared properties.

Despite being in the bar of the Thistle Hotel until the early hours of Saturday morning, Rayner, Winnett, Prince and Swaine had volunteered to work on Saturday to supply the *Sunday Telegraph* with stories on another eight MPs not covered in the material the Sunday paper had in its possession. They included the former Tory environment minister John Gummer, who had claimed for moles to be removed from his country estate; John Reid, the former home secretary and self-styled hard man of Labour, who had claimed for a pouffe and a glittery loo seat; and the junior minister Kitty Ussher, who had given her Victorian home a £20,000 makeover on expenses.

Ussher had written a letter to the fees office, which had been spotted by Prince in the early days of the investigation, in which she asked whether she could claim for various items, including having her ceilings replastered. She wrote: 'Most of the ceilings have Artex coverings. Three-dimensional swirls. It could be a matter of taste, but this counts as "dilapidations" in my book! Can the ACA pay for the ceilings to be plastered over and repainted?' The fees office refused, but Ussher was one of the first MPs to discover that the money didn't actually have to be paid out for public anger to erupt. The very fact that she had tried to claim for having the swirly Artex removed was enough to enrage her constituents.

There was also a blast from the past in the form of Tony Blair, whose final expenses claims showed that he put in a bill for almost £7,000 of roof repairs just two days before he left Parliament in 2007. (Mr Blair's expenses file was incomplete, however – parliamentary officials had shredded many of his claims forms in error more than a year earlier after they had been requested by journalists Heather Brooke, Ben Leapman and Jan Ungoed-Thomas.)

While the investigation team was preparing stories for the *Sunday Telegraph*, William Lewis was spending Saturday at a garden party in Wiltshire where fellow guests including the novelist Robert Harris and newsreader Jon Sopel warmly congratulated him on his newspaper's audacious scoop. The host of the garden party, however, found himself in a rather unenviable position. Just days before the *Telegraph*'s expenses story had broken, he had been approached by Gordon Brown, who wanted him to replace the outgoing Michael Ellam as his communications chief. Unbeknown to all but a handful of the guests who had gathered to celebrate his fiftieth birthday, the host was having to slap Lewis on the back for a job well done, knowing full well that if he accepted the offer from Brown, he would not only have to help clear up the wreckage caused by Lewis's newspaper, but would also have the job of trying to protect Brown from any future attacks by Lewis or his staff.

That would have been irony enough, but what made this confluence of events even more remarkable was that the party host and prospective prime ministerial spin doctor was none other than Simon Lewis, William's elder brother. William was one of the few people who knew about the job offer from Brown, and the brothers exchanged knowing glances as the congratulations kept coming. Simon had recently left the telecommunications giant Vodafone, where he had been director of corporate affairs. To the Prime

Minister's credit, he didn't hold Simon Lewis's family connection against him; the job offer remained, and Lewis decided to accept, though he would not start work at No. 10 until the worst of the expenses scandal had blown over.

By Sunday the entire bunker team was back in harness, in readiness for the assault on the Shadow Cabinet's expenses claims which would appear in Monday's paper. For Christopher Hope, working on Sunday had meant a particularly early start, as he had to get to London from his family home in Norfolk on a day when there was no regular train service. Like the majority of his colleagues, Hope had lived in London for most of his career, but his life had been turned upside down in 2007 when his family was involved in a horrendous accident. His wife, daughter and mother-in-law had been on their way to visit his wife's sister, who had just had a baby, when they were hit by a bus which ran out of control in a terminus near their home. Hope's mother-in-law was killed, his daughter Pollyanna, then aged two, lost a leg below the knee, and his wife Sarah also suffered terrible leg injuries. As they tried to rebuild their lives, the Hopes had decided to get away from London in favour of the tranquillity of rural Norfolk, leaving the *Daily Telegraph*'s Whitehall editor with a punishing commute.

Hope had earned immense respect from his colleagues for the dignity and quiet determination with which he went about getting on with his life, regularly bringing in superb exclusives for the newspaper while coping with the ever-present consequences of the accident. The expenses story had come along at a particularly difficult time, as Hope had just gone through the painful process of reliving the accident and its aftermath for a lengthy article in the *Telegraph* magazine. On the day when the *Telegraph* published its first revelations about MPs' expenses, Hope, in between writing letters to government ministers, had left the office to record an interview about the accident with BBC Radio Five Live, and he had also been asked to write an article for the *Daily Mail*, which he did in what little spare time he had. His articles and interview, which were aimed at raising awareness of the Limbless Association, drew a huge response from the public, and Hope's days in the bunker always began with opening letters and cheques from well-wishers, who sent in nearly £70,000 for the charity.

Leaving his wife and three children to work on a Sunday was always a wrench, and on this particular day he had to leave home at dawn to get to the office for 8 a.m. The only way he had of getting to London without taking the train was to borrow his wife's bright pink Nissan Micra convertible, and as he started the engine his mind wasn't entirely on the task in hand. Hope put the car in reverse, pressed the accelerator – and drove straight into a lamp-post.

'Sod it,' he thought, as he checked there wasn't any visible damage to the lamp-post. 'Not the best start to the day.'

Hope had spent much of his time in the previous week looking through the expenses of the Shadow Cabinet. The investigation team had expected the expenses of the Tory front bench to be among the cleanest of all: after all, not only were they at the head of a party preparing for government, they were also, traditionally, better off than their Labour counterparts and so would surely have less need to claim money back from the taxpayer. This was an assumption which turned out to be spectacularly wide of the mark, and Hope, together with other members of the team, had made some startling discoveries.

Chris Grayling, the shadow home secretary, who had built his reputation as the Conservatives' 'attack dog' when it came to the propriety of Labour MPs' conduct, had made a series of questionable claims. Grayling's constituency was in Epsom, just 17 miles from the House of Commons, yet he had claimed expenses for a second home in central London. He also owned two other properties within the M25 which he rented out to supplement his income.

Alan Duncan, the Shadow Leader of the House of Commons, was a millionaire, having worked as an oil trader before entering politics. Surely he didn't need to claim expenses for his second home? Wrong again. Hope discovered that Duncan had spent almost £5,000 of taxpayers' money on gardening, including £598 for the cost of having his ride-on lawnmower serviced. Hope branded him 'the constant gardener' as he found invoice after invoice relating to work on Duncan's second home in Rutland. At one point – highlighted in the files – the parliamentary fees office had even warned Duncan that his claims might appear excessive. The discoveries were particularly embarrassing as Duncan was the Conservative charged with leading the party's drive to clean up the expenses system. He had also made a recent appearance on the BBC's satirical current affairs quiz show

Have I Got News for You, when he had joked about the generosity of expenses available to MPs. Asked by team captain Ian Hislop if he claimed expenses on his second home, despite his personal wealth, Duncan had smugly replied: 'It's a fabulous system, isn't it. It's a great system.'

Hislop asked: 'You don't feel that's a bit dodgy?'

'No.'

The clip would come back to haunt him when it was replayed endlessly on television and posted on YouTube after his gardening claims came to light.

Other members of the Shadow Cabinet had made claims that were simply embarrassing. The shadow universities secretary David 'two brains' Willetts had claimed £132 for a workman to change the light bulbs at his London house. The chairman of the Conservative Research Department, Oliver Letwin, claimed more than £2,000 for a plumber to replace a leaking water pipe under his tennis court. Cheryl Gillan, the shadow Welsh secretary, even claimed £4.47 for dog food for her Lhasa apso bitch, Curby.

Nor were the expenses claims of the party leader, David Cameron, or the Shadow Chancellor, George Osborne, squeaky clean. Cameron, whose blue-blooded wife Samantha is the daughter of Sir Reginald Sheffield, a landowning baronet, had claimed around £20,000 per year to help pay the mortgage interest on his constituency home in Oxfordshire. He had also submitted a £680 repair bill which included the cost of removing wisteria from his chimney. Osborne, meanwhile, had claimed £400 for the cost of a 'chauffeur' to take him from Cheshire to London.

As the reporters compiled formal letters to send out to the senior Tories, Evans and Winnett discussed which of the stories were potential front-page material. The *Telegraph*'s undertaking that all political parties would be treated equally meant that, ideally, Cameron should appear on the front page, in the same way that Brown had done three days earlier. But there was no escaping the fact that Cameron's expenses claims were pretty straightforward compared to those put in by several of his frontbenchers. Boring, even. Cameron had gone public the previous year with the fact that his second-home claims related to mortgage payments (the total amounts for second-home claims were already in the public domain), so there was nothing earth-shattering about what the *Telegraph* had found in Cameron's file. There was the wisteria bill, but hammering him over that would be stretching the point, Evans and Winnett both felt. So in the end it was decided that Cameron's expenses would appear on page five of the paper – enraging Labour and eliciting ever louder accusations of party political bias.

However, there was one senior Conservative whose claims particularly surprised Winnett – and would be at the centre of the first real threat of legal action since the investigation had started. Michael Gove, the shadow schools secretary and paid-up member of Cameron's 'Notting Hill set' of trusted friends, had spent thousands of pounds kitting out two different houses after flipping his second-home designation.

Gove, a former *Times* journalist who had become an MP in 2005, had helped overhaul and modernize the

Conservative Party and was widely regarded as a man in line for one of the very top Cabinet jobs in the next Tory government. Of all the senior Tories who had made questionable claims, Gove had the most to lose, which made his behaviour all the more remarkable. Christopher Hope discovered that in the months after Gove was elected to Parliament he had spent thousands of pounds kitting out his house in west London before flipping his second-home designation to a semi-detached house in his Surrey constituency and claiming £13,000 in moving costs. Then, over a five-month period between December 2005 and April 2006, he had spent more than £7,000 on the Surrey house, which Gove and his wife Sarah Vine, a journalist at *The Times*, had bought in 2002.

Much of the cash was spent at Oka, an upmarket designer store run by Lady Astor, David Cameron's mother-in-law. Gove bought a £331 Chinon armchair from there, as well as a Manchu cabinet for £493 and a pair of elephant lamps for £134.50. He also claimed for a £750 Loire table – although the Commons authorities only allowed him to claim £600 – a birch Camargue chair worth £432 and a bird-cage coffee table priced at £238.50. Other claims in the five-month period included Egyptian cotton sheets from the White Company, a £454 dishwasher, a £639 range cooker, a £702 fridge–freezer and a £19.99 Kenwood toaster. In February 2006 Gove even claimed for a £34.99 foam cot mattress from Toys 'R' Us – despite children's equipment being among the few items excluded from claims under Commons rules.

Appropriately enough, Gove's wife wrote a regular

column in *The Times* called 'How Not To Spend It', in which she had previously observed that 'Like it or not, shopping is part of our cultural DNA: we can no more resist the urge to spend than we can the need to eat.'

As Hope read out a list of the items Gove had claimed for, Winnett shook his head in disbelief. As a former journalist, Gove was surely savvy enough to realize that this information might one day become public and would embarrass him.

'Are you absolutely sure about all this, Chris?' Winnett asked over the top of his computer screen. 'There's no way someone else's claims have got mixed up with his file? What on earth was he thinking?'

There was only one way to find out.

Winnett picked up his BlackBerry and looked up the number for Henry Macrory, the Conservative Party's head of media. Macrory, now in his mid-fifties, was a Fleet Street legend who had covered Parliament for the *Daily Express* and the *Daily Star* and had been famous for taking his own food – usually pork pies – when travelling abroad to exotic locations with the Prime Minister. He had also been responsible for an agony column, written under the nom de plume of Uncle Percy, where on quiet days he would mischievously make up letters from 'readers' with names that sounded remarkably similar to those of his bosses. A typical example, from a 'Dave Stevens', asked: 'A bird crapped on my car, what do I do?' Uncle Percy replied: 'Get a new bird, Dave.' Lord (David) Stevens, the then boss of Express Newspapers, was distinctly unimpressed.

Macrory, or Uncle Percy as he was universally known within the Westminster press corps, had made the switch to press relations almost a decade earlier, but loved nothing better than to be at the centre of a big political story. So when Winnett interrupted his holiday in his native Ireland, he was more than happy to take the call.

'It's the moment you've been waiting for,' Winnett said.

'Ah yes, I thought this might be coming,' Macrory replied.

'As you've probably guessed, tomorrow is Shadow Cabinet day. We're going to be whacking out some letters to a lot of the frontbenchers with questions about their expenses.'

'Right, I'm on my way to a computer. It looks like it's going to be a busy day,' Macrory said. 'How bad – on a scale of one to ten – is this going to be?'

Winnett replied: 'It's not looking good, but there's nothing much we didn't know on Cameron, Osborne or [William] Hague [the shadow foreign secretary].'

Macrory said he already had permission from Cameron and the Shadow Cabinet to have the letters for each MP copied to him. Macrory's questions to Winnett made it clear that the Tories – who knew as soon as the *Telegraph* had begun running its stories about MPs' expenses that the spotlight would inevitably be turned on them – had done their homework on the claims made by the Shadow Cabinet.

'With David [Cameron] it's just that one repair bill, isn't it?' said Macrory.

Winnett was slightly taken aback by such a direct question.

'Er, yeah,' he replied.

'The Tories have already been through all the Shadow Cabinet's expenses by the sound of it,' Winnett told the reporters in the bunker team. 'They seem pretty organized, so hopefully we'll get some answers fairly quickly.'

Unbeknown to the reporters, within minutes of the *Telegraph*'s expenses story breaking the previous Thursday evening, Andy Coulson, the former *News of the World* editor who was now the Conservatives' head of strategy, had been on the phone to Cameron at home. Both men had agreed that the newspaper would be turning to them shortly and that they should start preparing their response. Oliver Dowden, recently installed as the party's director of political operations after a period advising companies as a public relations consultant at Hill & Knowlton, was nominated as the man who would become the party's expenses expert. During the course of the previous Friday, Dowden had been installed in a special office in the Norman Shaw South building in Parliament – adjacent to the offices of Cameron and Osborne. It was an early sign of how central the party's response to the expenses crisis was to Cameron's prime ministerial ambitions.

From his new base, Dowden formed a team made up of several members of the press office and specialist researchers – later expanded to a total of fifteen – to comb through the expenses files of every Conservative MP. This was the Conservatives' own bunker, whose inmates were also working from dawn until dusk in a bid to beat the *Telegraph*'s investigators. Cameron, whose office was only feet away, would regularly pop in to see how his team were progressing.

The Tories' team began with the Shadow Cabinet and would later examine the claims made by MPs about whom the *Telegraph* had been asking questions. This approach would put Macrory and Coulson in a far stronger position to answer questions than their Labour counterparts – as was already clear by the time Winnett and Macrory had spoken little more than forty-eight hours later.

By noon on Sunday the letters to the Tory frontbenchers had been sent, but it would be nearly six hours before the Conservative Party's coordinated responses came back. It was a far from quiet day, however. In the television studios MPs went on the attack in the Sunday morning political shows – among them Margaret Moran. The Queen of the Flippers had taken to the airwaves to tell the BBC that she had been 'misrepresented' and the *Telegraph*'s story was 'actionable', without ever managing to specify what was inaccurate. She claimed she was justified in spending £22,500 of taxpayers' money on the home in Southampton because she was 'entitled to a family life'.

She said: 'My partner works in Southampton. He has done for twenty years. He, if I'm ever going to see my partner of thirty years, I can't make him come to Luton all the time, I have to be able to have a proper family life sometimes, which I can't do unless I have er, you know, I, I share the costs of the Southampton home with him.'

It had clearly never occurred to her that her partner should pay for his own house if the couple chose jobs which meant they lived 100 miles apart, as anyone else would have to do.

The interviewer asked her why the taxpayer should pay for the property. 'Well I, you, you could argue that I use it to be able to sustain my work,' she replied. 'Any MP has to have a proper family life, they have to have support of their partner. How can an MP, I mean I defy anybody to try and do a proper job, it, it – much less an incredibly pressured job, in which you work all hours all, all over you know, in the constituency, in Westminster and incredible pressure all the time.

'It is all within the claims policy and that's why I'm angry about this because not only has it been very stressful for me and my family, it gives the incredibly misleading impression that somehow we've been dodgy, that we've been fraudulent or we've been corrupt. Nothing is further from the truth. As I say, there are – I've done everything by the rules. There are inaccuracies, some of which I think are probably actionable and I think that it's deeply irresponsible and actually the invasion of privacy, not just my privacy but my partner's privacy.'

Her self-pitying interviews were greeted with disbelief by her constituents, many of whom bombarded internet message boards and some of whom branded her 'insane'.

Reporters are used to being criticized and threatened with legal action, but if there's one thing guaranteed to raise their hackles it's an unfounded accusation that they've got a story wrong. Moran was about to find herself at the centre of a daily battle with the bunker team, during which the previously obscure backbench MP became one of the most infamous women in Britain.

Martin Beckford, who was tasked with finding a suitable follow-up story on Moran, discovered that her neighbouring MP Kelvin Hopkins, who represented Luton North for Labour, had made virtually no claims on his second-home allowance despite living in the very same street as Moran. Hopkins had chosen to commute into London every day, just like thousands of his constituents, rather than boarding the gravy train. In one year he had claimed just £296 in second-home allowances, covering a handful of hotel stays.

When he was contacted by Beckford, Hopkins said he was 'astonished' at what had been going on, adding: 'I frankly didn't know that all those things were possible within the rules. I've never had a second home, so I didn't know you could switch them.'

As the week went on, Moran continued to take issue with the *Telegraph*'s coverage, and so Beckford continued to dig up more revelations about her extraordinary behaviour. It turned out that she had not three but four homes, the fourth one being a villa in Spain, where she had angered locals by cutting off access to a footpath by having a mound of earth dumped across it. She had even pinned a letter on her gate in Spain, using House of Commons notepaper, warning people away from her land. Moran denied misusing Commons notepaper by using it for personal correspondence, so the *Telegraph* sent its Spanish correspondent, Fiona Govan, to the village, where Govan found that one of the neighbours had kept a note written on Commons notepaper which he had found pinned to his motorbike, telling him to move it.

Moran – who never contacted the *Telegraph* directly after the first call with Rosa Prince – finally agreed to repay the £22,500 dry rot money, but her constituents made it clear they would settle for nothing less than her resignation.

Meanwhile, another department at the *Daily Telegraph* was becoming almost as busy as the bunker. On a typical day, the readers' letters department might receive scores of emails and letters, but as the expenses investigation got into full swing Christopher Howse, the *Telegraph* columnist and letters editor, was deluged with between 1,800 and 3,000 pieces of correspondence a day – more than twice the previous record for any story in the newspaper's history. Peter Green, of Somerset, summed up the mood when he wrote: 'We are constantly told by MPs that if they were in mainline business they would be earning more. I don't think so: they would be in gaol.'

Sales of the *Telegraph* had gone through the roof, outstripping even the wildest hopes of executives at the paper. For years there had been little evidence that major scoops could lead to a significant rise in newspaper sales – the advent of the internet meant that millions of potential readers simply went online to cherry-pick stories they were interested in seeing. The accepted wisdom was that promotions such as free DVDs were the only way to give sales a boost. Before the expenses stories started running in the *Telegraph*, executives believed the investigation might sell a few thousand extra copies each day, on top of the average

Monday to Saturday daily sale of just under a million. But on the day the paper revealed the expenses claims of the Cabinet an extra 87,000 copies had been sold, one of the biggest daily increases in the newspaper's history. By the end of the expenses investigation, an extra 1.26 million newspapers had been sold, with particularly large sales rises in Scotland and London – and a very localized rise in sales in the Welsh county where the tax office which deals with MPs' expenses is situated.

In the early days of the investigation, however, William Lewis couldn't shake off the fear that somehow or other the operation would be closed down by the authorities, through a police investigation, an injunction or some other means. There was also the danger that the public, and in particular *Telegraph* readers, might decide after a few days that they had had enough of the story, or that the newspaper was being unduly harsh. These concerns meant that every day the subject of an 'exit strategy' came up in editorial meetings.

'Do we call a truce next week to let them sort out the problem?' Lewis asked his deputy, Tony Gallagher, shortly after the stories had started running. 'We need to make sure that we think through what happens every step of the way,' he went on. 'We've had the shock and awe, now we need to win the battle for hearts and minds.'

But no matter how many times Lewis raised the issue, neither he nor his executives could come up with an obvious answer. All they could do, they decided, was to monitor reactions to the story and be ready to react if public opinion started to turn.

The public, however, couldn't get enough of the story. As well as the readers who wrote and phoned to encourage the paper to keep going with the investigation, Lewis received emails from fellow editors and media executives urging him to press ahead. The exit strategy, it seemed, wouldn't be needed after all.

Shortly after five o'clock that first Sunday afternoon, the Conservative frontbenchers began responding to the questions which had been put to them earlier in the day. Most issued short statements – via the party's press office – simply saying that they had acted within the rules. The notable exception was Michael Gove.

Gove was acutely aware that he could be damaged by allegations that he was a 'flipper' of his Commons allowance. In the febrile atmosphere which was building after three days of the expenses investigation, such a charge could mean political death. He firmly rejected any allegation of wrongdoing in his reply to the *Telegraph*, but that was just the opening shot in what would prove to be a desperate attempt to kill off the story. At 7.07 p.m. Christopher Hope received an email from Anthony Julius, the late Princess of Wales's divorce lawyer and a consultant to solicitors Mishcon de Reya.

The email stated that Julius was acting for Gove, who had 'complete and compelling' answers to each of the reporter's questions. It warned Hope that any piece criticizing the shadow minister for breaching even the spirit of the rules would lead Gove to take 'appropriate steps to defend his reputation'.

This email significantly raised the stakes. Lewis called Hope into his office to discuss the Gove story, aware that it was one of the most damaging because of Gove's closeness to Cameron.

'We're getting right into Cameron's circle here,' he said, before grilling Hope on the facts underpinning the story. Hope stuck to his guns. After consulting with Winnett and Evans, Lewis was confident that the shadow schools secretary had behaved in a questionable way and decided to push ahead with the story.

It was starting to look as though the *Telegraph* might find itself in an even bigger fight with the Tories than with Labour – an ironic possibility, given the newspaper's traditional if somewhat outdated reputation as the 'Daily Torygraph'. But there was a welcome surprise to come before the night was out. More in hope than expectation, Winnett had asked Andy Coulson whether David Cameron would like to make a comment on the conduct of his senior team. To the reporter's surprise, shortly after 8 p.m. a spokesman for Cameron telephoned to say that the leader would be providing a quote for inclusion in the newspaper's main story the following day. Although it did not specifically address the allegations, it containedthe word 'sorry' and gave the first indication that Cameron – unlike Brown – was preparing to tackle the expenses scandal head-on. He said:

> We have to acknowledge just how bad this situation is and just how angry the public are. We have to start by saying that the system we had and used was wrong and that we are sorry

about that . . . Claims should in my view be published online immediately they're made. That would be a step towards rebuilding the trust between Parliament and the people it's meant to represent.

Far from defending the claims as being 'within the rules', Cameron had apologized and effectively endorsed the *Telegraph*'s investigation. What he didn't know, however, was that the real scandal involving Tory MPs was yet to come.

Meltdown

Monday, 11 May

'I call him the Speaker
because half the house
is against him'

CHAPTER 13

BY THE TIME MPs returned to Parliament from their weekend break on Monday, 11 May, the expenses investigation was into its fourth day of publication, and with the exposure of the Tories' claims it had become clear to members of all political parties that no one was immune from the *Telegraph*'s disclosures. Panic began to grip MPs, who took to waiting by the phone every day, dreading a call from the *Daily Telegraph*. Only when mid-afternoon had come and 'the call' hadn't could they relax, knowing that they were safe – for another day at least.

The Labour MP Stephen Pound later described the atmosphere as being 'like a slasher movie where every morning we come in and see who's still alive. It really is very desperate and very dark, but what makes it worse is that it's nobody's fault but their own.'

Ann Cryer, another Labour MP, later said: 'It was a very, very grim two or three weeks and there were a lot of very depressed people. People were in such a state. You know, the saying is, if you can't stand the heat, get out of the kitchen. Well, I had no idea just how hot that kitchen was going to get.'

A third MP, who wanted to remain anonymous, told the *Telegraph*: 'It was the most subdued I have ever seen the Commons other than in the wake of a terrorist attack or disaster. Everyone was shell-shocked, casting furtive glances at each other and wondering if they had anything to hide.'

Lobby journalists from all newspapers found that with each new day, a new group of MPs with whom they had enjoyed good working relationships for years would suddenly refuse to speak to them. The *Telegraph*'s James Kirkup sent regular text messages to Winnett and Rosa Prince charting the disintegration of his contacts book. 'Deleting another number from my phone,' said one typical text.

Some MPs were confrontational. Kirkup was shouted at by one Tory frontbencher who fumed: 'My son is being bullied at school because of you!' Others were more reflective. Another Tory frontbencher, whose claims had caused him considerable trouble with his constituents, told Kirkup: 'This is the way the game is played. And when I looked at [the claims] from my constituents' point of view, I realize why they're not happy. It's my responsibility so I have to deal with it.'

The public had little or no sympathy for the MPs, and *Telegraph* staff even found themselves being applauded by total strangers simply because of their association with the paper. When one senior *Telegraph* staffer went into his local newsagents, the friendly shop-owner behind the counter congratulated him on the paper's success at exposing MPs. The queue of people behind him erupted in spontaneous applause as he turned bright red and hurried from the store, nodding his thanks. Benedict Brogan, the *Telegraph* political columnist who was rapidly becoming one of the public faces of the investigation after countless TV interviews, found himself for the first time in his life being stopped in the street by people asking: 'Aren't you that bloke I saw on the telly last night?' and shaking his hand in approval.

One of the most immediate barometers of public opinion – the London cab driver – also backed the *Telegraph* to the hilt. As consulting editor Rhidian Wynn Davies took a taxi home to north London, he was treated to an expletive-ridden tirade by one cabbie, who had taken a particular dislike to Alan Duncan and 'his effin' garden'.

'It's about bleedin' time these people were taken down a peg,' the cabbie said. 'They lord it over us but they don't like it when people find out what they've been up to, do they?'

The following night, Wynn Davies was coming out of a meeting in Holborn when he raised his hand to call a taxi. He was slightly alarmed when a black cab braked sharply and swerved towards him, apparently desperate for his business. Incredibly, it turned out to be the same cabbie that had picked him up the night before.

'Hop in, mate,' said the driver, looking pleased as Punch. 'You can tell me who the *Telegraph*'s having a go at in tomorrow's paper!'

Telegraph staff who were churchgoers even found the expenses story being quoted from the pulpit, as vicars used MPs' greed as an attention-grabbing way to kick off sermons on morally upstanding behaviour.

The story was beginning to ingrain itself in the national consciousness in a way that few other stories had the power to do. At bus stops, in pubs and in workplaces up and down the country, people were talking about MPs' expenses.

After four days of relentless criticism, Gordon Brown finally appeared to be recognizing that his and Labour's response to the growing scandal might have failed fully to address the growing public anger. Cameron's apology, published in that morning's *Telegraph*, was receiving significant airplay and Downing Street realized that the Prime Minister also needed to express remorse. However, Brown – still stung by the criticism of his own claims – could not bring himself to offer a personal apology. Instead, in a late addition to a speech to the Royal College of Nursing conference, he apologized on behalf of all politicians.

'Just as you have the highest standards in your profession, we must show that we have the highest standards for our profession,' he said to the hall of nurses. 'And we must show that, where mistakes have been made and errors have been discovered, where wrongs have to be righted, that that is done immediately. We have also to try hard to show people and think hard about how a profession that, like yours, depends on trust – the most precious asset it has is trust – how that profession too can show that it is genuinely there to serve the public in all its future needs.'

He then added: 'I want to apologize on behalf of politicians, on behalf of all parties, for what has happened in the events of the last few days.'

Elsewhere, politicians from all parties were beginning to

question whether the public's trust in Parliament could ever be restored. The Liberal Democrat Norman Baker warned that the public's relationship with MPs might have been 'irrevocably damaged'.

But one man remained unrepentant. Michael Martin, who had for so long tried to block the release of MPs' expenses claims, made it clear that in his view there was only one way to resolve the crisis: by shooting the messenger. In an extraordinary stand-off during an emergency debate on expenses in the Commons chamber on that Monday afternoon, Martin – who as Speaker was supposed to be the imperturbable, politically neutral referee of Commons debates – not only tried to make the *Telegraph* the villain of the piece but also rounded on MPs who dared to suggest that the *Telegraph* might have been serving the public interest by holding up Members' expenses claims to scrutiny.

Closely watched by an incredulous bunker team, as well as the wider world, Martin rose to his feet and began steadily to dig his own political grave.

'Members will be aware of the unauthorized disclosure of material relating to their allowances, which has appeared in the press on Friday and over the weekend,' he said. 'This has caused great public concern.'

Was he about to apologize for MPs' avaricious behaviour? Not a bit of it. He stressed that there was 'some basis for considering that a criminal offence or offences may have been committed', adding: 'I can understand Honourable Members' concerns about the revealing of details of bank accounts, style of signature and verbal passwords and their concern that an individual who may have sold the data is capable of selling this information further. That is why the police have been informed.'

Martin then sat down and allowed other MPs to comment and ask questions. First on his feet was Julian Lewis, Conservative MP for the New Forest in Hampshire and the shadow defence minister. Lewis had been instrumental in ensuring that MPs' addresses would not be published when 'redacted' versions of their expenses claims were made public later in the year, by the introduction of legislation which exempted Parliament from having to publish MPs' personal details. Now, however, the *Telegraph*'s disclosures of how MPs had 'flipped' their second-home designations cast doubt over the motives of those voting to keep addresses secret. The MP had written to the *Daily Telegraph* earlier asking what steps the newspaper was taking to ensure that what he described as 'stolen' personal data did not fall into the wrong hands. Arthur Wynn Davies had been concerned from the outset that MPs might try to use an obscure and ancient legal concept, contempt of Parliament, to bog down the *Telegraph*'s investigation by accusing the newspaper of hindering MPs in going about their duty. To reassure Julian Lewis, consulting editor Rhidian Wynn Davies wrote back to the MP pointing out that the information had not been stolen, and that 'exceptional steps' had been taken to ensure sensitive information was not published.

As Lewis rose to his feet in Parliament, Wynn Davies stood with William Lewis and Tony Gallagher in the editor's office waiting to see whether the MP would accept the assurances given in the letter, or whether he would go on the attack.

Lewis began: 'May I say something of a more positive nature about this matter? I was pleased to see that, in publishing some of the material, the *Daily Telegraph* has been careful to black out such information as Members' home addresses.' He then read out an extract of the letter from Rhidian Wynn Davies, and that was that. A wave of relief passed through the bunker. Another potential crisis had been averted. But as the reporters began to rib Wynn Davies about his fifteen seconds of fame in the Commons chamber, Michael Martin was just moments away from pressing the self-destruct button.

Kate Hoey, a Labour MP and former sports minister, went against centuries of parliamentary custom by openly criticizing the actions of the Speaker in calling in the police to investigate the leak to the *Daily Telegraph*.

'Many of us – I hope from all parts of the House – feel that bringing in the Metropolitan Police, who have a huge job to do in London at the moment in dealing with all sorts of problems, to try to find out who has leaked something when, as has been pointed out, the newspapers have handled the personal details very responsibly by blanking them out, is an awful waste of resources. Will the public not see this, whatever the intention, as a way of hiding . . .'

Martin had heard enough. 'Let me answer the Honourable Lady,' he said, jabbing his finger at her: 'I listen to her often when I turn on the television at midnight and I hear her public utterances and pearls of wisdom on Sky

News – it is easy to talk then. Is it the case that an employee of this House should be able to hand over any private data to any organization of his or her choosing? . . . I just say to the Honourable Lady that it is easy to say to the press, "This should not happen," but it is a wee bit more difficult when you have to do more than just give quotes to the *Express* – or the press, rather – and do nothing else.'

MPs looked stunned as Martin completed his attack on Hoey. The Speaker appeared to be losing control.

The Lib Dem MP Norman Baker suggested it would be best simply to publish MPs' expenses as quickly as possible, which earned him a blast of the Speaker's cold sarcasm, as Martin suggested some MPs were 'keen to say to the press whatever the press wants to hear'.

'What the hell is he doing?' Winnett asked no one in particular as the reporters watched in silent fascination.

'The bloke's a disgrace,' answered Beckford.

Hoey later suggested the Speaker had 'lost it', and in the following days murmurings in Parliament about Martin's behaviour would swell into ever louder cries for his resignation. For the first time, a senior political figure appeared to be on the ropes as a result of the *Telegraph*'s expenses investigation; but while Martin's performance amounted to great sport for the reporters watching in the bunker, none of them thought at that stage that he was in serious danger of losing his job. Speakers, after all, were elected for life, and no Speaker had been ousted from office for hundreds of years.

The fact that Martin had become so rattled did, however, take the *Telegraph*'s expenses investigation to a new level. Rather than simply embarrassing senior MPs, it had given the first real indication that the expenses story was starting to influence events, and there was a growing sense that this was only the beginning.

The reporters had felt from the outset that some of the most damaging revelations would probably lead to the resignation of one or more backbench MPs; indeed, there had been a certain amount of surprise that arch-flipper Margaret Moran had not already thrown in the towel. Some had even thought that at least one minister would have to resign, and that the only reason this had not yet happened was that damage caused to individual ministers had been diluted by the publication of so many individuals' details at once. No one involved in the investigation had made any predictions beyond guessing who might have to resign. But the events of Monday, 11 May, amounted to a tangible shift in the expenses scandal. For the first time, it was starting to become apparent that the greatest impact of the investigation might be not on individual MPs, but on Parliament itself.

Martin's outburst also had the unintended side-effect of marshalling media opinion squarely behind the *Telegraph*, with even the newspaper's habitual critics lining up to praise the investigation and pour scorn on the Speaker. Simon Jenkins, writing in the *Guardian*, the newspaper traditionally at the opposite end of the political spectrum, defended the *Telegraph* against Speaker Martin's attack, saying: 'I cannot see what the *Telegraph* has done wrong . . . publication was the only way to reveal a systematic fraud on the public accounts, whose perpetrators had already shown they were determined to use the courts to suppress it.' Stephen Glover, one of the *Telegraph*'s harshest critics over the years, used his column in the *Independent* to say: 'The expenses story will be written about by historians in a hundred years. It will become part of journalistic lore . . . the day-by-day present-ation of often complicated facts was a challenge which the paper brilliantly met. It could scarcely have been better done . . . the *Daily Telegraph* has pulled off a journalistic triumph of courage and skill.'

The bunker team, of course, decided such plaudits should be put on display to provide a fillip to morale in late-night moments of lethargy. Matthew Bayley got hold of a large packet of magnets and put the white-painted metal wall of the bunker to good use, transforming it into a 'wall of glory' which quickly became a giant scrapbook for the investigation team. It included letters of congratulation (the author Jilly Cooper wrote to the editor on lavender-coloured paper to tell him: 'I really think you've saved the country'), letters of thanks ('Keep up the good work!') and the best cartoons, jokes and quizzes that the investigation had spawned, such as *Private Eye*'s neat summary of the way the expenses system worked:

> Those expense claim rules in full:
> 1 All claims made by MPs are within the rules.
> 2 All rules are made by MPs.
> 3 Er . . .
> 4 That's it.

Rory Bremner, the country's leading satirist and impressionist, later suggested the story was beyond parody. 'People are getting their satire off the front page of the *Daily Telegraph* at the moment,' he said.

The only non-expenses-related material to appear on the wall was sports reports on Newcastle United's fortunes (or lack of them) put up by Newcastle fan Gordon Rayner, at a time when he was under the delusion that Alan Shearer's arrival at the club might save it from relegation from the Premiership. Rayner, a tall, wiry Geordie, liked to try to persuade colleagues (unsuccessfully) that he bore a passing resemblance to Shearer, though in truth all he shared with his footballing idol was his birthplace and a receding hairline.

Another Geordie who was regularly invoked in the bunker was Marcus Bentley, the man whose rather exaggerated north-east accent has described events in Channel Four's Big Brother house for almost a decade. With so many of them cooped up in such a small space for so many hours a day, the reporters were starting to feel like participants in a slightly twisted social experiment, and took to mimicking Bentley's accent each morning as they registered 'day seven hundred in the Big Brother house'. Although the public had been aware of the expenses story for just four days, the reporters had been on the case for a fortnight, and it was starting to become difficult to remember what life had been like 'pre-expenses'.

But some of the most shocking revelations were still to come.

The Moat

Monday, 11 May (still)

'Douglas Hogg has returned
some of his moat'

CHAPTER 14

WHILE MICHAEL MARTIN had been busily undermining the foundations of his own career with his outburst in the Commons chamber, the *Telegraph*'s investigation team was preparing to go public with a series of disclosures which they were sure would ramp up public anger to a whole new level.

From the very first day that the reporters had started looking through the Firestorm disks, it had become obvious that some of the most colourful – and breathtaking – expenses claims had been made by some of Parliament's most fabulously wealthy MPs. All of them were Conservatives, and several of them were knights or aristocrats. Despite having multi-million-pound fortunes and, in some cases, several privately owned homes, these 'Lords of the Manor', as they were dubbed by the bunker team, had been using the expenses system to help subsidize their sprawling country estates. Tens of thousands of pounds of taxpayers' money were being spent every year on gardeners, housekeepers, even swimming-pool maintenance.

The investigation team knew that these extravagant claims by Tory grandees were likely to be far more damaging to the Conservative Party than the flipping and the furniture claims by Tory frontbenchers which had already been exposed. After all, the antics of Michael Gove, Chris Grayling and other members of the Shadow Cabinet had only served to prove that the Tories were just as capable as their Labour counterparts of playing the system. At a time when the Tories were way ahead of Labour in the polls, David Cameron could live with that.

But in his three and a half years at the head of his party, Cameron had worked tirelessly to change the public's long-standing perception of the Conservatives as the party of the rich and privileged. Although his background was quint-essentially 'Old Tory' – wealthy parents, Eton and Oxford education – Cameron had achieved remarkable success in persuading a significant percentage of the British people that the Conservatives had become an inclusive party which cared about all levels of society. By moving his party to the centre ground and disowning the far right, Cameron had mirrored the winning formula used by Tony Blair to bring 'New Labour' to power in 1997. Now that new image of the Tories as a party for the people was at risk of being destroyed overnight by the evidence the *Telegraph*'s investigation team had in front of them. The British public was about to be confronted with a parade of 'toffs' whose claims for domestic staff, Aga servicing and horse manure would make them seem as grand, arrogant and out of touch as it was possible to imagine.

The reporters had been staggered not only by what the grandees had been claiming for, but by the spellbinding wealth of so many Tory MPs.

'I'd realized some of the Tories were rich, but I had no idea they were *that* rich,' said Rayner as he looked through the expenses claims of yet another 'Lord of the Manor'.

'The paper's going to be like an edition of *Country Life*,' added Watt, as she stared at a picture of one of the many dream homes owned by Tory MPs.

'This is going to be an absolute disaster for the Tories,' Hope grimly observed. 'Cameron's going to be livid.'

One of the most startling examples involved Michael Ancram, also known as the Marquess of Lothian. Ancram owned three houses worth a combined total of around £8 million, none of which was mortgaged: a £1.5 million flat near Parliament, a £5 million mansion in the Scottish borders which had been in his family for three hundred years, and a large country house in Wiltshire. Despite his enormous wealth, Ancram had claimed close to the maximum second-home allowance in 2006/7 to pay for gardening and maintenance at his Wiltshire property, which included £98.58 for having his swimming-pool boiler repaired and a £1,117 gardening bill which included 'cleaning up moss etc'. Ancram said he would repay the money for the swimming-pool maintenance, insisting it had been 'a mistake'. He would later be critical of Cameron's handling of the crisis and announce his resignation on health grounds at the next election.

Not that he was he alone in claiming for swimming-pool maintenance: James Arbuthnot, a senior backbencher, made claims relating to the swimming pool at his home, as well as recouping thousands of pounds to pay for gardeners and housekeepers. When challenged by the fees office over the necessity of his claims, he had replied: 'My house is very expensive to run.' And Stewart Jackson, a shadow communities minister, claimed £304 for work on the swimming pool of his second home in Cambridgeshire.

David Davis, the former Tory party leadership candidate who liked to remind people he grew up on a council estate, had claimed £5,700 for the cost of a new portico at his home in Yorkshire, as well as £2,000 for the cost of mowing and rolling two 'paddocks' and £400 for servicing his tractor mower. He was somewhat taken aback when he received the call from the *Telegraph* questioning his expenses, telling Christopher Hope: 'I thought I was bombproof!'

Other claims were almost beyond ridicule. Sir Michael Spicer, the chairman of the 1922 Committee of backbench Conservative MPs, charged more than £5,000 during one nine-month period for gardening, which included an invoice for a hedge to be trimmed around his 'helipad'. The taxpayer also stumped up £620 for the installation of a 'chandelier' at his Worcestershire home, where he made council tax claims for two separate houses within the grounds of his property.

David Heathcoat-Amory's claims for 550 sacks of manure would also be published.

All of these claims, however, would come to be overshadowed by the antics of the former environment secretary Douglas Hogg, alias Viscount Hailsham. One of the items he claimed for at his Lincolnshire manor house came to define the whole expenses saga in many people's eyes; yet it was a story which nearly, very nearly, was never told at all.

Rosa Prince had decided to examine Hogg's expenses claims, knowing that, although he was a backbench MP who had rather faded into obscurity since his time as a Conservative frontbencher in the 1990s, his aristocratic background put him squarely into the category of Tory grandees. Hogg, the MP for Sleaford and North Hykeham, had submitted the maximum allowable expenses claims for his 'second' home, the historic Kettlethorpe Hall, parts of which dated back to the thirteenth century. Previous occupants of the mansion included a sister-in-law of Geoffrey Chaucer; Margaret Beaufort, grandmother of Henry VIII; and Joan Beaufort, grandmother of Richard III. It had also featured in the 1954 novel *Katherine* by Anya Seaton. Prince guessed that Hogg would own the property outright and that he, like Ancram and others, could only be seeking the maximum ACA if he was claiming for gardeners, cleaners and other staff. She was not disappointed.

Rather than handing in receipts for expenses he had incurred, like other MPs did, Hogg saw no need to waste time filling in itemized forms. Pointing out that his grand manor house cost him well in excess of the maximum second-home allowance, he simply wrote to the fees office suggesting they should just pay him the full amount in twelve equal monthly instalments.

To illustrate just how expensive it was to run his stately pile, Hogg sent the fees office a ten-page letter setting out all his household costs over the course of the year. It included the cost of employing a full-time gardener at £18,000 per year, a salary package of £14,000 for a 'lady' who looked after the house (as well as the cost of running her car), a separate bill of almost £1,000 to have the lawn mowed regularly, and £671.17 for a mole-catcher.

He also paid £4,488.48 for 'machines and fuel', including a new lawnmower; between £200 and £300 a month for 'oil and coal'; £93.41 for tongs; £40 for piano tuning; £646.25 for 'general repairs, stable etc.'; £31 to have bees removed; and around £200 a year for maintenance to his Aga. He asked the fees office to agree simply to pay him the maximum on the basis of the 'accounts' he had provided, saying his running costs were 'greatly' in excess of the annual expenses limit and: 'It will certainly make my life a lot easier.'

He said he was not claiming for all of the sums involved, adding: 'Whilst some items may be disputable as to whether they do or do not fall within the allowance, I would suggest that it is certain that allowable expenditure exceeds the allowance by a sizeable margin and consequently we need not spend too much time on debate.'

After an exchange with the fees office, Hogg reluctantly agreed to cover 35 per cent of the housekeeper's salary from his own funds.

Hogg's complicated financial arrangements seemed to have caused something of a headache for the fees office. While his claims were initially allowed by senior officials, later attempts to implement a tougher regime were opposed by the MP. Asked to provide receipts, he responded, saying that his agreement meant documentation was not necessary. In December 2003, he wrote:

I am writing this formal letter in the hope that we can resolve this matter by the end of next week. I have received the letter dated 4th September 2003 and the pro forma rejection of my October claim dated 20th November 2003 (which was more than a little surprising . . .) I hope that you will agree that the matter cannot be left outstanding for any longer. I would be surprised if any other Member has provided fuller documentary evidence. These sums are significant and in the absence of some good and compelling reason I suggest that they should be paid without further delay.

Eighteen months later, when the system was queried again, he wrote:

Might I suggest that we continue with the present system. It is a system that was positively suggested by the Fees Office. It is to everybody's convenience. I am happy to let you have the supporting documents but to do it in a monthly way as you suggest was positively declined by your colleagues and I was happy to welcome their suggestion.

Prince was stunned by what she was seeing. Hogg appeared to be trying to wear down the resistance of fees office workers who were reluctant to accept what appeared to be questionable claims.

'This guy is unbelievable, is he having a laugh or what?' Prince said to Winnett, as she began preparing a formal letter for Hogg.

The MP responded to her letter within forty-five

minutes, saying his odd method of claiming had been 'initially at the suggestion of the fees office', which had been 'kept fully informed of all the expenditure incurred on the property'.

With Hogg's reply in hand, Prince began writing the story for the following day's paper, referring back to the documents in his expenses file to quote verbatim from them. As she did so, her eyes opened wide and she emitted one of her trademark involuntary gasps as she noticed a line buried in one of the letters which she had missed when she had looked at it the first time.

'Oh my God! Look at this,' Prince shouted across the bunker. 'He's claimed for someone to clean his moat!'

'What!!?' chorused the rest of the bunker team. All eyes turned to Prince, and within moments several of the reporters had crowded round her desk to see what she had discovered.

Sure enough, there, towards the end of one of his lengthy letters to the fees office, among Hogg's list of household expenditure was: 'moat clearing, £2,115'.

As the bunker erupted in gales of laughter, Prince brought up a Google Earth aerial photograph of Hogg's home. And there it was, snaking around three sides of the house to keep out the great unwashed: Douglas Hogg's moat. All of a sudden, the expenses claims of other MPs seemed dull by comparison. Hogg had gifted the *Telegraph*'s investigation the sort of story which you simply couldn't make up.

The beauty of the expenses story had been that it was a political scandal which everyone could instantly understand:

readers didn't need to get their heads around the complexities of obscure company directorships, government contracts or labyrinthine connections between MPs and big business – a child could grasp the fact that public representatives were spending public money on big houses, televisions and leather armchairs. With his claim for the moat, Hogg had been elevated to the position of standardbearer for arrogant excess; a man who, perhaps more than any other, appeared to inhabit an entirely different world from the little people he and his colleagues claimed to represent.

The reference to Hogg's moat was contained in a letter which was marked 'deleted' in the files, meaning it was not due to be published by Parliament. If Prince had not spotted the moat when she read the letter for a second time, it would have remained a secret to this day. The near-miss was a reminder to everyone on the investigation team of just how easy it would be to let a crucial detail slip through the net, given the breakneck speed at which the reporters were working.

As Prince sent off a second letter to Hogg asking him about the moat, Winnett was called into the editor's office to run through the top stories for the next day's edition. William Lewis was so taken aback by what Winnett had to tell him that he had to reach for his trusty polo mallet for extra emphasis.

'This is the best yet,' Lewis said. 'This will cause a revolution. People will go absolutely mad about this,' he added, waving the mallet in the direction of Parliament as he spoke. He had no idea how right he would turn out to be.

The grandees themselves also seemed to have sensed just how badly their claims would go down with the public, having already seen the fallout from other people's less extravagant claims. Several appeared to be on the warpath.

Hogg himself had sent Prince a detailed rebuttal of most of the claims, written as though he were preparing a legal case. In rather clumsy terms, he insisted that he had not claimed for his moat, saying: 'As explained in the schedule in whether claimed or not, I don't have records to hand when responding to this but I don't believe that the moat would have featured in the claim.' He then telephoned the reporter repeatedly in an attempt to close down the moat story, before attempting to call the editor.

Sir Michael Spicer adopted a similar stance with Holly Watt, phoning her to protest about the questions the *Telegraph* intended to raise over his expenses claims, then sending an email attempting to justify his actions.

'I have lived in my house for over thirty years,' he said. 'Recently it has needed more maintenance and decoration as wear and tear sets in. It is perfectly proper that I should claim this.' He also claimed that he did not have a helipad, and that the description was 'a family joke'. (Taxpayers failed to see the funny side when the claims were published.) The 'chandelier', meanwhile, was simply a light fitting with several bulbs, he said (despite the enormous cost of its installation).

Sir Michael was to be disappointed if he thought he had persuaded the paper to drop the story about him or leave out the details about the helipad and the chandelier. Later in the evening, he dashed out to Victoria station to get an early edition of the next day's *Daily Telegraph*. As he got into a cab, the driver, who had already seen the paper, remarked: 'You're that Michael Spicer, aren't you?' before barracking him about his expenses claims.

As the bunker team brought up the television news on their computer screens, the latest revelations in the MPs' expenses saga were brewing up to dominate the headlines for a fifth day running. ITN's political editor, Tom Bradby, had caught wind of the Tory grandees story by the time he appeared at 6.30 p.m., though he was unaware of the precise details. 'One may even have claimed for a butler,' said the breathless Bradby.

Within moments of the broadcast ending, Winnett's phone rang. On the line was Andy Coulson, the Conservative Party's head of strategy. Coulson had been hired by the Conservatives in controversial circumstances after resigning as editor of the *News of the World*. One of his reporters had been gaoled for paying a private investigator to illegally access voice messages on mobile phones belonging to members of the royal household, and Coulson, although he said he had been unaware of what was going on, accepted that, as editor, he bore responsibility for what his reporters were doing. Although David Cameron was criticized by his opponents at the time he hired Coulson, the former editor had repaid his confidence by helping to transform the party's image, just as another former red-top newspaper journalist, Alastair Campbell, had done for Tony Blair.

Coulson had been involved in going over the expenses claims of members of the Shadow Cabinet who were expected to feature in the *Telegraph*, but he and other members of Cameron's media team had not had the chance to bone up on what people like Ancram and Hogg had been up to.

Coulson sounded worried. 'Did you see the ITV news?' he asked Winnett.

'Yep,' replied the reporter.

'This butler stuff isn't true, is it? If not, I'd really appreciate it if you could close it down as a rumour.'

'No, it's not true,' Winnett replied. 'But it's not that far off the truth. There are housekeepers and so on and they are in the right area.'

'OK, I see,' said Coulson. 'I'd really appreciate it if you could give me a heads-up on the very worst of it tomorrow. I will only tell David [Cameron].'

'Erm, OK,' Winnett said. 'As long as this is strictly not for repetition, the worst thing is someone claimed for a moat to be cleaned.'

There was a pause at the other end of the line. 'F*** me. A moat?' Coulson finally spluttered.

He quickly ended the call and picked up the phone to David Cameron to warn him that all the work they had done to dispel the image of the Tories as 'toffs' was at risk of unravelling.

Hogg, meanwhile, was fighting for his reputation – and his career. When Rosa Prince booted up her computer early the next morning, one of the first emails she received was from Hogg, evidently written in a rush, judging by the poor spelling and grammar.

'I enclose the comments that I make as to you [sic] article,' the email began. 'You will see that I did not claim for either the moat (about which we spoke last night) or for the piano tuner.'

He continued:

> The stable lights [referred to in one of Hogg's letters to the fees office] are in facts the security lights in the back yard which were advised by the police and the installed by the home office; after 10 years or so they needed to be replaced; I was one of those on the IRA list and for about 6 weeks or so after the murder of [Conservative MP] Ian Gow I had a squad of police in the house. You might care to correct the article
>
> Yours, Douglas Hogg.

Hogg had also begun phoning the editor's office to demand a correction, insisting he had not claimed for the moat. Instead, William Lewis agreed that Hogg's letter to the fees office which included the reference to the moat should be published online so the public could decide for themselves.

To the horror of Conservative Central Office, Hogg then conducted a bizarre four-and-a-half-minute interview with *Channel 4 News*, who had waited outside his London flat for him to emerge in the morning.

Wearing a dark green shooting cap, a blue raincoat and a rucksack, Hogg walked briskly towards Parliament, denouncing the *Daily Telegraph*'s story as he went, but never breaking his stride as the television cameraman struggled to keep up. Tory spin doctors watched through their fingers as Hogg broke three of the golden rules of television interviews: don't walk and talk, don't wear a hat and don't defend the indefensible.

'I agreed with the fees office that a proportion of the maintenance and cleaning of my house, hence the housekeeper, should be claimed on the parliamentary allowance,' he said.

Did he claim for a moat?

'That is not correct. In the interests of transparency I sent them a complete schedule of expenses incurred on the house. The letter was not a claims schedule.'

But the publication of the documents on the *Telegraph* website showed that while Hogg may not have specified that he was claiming for the moat, he didn't specify that he was not. By lunchtime, Hogg had changed his position and had accepted that he had 'not positively excluded the items'.

'You slippery so and so!' Prince exclaimed as Hogg changed his statement.

If Hogg thought the public would accept his clear-as-mud explanation for the moat claim, he was sorely mistaken. The public seized on the moat story as a form of shorthand for the entire expenses scandal, he received the full force of David Cameron's ire, and the newly installed Poet Laureate, Carol Ann Duffy, was inspired to write a verse about it:

What did we do with the trust of your vote?
Hired a flunky to flush out the moat.

In the corridor outside the bunker, Mark Skipworth was discussing the reaction to the story with Winnett and Rhidian Wynn Davies.

'The funny thing is,' said Skipworth, 'if he'd just called it a drainage ditch instead of a moat, he would have got away with it.'

The Tory grandees story provided helicopter firms up and down the country with a sudden rush of business as television crews flew over the spectacular mansions to film much-needed 'visuals'. Hogg himself became, for a while at least, world-famous as his moat claim captured the imagination of journalists and satirists across the globe.

In America, Jon Stewart, host of the top-rated *Daily Show*, mercilessly milked the Hogg story, calling it 'the real Watergate' and describing the expenses scandal as 'Scamalot'. He was particularly tickled by Hogg's name ('neither I nor J. K. Rowling are making this name up!') and painted a picture of England as a country where every householder has a medieval moat to keep out invaders.

Some American viewers, however, were unclear exactly what was meant by a moat. In one interview with the cable news channel CNN, the *Telegraph*'s Andrew Pierce was asked by a news anchor: 'What exactly is this moat?'

Pierce replied: 'Well, do you know who Robin Hood is? The chap who robbed from the rich to give to the poor, unlike our MPs. His arch-enemy was the Sheriff of

Nottingham, and he lived in a castle with a drawbridge, which went over . . .'

'Oh, that's over the moat!' replied the newsreader.

Newspapers in Australia, Canada, Iran and South America delighted in picking over the bamboozling array of fripperies which MPs had spent public money on, while communist countries, including China, happily reported the excesses which come with democracy. The *China Daily* reported: 'Disclosures that MPs have claimed everything from an adult movie to a chandelier on expenses have infuriated voters, eroding faith in the country's ancient democratic institutions and causing Britain's worst political crisis for years.' And in Zimbabwe, the *Herald* newspaper suggested that politicians in the parliament controlled by the despotic Robert Mugabe should be given higher salaries in case they were tempted into corrupt activities like British MPs (yes, really).

Writing in the *New York Times*, the novelist Garrison Keillor, who was on a visit to London, described the *Telegraph*'s story as 'the best show in town', while an editorial in the same newspaper noted that 'The British public is not amused.'

The man who was the least amused by the behaviour of the Tory grandees, however, was David Cameron. His MPs were about to find out what can happen when Cameron gets angry.

Payback

Tuesday, 12 May

'I'm only a Premiership
footballer, love. You spend
money like I'm an MP'

CHAPTER 15

DAVID CAMERON'S FURY when he was told about the expenses claims of some of his wealthiest backbenchers had reached boiling point on Monday evening when Andy Coulson told him about Douglas Hogg's moat. He spent more than two hours taking soundings from members of his Shadow Cabinet about how the party could limit the fallout from the grandees story, and by the time he saw the headlines on the television news that evening he knew that the following day would be one of the most testing yet of his leadership.

Shortly after dawn on Tuesday, 12 May, television crews had started to gather outside the Camerons' west London townhouse. After a family breakfast Cameron had spoken to his advisers, who agreed that the Conservative leader should reveal his anger to the waiting press. He was heading for what he would later describe as his 'John Wayne moment'.

At around 8 a.m. Cameron marched purposefully out of his front door towards a car that was waiting to drive him to the Commons. When reporters asked him about the morning's revelations in the *Daily Telegraph*, he let rip, with a thunderous look on his face.

'I am angry about what has happened. It is out of order, some of this is an abuse of taxpayers' money and I'm going to deal with it.' Then he ducked into his chauffeur-driven silver Lexus, slammed the door and was driven away, one of the more tenacious reporters narrowly avoiding getting a microphone caught in the car door.

As Cameron sat in the back of the car, he knew that the only way to protect the image of a caring Conservative Party he had taken such pains to construct was to be ruthless with those who threatened to destroy it. If that meant terminating the careers of long-serving Tory MPs, then so be it. Several of the MPs who had been guilty of the worst excesses – Hogg included – were, in any case, 'bed-blockers': ageing MPs whose best days were behind them but who refused to give up their safe seats for new blood that could bring freshness and vigour into the parliamentary party. The one consolation for Cameron was that he would have the chance to get rid of some dead wood.

That morning, the MPs who had appeared in the paper received the one phone call they had been dreading more than that from the *Telegraph*: the call from their party leader. Cameron spoke to each of the worst offenders in turn to confront them with the details of what the *Telegraph* had reported and find out at first hand what, if any, explanations they had. On the whole, he was far from satisfied with their answers.

At lunchtime, he summoned all Conservative back-bench MPs to a meeting of the 1922 Committee in a private room in Parliament. Cameron felt that the growing public fury over the continuing expenses revelations was justified, and realized that he had to align himself with this mood – rather than taking a defensive attitude of the kind which had got Labour off on the wrong foot when they first responded to the *Telegraph*'s disclosures. He told his backbench MPs that he had decided to take a lead on the expenses scandal, and would be establishing a 'Star Chamber' committee that would analyse the claims made by every Tory MP over the previous four years. The name – coined by the press – was an apt analogy; it referred to a court which sat in Parliament in the fifteenth century to try men so powerful that their cases could not be left to the ordinary courts. The original Star Chamber, which took its name from the night sky design on the ceiling of the room in which it sat, held its sessions in secret, with no right of appeal. Cameron's modern-day equivalent would run on similar lines: anyone who refused to cooperate with the inquiry would be expelled from the party, and the committee would decide whether MPs needed to repay money – and how much.

There was more. The Conservatives would be introducing new rules over expenses claims made by the party's MPs which were far tougher than those applied by the parliamentary authorities. There would be a ban on 'flipping' the second-home designation between properties; Tory MPs would be prohibited from claiming for furniture, household items and food – and they would have to pay capital gains tax on the sale of homes against which they made claims.

Many MPs in the room did not like what they were hearing. They cast sideways glances at each other, looking for signs that others were feeling vaguely mutinous, but realized they had little choice but to agree to what their leader was announcing. After all, anyone who dissented was liable to see their political career come to a premature end.

Once Cameron had finished addressing the back-benchers, he walked the short distance to St Stephen's Club, a private club for Conservatives in a nearby Westminster townhouse, where the media had been told to gather for a press conference.

'I want to start by saying sorry,' he said. 'Sorry that it's come to this. And sorry for the actions of some Conservative MPs. People are right to be angry that some MPs have taken public money to pay for things that few could afford. You've been let down. Politicians have done things that are un-ethical and wrong. I don't care if they were within the rules – they were wrong.'

The reporters watching on in the bunker were impressed.

'He's always good when he's angry,' Prince observed.

'Bet Brown's wishing he'd done this,' added Rayner. Then came a surprise announcement which was greeted with roars of approval in the bunker.

Cameron said virtually his entire Shadow Cabinet would be repaying money – including himself – for claims which had been disclosed by the *Telegraph* the previous day. To leave no room for ambiguity, he named each Tory front-bencher in turn and gave the amount they would be repaying, and why.

'Alan Duncan will repay £5,000 for gardening bills,' he said.

'Yes!' shouted Christopher Hope, as he received slaps on the back from his colleagues.

'Michael Gove will repay £7,000 for furniture.'

'Good stuff!' interjected Hope, clenching his fist, recalling Gove's futile threats of legal action.

'Oliver Letwin will repay more than £2,000 for replacing a pipe under his tennis court.'

Thumbs up from Rayner.

Cameron himself said he would be repaying the £680 bill for repair work on his house, while Chris Grayling and others would stop claiming the additional costs allowance altogether.

One by one, the reporters who had written stories questioning the expenses claims of Shadow Cabinet members – and whose stories had in many cases been publicly challenged by the MPs themselves – were being vindicated, on live television, by the probable future Prime Minister. For a reporter, there are few things more satisfying than seeing the subject of a potentially risky story holding their hands up and admitting to the allegations concerned. For a whole roomful of reporters to experience that buzz simultaneously, in such high-profile circumstances, was the high point of the investigation to date.

As the team shook hands and exchanged congratulations on a job well done, Hope grabbed a red marker pen and began writing down on a whiteboard the amount each MP was paying back, next to the name of the reporter who had written that story. A handful of MPs, including Michael Ancram and Stewart Jackson, had already made clear their intention to pay money back (for swimming-pool maintenance, in both cases) and suddenly it was becoming clear that the rush to pay back money was going to be a whole new story in itself.

Back in the press conference, parliamentary reporters were surprised by the directness of Cameron's approach. Once he had finished listing the names of the MPs who were paying money back (right down to David Willetts's light bulbs and Cheryl Gillan's dog food) he took questions from the floor, and answered them head-on.

The watching press pack began to think that, despite the atrocious behaviour of many of his fellow Conservative MPs, they might be witnessing the moment when Cameron showed that he was ready to become Prime Minister. Gordon Brown had dithered and dodged; Cameron was grasping the nettle with both hands. In short, he was show-ing ruthless, decisive leadership.

The significance of Cameron's performance was not lost on the prime ministerial advisers watching with growing alarm in Downing Street. In front of their eyes, Cameron was seizing the initiative on the expenses issue while Brown was still struggling to connect with the public. Earlier in the day, the Prime Minister had attempted to move the agenda on with a major speech about crime. But it had largely been ignored, and Downing Street aides now decided they had no choice but to follow Cameron's lead and tackle the expenses scandal directly.

Within minutes of Cameron's press conference ending, deputy Labour leader Harriet Harman hit the airwaves to announce that a Commons committee was meeting to discuss new rules, immediately applicable, to stop the abuse of the expenses system. Aides to the Prime Minister briefed reporters by saying that these would include rules to limit the amount of mortgage interest that could be claimed. (Many Labour MPs were angry that their Conservative counterparts were apparently able to fund huge properties at taxpayers' expense without criticism.)

But the public wasn't interested in 'the system', no matter how flawed it might be. British voters were angry with the MPs themselves. If they could have done, the public would have put their MPs in the stocks on the local village green and taken out their frustration by throwing rotten eggs at them. Cameron had come close to a modern-day equivalent by naming and shaming his own Shadow Cabinet on live television, and Brown realized that if he was going to keep up with the game, he needed to hang some of his own ministers out to dry. And he knew exactly who should be first.

Hazel Blears, the communities secretary, had over the previous few months gone from being the Cabinet's feisty 'ginger chipmunk' to something of a poison dwarf. Shortly before the *Daily Telegraph*'s expenses revelations began, Blears had mocked Brown in a newspaper article, making reference to his disastrous attempt to connect with young voters by announcing a botched plan to reform the expenses system on the internet video site YouTube. Brown's attempts to smile and speak at the same time had resulted in the usual sinister facial contortions, and instead of getting his message across, the Prime Minister had once again left himself open to ridicule. Blears had poked fun at her leader's inept performance by saying: 'YouTube if you want to . . .' – simultaneously committing the cardinal sin of making a nod to Margaret Thatcher's famous 'U-turn if you want to; the lady's not for turning' speech.

Blears was fast becoming the Prime Minister's biggest Cabinet opponent, and she had also been guilty of gross hypocrisy in Brown's eyes when it came to her expenses. The *Daily Telegraph* had disclosed that Blears had flipped the designation of her second home between three different addresses in the space of a year. She had avoided paying capital gains tax by telling HM Revenue & Customs that the London flat she was selling was her 'principal residence' while telling the parliamentary authorities it was her 'second home'. Although she had not broken any tax laws or parliamentary rules by doing so, such behaviour was regarded as morally wrong by many members of the public, as well as many Labour MPs. Roy Hattersley, the former deputy leader of the Labour Party, summed up the feeling of many long-serving members of the party by saying: 'It's inconsistent to be a member of the Labour Cabinet if you consciously try to avoid paying taxes.'

Brown decided that Blears should pay capital gains tax retrospectively on the profit of around £45,000 she made when she sold her taxpayer-funded second homes. The BBC's Nick Robinson and Jon Craig of Sky News were called into Blears's Whitehall office, where she apologized for her behaviour and provided one of the defining images of the expenses scandal by holding up a cheque she had written out to HM Revenue & Customs for £13,332 in lieu of the capital gains tax she would have paid, had she been legally obliged to. In one of the interviews, tears welled up in the Cabinet minister's eyes.

In the bunker, it all seemed too dramatic to be true. First, virtually the entire Shadow Cabinet had been ordered to pay back the money the *Telegraph* had highlighted; now a Cabinet minister was holding up a personal cheque, made out to the taxman, for more than some people earn in a year. Things like that just don't happen in the real world.

'This has got to go on the wall of glory,' said Christopher Hope, as he asked assistant picture editor Veronica Hale to print off a blown-up image of Blears with the cheque.

Editor William Lewis decided that the repayments, rather than the new expenses revelations the team was working on, had now become the story, and the next day's newspaper would lead with the headline 'Payback time'. It turned out, in fact, that the great payback had only just begun.

The following day would see the biggest single repayment by any of the MPs, when the care services minister Phil Hope unexpectedly announced he would be repaying £41,709 for furniture, fittings and other items he had claimed for his second home, a flat in south London. The *Daily Telegraph* had featured Hope's expenses the previous Saturday, along with those of other ministers, and had questioned whether it was physically possible for him to have squeezed all the furniture he had bought on expenses into his 511-square-foot flat. Almost a week on, the *Telegraph* had covered the expenses claims of dozens more MPs, and Hope was a distant memory. But the MP's local newspaper in Corby had picked up the story, generating a huge response from its readers. The Northamptonshire *Evening Telegraph* published six pages of readers' letters on the subject, which were overwhelmingly critical of the MP.

Jeremy Clifford, the newspaper's editor, said: 'It has made people realize that their MP leads a completely different life to them when he is in London.' On the council estates where many houses stand empty in the former steel town, Hope's constituents did not hold back. Aran Stephen, an unemployed 26-year-old who lived with his mother, told the *Daily Telegraph*: 'I haven't got a home but [houses on the estate] have been empty for 10 years. What has Phil Hope done for me except spend money on posh furniture?' John McShefferty, an unemployed former steel worker, said: 'It's disgusting. And to think he's Labour. Paying it back is like saying he broke my window, but if he fixes it, is that OK? No, it's not OK.'

Hope, who had a slim parliamentary majority of 1,517, realized that the only chance he had of retaining his seat was to pay back the money highlighted by the *Telegraph*, though the *Telegraph* had accused him of spending only £37,000 on furniture, not the £41,709 he repaid. He had to remortgage his house to find the money. Although it was politically expedient for Hope to come up with the cash, he appeared to have been genuinely stung by the criticism when he appeared on television to announce his repayment. Tears welled up in his eyes as the shell-shocked MP said: 'The anger of my constituents and the damage done to the perceptions of my integrity concerning the money I have received . . . has been a massive blow to me.' The tears may have been more in self-pity than remorse, but they were genuine none the less.

The effect of persistent local newspaper coverage of Hope's expenses was typical of what was going on up and down the country. The *Daily Telegraph* would highlight an MP's expenses; the story would then be picked up by local media who could then develop new angles – which the national newspapers did not have the time to do, because of the breakneck speed with which the *Telegraph* was printing more and more new revelations. The expenses story was also providing a boost to local newspaper sales, just as it was with the *Telegraph*'s. Radio phone-in hosts, meanwhile, gave up trying to think of alternative topics for their shows, because all the public wanted to talk about was MPs' expenses.

While Hazel Blears and David Cameron had been arranging for taxpayers' money to be refunded, the *Telegraph*'s investigations team still had to get on with the daily task of lifting the lid on the expenses claims of more MPs. And after five days of revelations about Labour, the Conservatives and Sinn Fein, it was high time the Liberal Democrats had their day in the heat.

The fact that the Lib Dems had not so far featured in the *Telegraph*'s coverage had resulted in a four-point increase in their opinion poll ratings. A rough calculation suggested that the articles during the previous five days had swayed the voting intentions of nearly two million people – more than the typical number of 'swing voters' targeted by the tens of millions of pounds spent during election campaigns.

The Lib Dems, of course, knew their turn was coming, and ever since the expenses scandal had first appeared in the *Telegraph*, Lena Pietsch, one of the most senior aides to the Lib Dem leader Nick Clegg, had been anxiously texting Rosa Prince on a daily basis asking when the party's MPs would appear in the paper. Clegg and his team had spent the weekend on tenterhooks waiting for their claims to be exposed, and on Tuesday morning, when Prince texted Pietsch to say the time had come, it was almost a relief to some Lib Dem party workers, who cleared their schedules to deal with incoming emails from the *Telegraph*.

The Lib Dems prided themselves on the party's carefully built reputation for personal accountability. For example, it had unilaterally decided years earlier that all seven of its MPs representing outer London constituencies would forgo their entitlement to the ACA, an admirable move which had not been replicated by the Tories or Labour. The Lib Dems also tended to be among the first to criticize any MP who was seen as being 'on the make', and were advocates of transparency and open government. Nick Clegg had championed the reform of MPs' expenses and, after the first stories had appeared in the *Telegraph*, had been one of the most outspoken critics of the excesses of his colleagues, saying: 'People will just simply despair that all politicians look either ridiculous at best or corrupt at worst.' Clegg had, until now, been having a good war.

Yet it turned out that some of the most high-profile Lib Dem MPs had been quietly filling their boots from the generous ACA in similar ways to MPs from other parties.

Prince was surprised to discover that Clegg himself had claimed so much for his second home that he exceeded the annual limit of £23,083 by £100 in 2007/8. He submitted claims for food, gardening, furniture and decorating at his constituency home in Sheffield, and also put in phone bills which included calls to Colombia, Vietnam and Spain. When he had bought his second home he had claimed almost £10,000 for stamp duty and other legal costs associated with the purchase, then billed the taxpayer for new carpets, tiling, curtains, blinds and even work to 'build small wall in rose garden'.

The honeymoon period the Liberal Democrats had been enjoying during the scandal so far was about to come to an abrupt end.

Clegg was in the process of announcing his party's manifesto for the European elections when his staff picked up an email from Rosa Prince at 11.29 a.m. with a detailed series of questions about his expenses claims. Clegg was quick to respond, saying he would pay back the £80.20 he had spent on international calls, which 'should never have been charged to the taxpayer'. He apologized, and gave a commitment that any profit he made when he sold the house in Sheffield would be given back to the taxpayer.

Other senior Lib Dems were also about to find themselves embroiled in the furore. Sir Menzies Campbell, a former leader of the party, had hired an interior designer –

who also happened to be a family friend – to refurbish his central London flat, spending almost £10,000 on items including scatter cushions, a king-sized bed and a flat-screen television. He decided to pay back almost £1,500 for the cost of the designer.

Chris Huhne, the Liberal Democrats' home affairs spokesman and former party leadership candidate, had claimed £119 for a Corby trouser press, finished in mahogany, despite being a millionaire who owned a total of seven properties, having made a fortune during his previous career as a City economist. His meticulously typed office expenses also included claims for chocolate HobNobs (79p), tea bags (89p), a bus ticket (£3.20) and semi-skimmed milk (62p). To the amusement of the bunker team, the items which Huhne had not claimed for, but which appeared on the same receipts, showed that the sombre MP had a taste for cheese muffins, bacon flavour Wheat Crunchies and Ready Brek. He had even claimed £85.35 for the 'mounting, framing and inscription of photo of Chris Huhne' (it had been requested by the local council for use in the civic centre).

Huhne was not amused when he received an email from Gordon Rayner querying his expenses, and rang the reporter to point out that he had claimed less than 20 per cent of the allowable maximum. He did, however, decide to repay the cost of the trouser press, later admitting that buying it had been 'a bit Alan Partridge'.

There was further comedy value in the claims made by the colourful Lib Dem housing spokesman and 'human anagram', Lembit Opik, a man better known for his ability to woo (and then usually break up with) famous and beautiful women such as the television weather presenter Siân Lloyd, an underwear model called Katie Green and, most improbably of all, the Cheeky Girls singer Gabriela Irimia. Holly Watt had discovered what appeared to be a hidden gem in Opik's expenses during her trawl for MPs' addresses. He had claimed for a 'triple mirror', and the reporters immediately started to wonder what the amorous MP would do with such an item. Was it for his bedroom? Would it be going on the ceiling? The truth, for once, turned out to be rather disappointing. Jon Swaine discovered that the triple mirror, bought at Argos, was nothing more than a folding, free-standing mirror to be placed on a dressing-table.

Swaine also discovered that the hapless Opik had managed to mistime the purchase of a £2,499 plasma television in such a way that he had to pay for it himself. Opik had bought the TV in 2005, after the dissolution of Parliament for the general election. As soon as Parliament has been dissolved MPs technically lose their jobs until they are re-elected; as they are not strictly speaking MPs, they can't claim any expenses, and so the fees office refused to pay him anything for his new television.

None of these claims by well-known party figures, however, were considered sufficiently scandalous to make front-page stories, and head of news Chris Evans wanted to know what else had been uncovered on the Lib Dems.

Over the previous few days, Martin Beckford had been intrigued by the expenses claims made by Andrew George, a little-known Liberal Democrat who represented St Ives in Cornwall. His files showed that he had bought a flat in Rotherhithe, south London, as his second home, but one page of a Post Office home insurance invoice showed that the person covered was a 'Miss M. George'. Beckford soon discovered that George had a daughter called Morvah, who had started university in London just months after he bought the flat. The reporter suspected she was using the taxpayer-funded property as her student digs.

John Bingham, who had recently joined the *Telegraph* from the Press Association, where he had distinguished himself by conducting a series of interviews with Prince Harry in Afghanistan, was sent to the flat. He discovered from neighbours that Morvah was regularly seen at the flat with her boyfriend, suggesting that the MP's 'second' home was in fact his daughter's main home. When George was contacted by the *Telegraph*, he admitted that his daughter, a part-time professional model who had also worked as a parliamentary intern for her father, used the flat as a 'bolt hole' and stored some of her possessions there. He later admitted she had lived there exclusively for several months.

Andrew George and his daughter's living arrangements took a prominent place on the *Telegraph*'s front page the next day, below the main story about MPs paying back money. George was outraged, and appeared on *Channel 4 News* to deny the *Telegraph*'s story, calling John Bingham a 'snooper'.

Beckford also found himself under attack from a rather more unlikely source – the Bishop of Croydon. In the course of his 'day job' as social and religious affairs correspondent, Beckford followed the musings of several bishops and vicars via their internet blogs or Twitter accounts. Some Anglicans criticized politicians' greed and abuse of public funds, among them the former Archbishop of Canterbury, Lord Carey, who attacked MPs from his unorthodox 'pulpit' in his *News of the World* column. The liberal and media-savvy Bishop of Croydon, the Rt Revd Nick Baines, however, concluded that the real scandal was the hypocrisy of journalists. 'I can't help feeling that, despite the awfulness of exploitative MPs, the awfulness of the media coverage is also nauseating,' he wrote in his blog.

The normally quiet and unassuming Beckford had already shown an entirely different side to his character when he had become embroiled in a heated, no-holds-barred row with Phil Woolas over his claims for tampons and other women's items, and the red mist descended once again when he read the bishop's haughty comments. 'Your blog is more outrageous than anything our MPs have claimed. If only the public could vote out bad bishops,' Beckford wrote on his Twitter page.

The prelate shot back: 'What constitutes a bad bishop? Questioning the media?'

Beckford pointed out that public money was being repaid as a direct result of the investigation and asked: 'Do you really think that is hypocritical and nauseating?'

Bishop Baines responded that the issue was about the 'wider cost' of the 'corrosive nature' of the reporting.

'The reporting is corrosive b/c of what the MPs have

done!' Beckford angrily tweeted. 'Would you really rather have a tame press and untouchable politicians?'

The bishop agreed that 'good journalism is vital for democracy' but added: 'It does not give licence for anything.' He claimed 'all [MPs] are damned' as a result of the *Telegraph*'s revelations, though he later conceded that his tone had been 'harsh' in his earlier postings.

As the *Telegraph*'s investigation continued, the internet was playing an increasing role in building up the public's expectations each day for the following day's paper. The reporters would first write a 'taster' story, with no names in it, announcing that the following day's paper would contain details of prominent Tories, government ministers or whatever the top story was going to be. Within seconds of the story appearing on the paper's website at around eight o'clock each evening, it would be picked up by the 24-hour news channels and become 'breaking news' until the first edition of the paper appeared late that night. The strategy ended up driving broadcasters potty, with television reporters desperately trying to second-guess what the *Telegraph* had in store (and often getting it completely wrong); so instead the *Telegraph* started publishing on its website a story which would appear on the inside pages of the next day's paper, giving the broadcasters something specific to get their teeth into while they waited to find out what the main story would be in the next day's edition.

For the unfortunate MPs who featured in the 'tasters', it meant an uncomfortable few hours to endure while they temporarily became *the* story. Other MPs decided that they didn't want to wait for the call from the *Telegraph*, and voluntarily decided to pay back thousands of pounds before the reporters had even had a chance to open their files. Ronnie Campbell, the Labour MP for Blyth Valley, announced he was paying back £6,000 for furniture he had bought to kit out his second home (Jon Swaine was swiftly tasked with looking at his expenses claims to turn around a story for the next day's paper).

So far, the *Daily Telegraph* had exposed greed, excess, hypocrisy and cupidity. What it exposed next would border on the downright criminal.

The Phantom Mortgage

Wednesday, 13 May

'I'm your local MP and
I've come to sneer at your
ghastly little house'

CHAPTER 16

IN A NONDESCRIPT office block overlooking the Mersey, the staff of the Land Registry's Birkenhead division were among the first people outside the *Telegraph*'s bunker room to get a hint that something was brewing in the days before the first stories were published.

The civil servants working in this government agency provide one of the most valuable services of all to journalists carrying out investigations into an individual's finances, as they hold public records on the ownership and mortgage details of millions of properties dating back several decades. For a small fee, any member of the public can get hold of information on who owns a particular property and, if it changed hands in recent years, how much they paid for it. Copies of mortgage documents held for the property can also be accessed, and, since a recent change in the law, the details of previous owners and their mortgage arrangements are also publicly available. It amounts to an absolute gold mine for reporters; and for the expenses team, it was invaluable.

In the days after the *Telegraph* obtained the expenses disk, one of the most regular callers to the Land Registry's customer information service had been Holly Watt. Watt had been given the task of compiling a list of the past and present addresses of all 646 MPs, which would provide a unique database against which their second-home claims could be compared. Once the information had been keyed into a spreadsheet, any MPs who might be claiming for the same address – as it had been rumoured some were – would quickly be found out. But having the addresses was only the start. What if an MP was claiming for an entirely fictitious address? What if they were claiming for a property they didn't actually own? What if they were claiming more for their mortgage interest than they actually paid? The only way to find out was to delve into the Land Registry's records to establish whether the MPs' claims tallied with the public records held in Birkenhead.

Watt ran up a bill for thousands of pounds on her credit card (and later claimed it back on expenses, naturally) as she carried out hundreds of searches. The work was tedious and time-consuming, but it gave her a unique overview of all the MPs' claims; and out of all these claims she had spotted several relating to mortgage interest payments which, on the face of it at least, didn't seem quite right.

Working on a laptop computer, Watt had set up a spreadsheet which listed MPs' names, the addresses of properties on which they had claimed, whether each was rented or mortgaged, and notes of other points about their claims. By the middle of the second week in the bunker, she had reached the letter 'I' in her list of MPs when she had a potential breakthrough. As she typed in the address of the second home of Ian Cawsey, an obscure Labour MP (the Firestorm disk listed MPs according to the first letter of their first name), a box popped up on her screen with the rest of the address. This 'auto-complete' function meant she had already typed in the address for another MP.

'Bingo!' Watt shouted across the office.

Scrolling back up through the spreadsheet, Watt found that Cawsey's London address was shared with Elliot Morley, another Labour MP and a former agriculture minister. Morley was paying the mortgage on the house and claiming back the interest on his parliamentary expenses – but Cawsey was paying rent to him and claiming the rent back on his parliamentary expenses. In other words, the taxpayer was being billed twice for the same property. Morley had also spent several years claiming expenses for a property in his Humberside constituency before 'flipping' his second-home designation to London in November 2007; he even appeared to have attempted to claim for a £14,000 wet-room (an upmarket type of bathroom) to be installed in the London property in 2008.

Clearly, Watt thought, this was going to require further investigation.

A quick search of the men's names on Google revealed that they were long-standing allies and friends. Cawsey used to work as a researcher for Morley before he became an MP, and represented the neighbouring constituency to his former employer's. The pair lived in the same small Humberside village and their children played with one another. Now, it appeared, they were also claiming expenses for the same London property.

It was time to phone the Land Registry. Watt felt strangely tense as she picked up the receiver, sensing that it might be one of the most important calls of her career.

'Morning, it's Holly Watt here again,' she breezily said as a familiar female voice answered the phone in Birkenhead. 'Sorry, couple more checks to do.'

Watt gave the civil servant the address of Morley's London house.

'That's owned by an Elliot and Patricia Morley. There's a charge [mortgage] on it with Nationwide,' the official said.

'Great, thanks,' replied Watt. 'Sorry, just one more – a house in Winterton, near Scunthorpe – the address is—'

'Yes, got that as well,' the Land Registry official said. 'Also owned by an Elliot and Patricia Morley. No mortgage on that one since March 2006.'

Watt sat up straight. 'Sorry, can you repeat that?'

'There hasn't been a charge on that property since March 2006,' the Land Registry official repeated.

Morley had been claiming mortgage interest of £800 per month for the property near Scunthorpe until November 2007. But the mortgage had been paid off in March 2006. Over almost two years, Morley, it seemed, had claimed thousands of pounds of taxpayers' money for a mortgage that did not even exist.

Watt struggled to keep the excitement out of her voice as she asked the Land Registry official to fax over the documents detailing Morley's mortgage arrangements. Only when she saw it in black and white would Watt be certain she had got the story straight. As she spoke, she did a quick mental calculation: £800 for twenty months equalled £16,000.

'We don't have those documents here,' the official said. 'We'll have to order them from the archives. It'll take a couple of days or so.'

So be it, thought Watt. As she put the phone down, she turned to Winnett, sitting at a desk at right angles to hers.

'I've found something pretty incredible,' she said. 'Elliot Morley's been claiming for a mortgage that he'd already repaid. By my reckoning, he made at least £16,000 and it's probably a lot more. Could that be a criminal offence?'

'Blimey,' Winnett replied. 'Sounds like he could be in all sorts of trouble.'

Watt had to endure an anxious few days as she waited for the documents to arrive from the Land Registry. In the meantime, the bunker team decided not to tell the news executives about the Elliot Morley story until they were absolutely sure it was correct. They were all experienced enough to know that one of the first rules of journalism is that you don't tell news editors about possible scoops until they're completely nailed down – because you'll end up looking a complete idiot if the story falls apart.

It was the following Monday – the day the first stories about the Conservatives appeared in the paper – before a fax machine on the floor of the bunker (there hadn't been one at all to begin with) whirred into action and deposited several pages of documents from the Land Registry on to the carpet.

Watt snatched up the papers and spread them out on the floor, together with Morley's expenses claims, then sat cross-legged in front of them as she checked the documents against each other. Sure enough, the Abbey National mortgage on Morley's constituency home had been paid off in March 2006, confirming what the official had said on the phone. Morley had, as Watt already knew, carried on claiming exactly £800 per month for mortgage interest on the property until November 2007. It struck her that mortgage interest was unlikely to come to such a neat, round figure. And there was more.

Watt had found a letter to Morley from the parliamentary fees office asking him for documentation to back up his mortgage interest claim, as he had failed to include a copy of his mortgage statement, as required by the fees office. Shortly after being asked for documentary proof of the mortgage, Morley flipped his expenses claims to his London address (where he did still have a mortgage).

The only document Morley had ever given the fees office to back up his mortgage claim was a copy of a 2005 bank statement showing a payment of £800 to Cheltenham & Gloucester. But the Land Registry documents showed that his mortgage was with Abbey National.

What on earth is going on? Watt thought.

Nor did the mystery end there. Morley had bought the house in 1986, the year before he became an MP. It was too long ago for the Land Registry to have a record of how much he had paid for it, but other houses in the same street had cost around £20,000 at that time. Yet mortgage interest of £800 per month, at a typical rate of 5 per cent, would equate to a loan of around £195,000. Curiouser and curiouser.

Watt couldn't wait to find out how Morley was going to explain what the bunker team had begun to refer to as his 'phantom mortgage'. Together with Winnett, she broke the news of Morley's suspect claims to news editor Matthew Bayley and head of news Chris Evans. They were astonished by what they were told, but felt that Morley's story would have to wait, as the *Telegraph* had only just started exposing the Tories' expenses, and had the Lords of the Manor edition to come, which would have to be followed by the Lib Dems for the sake of even-handedness. Publishing Morley's story at this stage would shift the focus straight back on to Labour; so it would just have to wait until later in the week. Also, the paper's editor, William Lewis, wanted to be at the helm on the day such serious allegations were put to Morley; but he was due to leave the country the next day on a flight to Milan, where he had been told by consulting editor Rhidian Wynn Davies that his presence was required at a World Association of Newspapers conference. Lewis had been reluctant to leave the office when there was so much going on, but Murdoch MacLennan, the *Telegraph*'s chief executive, had insisted he should be there.

In fact, Lewis was going nowhere near the conference. MacLennan had hatched a plan weeks earlier with Simon Greenberg, Chelsea FC's director of communications and a close friend of Lewis, for the football-mad editor to spend the day training with the former Chelsea manager Jose Mourinho and his new club Inter Milan as a surprise fortieth birthday present. (Not that this was on expenses, of course; Lewis and Wynn Davies paid for the trip out of their own pockets.)

After arriving in Italy on the Tuesday night, Wynn Davies told his boss that he would be spending the next day in the company of some of the world's most famous footballers, including Patrick Vieira and Zlatan Ibrahimovic, and that he would be put through his paces by Mourinho.

When the pair turned up at the training ground the next day, the former Chelsea manager shook Lewis's hand and said: 'I hear you're bringing down the government!' Mourinho, coach Rui Farias and the Inter Milan club doctor then began Lewis's personal training session, making him spend forty-five minutes on a running machine under the watchful eye of the 'special one', as Mourinho famously referred to himself.

'Jesus!' Mourinho muttered as the sweat poured off Lewis and he struggled for breath. The late nights of the previous few weeks had clearly taken their toll on the editor, the former captain of his university football team. However, miraculously, Lewis was passed fit by Inter's top medical team.

After sharing with Mourinho a footballers' lunch of pasta and salad in the Inter Milan canteen, Lewis and Wynn Davies headed to the bar of an upmarket hotel on the banks of Lake Como to enjoy a glass of chilled rosé.

The glorious peace was interrupted by a seaplane coming in to land on the lake. 'Right, time to go,' Lewis abruptly announced, and they headed to the airport.

Meanwhile, as Evans, Bayley, Winnett and deputy editor Tony Gallagher met to discuss the Elliot Morley story, they had to decide whether the *Telegraph* should pass a file on

Morley's claims to Scotland Yard later that day. Richard Edwards, the *Telegraph*'s crime correspondent, was asked to sound out his sources at the Yard to ascertain how they would respond to being passed a file from the newspaper. They said they would be interested, though ultimately the newspaper decided it was up to Scotland Yard to request a file, rather than the other way round.

As Elliot Morley set off for a long-planned engagement on Wednesday morning, he had no idea of the maelstrom that was about to envelop him. The former minister, who had been appointed a member of the Privy Council in 2006 (making him, in theory, an adviser to the Queen), was one of the guests of honour at the annual conference of the Parliamentary Renewable and Sustainable Energy Group, where he was scheduled to take his place on the panel for a debate that afternoon on 'fiscal and regulatory issues'. In the event, he would never give his speech, and within hours would have become a virtual political pariah.

As Morley arrived at the conference venue across the road from the House of Commons, Holly Watt was beginning to draft the letter that would shortly be sent to the Labour MP. Considering the severity of the allegations, the letter was even more direct and forthright than normal.

'Dear Mr Morley,' began the letter, which was sent at 10.07 a.m.

You claimed £800 a month in respect of the interest on a mortgage on your home at [address] between March 2005 and November 2007.

The Land Registry records – dated 1 March 2006 – show that this registered charge [the mortgage] was removed. There has therefore been no mortgage on [the address] since that date, according to the official record. However, between March 2006 and November 2007, you claimed £800 a month – a total of £16,800 – in mortgage interest on this property. How can you explain this claim?

And then came the killer line: 'This would appear to be prima facie evidence of the offence of false accounting under the 1968 Theft Act (section 17); and/or offences under the 2006 Fraud Act (multiple sections). What is your response to this?'

Watt breathed deeply after pressing the 'send' button, and prepared for what she expected to be a long wait. By noon, there had been no reply, so Watt started eating her rather unorthodox lunch, consisting of a small loaf of bread, a whole cucumber and a bag of tomatoes. Watt had been relentlessly mocked by her colleagues over her peculiar eating habits, for which her only explanation was: 'I never cook; I prefer food in its constituent parts.'

It was at 12.35, as she snapped her cucumber in half to begin her 'second course' that Morley's response flashed up in Watt's email inbox.

Amazingly, he failed to answer the question about whether he had broken the law.

Morley offered a convoluted explanation about how the £800 a month involved payments being made into an endowment investment policy. However, what seemed to concern him most was a question about whether he had claimed for the £14,000 wet-room. In fact, he explained, he had had to pay for an estimate for the work and the taxpayer had simply covered the cost of the estimate.

'I did not submit a bill for £14,687,' Morley wrote, underlining apparently random sections.

> I had a quote from a local plumbing firm to do some repairs to the bath and install a new shower. That was their estimate. I considered the quote completely outrageous though they are excellent plumbers. Unfortunately as a condition of the quote if I did not proceed with the work I had to pay for the estimate which I think was £90. That's why the Bill was submitted. Please don't accuse me of that.

Watt was stunned. A senior MP had just effectively been accused of fraud, yet had not even addressed the allegation.

Chris Evans, Arthur Wynn Davies and Winnett gathered around Watt's screen to read Morley's email. They shared Watt's surprise.

'Hit him again,' said Evans. 'Give him another chance to answer the question.'

Watt began to draft an even more strongly worded letter in reply to Morley. 'Thank you for your response,' she began. 'We now understand the situation regarding the "wet-room".'

> However, I note that you have not directly addressed many of the points we raised in our letter.
>
> Serious allegations – including the potential breach of

criminal laws – are being made about your conduct when making claims under the parliamentary additional costs allowance.

As set out in our previous letter, we intend to state that you did not have a mortgage on [address] after 1st March 2006. You state that you were paying £800 to a C&G endowment policy. This is not a mortgage but an endowment policy. Your expense claim was for mortgage interest costs. How do you justify this anomaly between what you claimed and what you are now stating in your letter? What was the cost of your mortgage interest per month before 1st March 2006?

We repeat that the situation would appear to be prima facie evidence of the offence of false accounting under the 1968 Theft Act (section 17); and/or offences under the 2006 Fraud Act (multiple sections). What is your response to this?

Watt sent the email just after 3 p.m., by which time Morley had taken his seat on the podium at the energy conference as part of the afternoon's panel. According to others present, his face dropped as he checked his BlackBerry and saw Watt's email. 'He went white,' said one of the conference attendees. 'He then stood up and walked straight off the stage without saying a word. We didn't see him again.'

Morley's response, when it arrived at just after half past three that afternoon, was gibberish. The email looked as if it had been sent by someone in such a panic that he couldn't spell or type the words correctly.

'I do not believe any offence has been committed,' began the email. 'The claim by Mr Cawsey was enterily legitimate.

The mortgage then was 900 per month council tax 100 I paid for furnishing and other costs. It had to my main home as a minister. When I claimed on London I renogiated the mortgage.'

Meanwhile, Morley's long-standing friend Cawsey was doing little to help the beleaguered former minister's cause. Watt had also sent Cawsey, the vice-chairman of the Labour Party, a letter asking about his rental of Morley's London home. The other Labour MP had given succinct answers to the questions posed.

'Were you renting one room or the whole property?' Watt asked.

'Whole property,' Cawsey replied.

'Are you aware that Mr Morley nominated [London address] as his main home for the purposes of claiming the ACA until November 2007?'

'No,' the MP said.

The next question from Watt asked: 'Did you know he designated [address] as his "second home" after this date?'

The MP replied: 'No – Elliot told me in March 08 when he received communication from the Fees Office that they were deducting my rent from his ACA claim. From that point on I have not claimed anything.'

Cawsey's response created whole new problems for Morley. Not only had he claimed for a mortgage that did not exist on his second home in Scunthorpe, he had rented out his 'main' London home in its entirety to his friend. Essentially, he was claiming for a 'second' home despite not having the use of a main home.

Watt and Winnett studied the various responses. The planned story was accurate – the first phantom mortgage had been uncovered. The pair began to write the first three pages of the following day's *Telegraph*.

Away from the drama of the Morley investigation, the rest of the team were preparing other stories for the newspaper, some of which provided a light-hearted counterpoint to the possible fraud uncovered by Watt.

Nick Allen, who had been preparing an article about Austin Mitchell, the veteran Labour MP for Great Grimsby, was laughing out loud as he read a response which Mitchell had sent him.

Allen had discovered that Mitchell had attempted to claim £1,296 for bespoke shutters to be installed at his London home. His claim had been rebuffed by the fees office. He had, however, successfully managed to claim £1,200 to reupholster his sofas; 67p for Ginger Crinkle biscuits; 68p for Branston Pickle; and more than £20 for a bottle of Laphroaig malt whisky, as well as a bottle of gin. Allen had sent Mitchell a letter asking him to justify some of the claims. The reporter now summoned the other members of the bunker over to his computer to read the sarcastic response he had just received from the MP.

'Thank you for dredging up the horrors of my expenses,' wrote Mitchell.

I am now arranging for my wife to commit ritual suttee on a burning pyre of furniture coverings as soon as the divorce comes through.

To answer your points:

Security shutters. I can't see why you raise this. No money was paid for them by the fees office. We had two break-ins at our flat with entry effected through the windows. In each case cameras were stolen along with the film which could have had on it some of the greatest pictures ever taken and won me first prize in the Jessops Parliamentary Photography Competition. Alas this was not to be as the cameras were never recovered.

Incidentally there had been an earlier break-in when an intruder had smashed the window into what was then my daughter's bedroom. He did not enter when she screamed. Security shutters were appropriate. Who knows, terrorists could have stolen information on my desk about council house transfers in Grimsby. We had the shutters fitted at our own expense with no support from the fees office. This was done by a firm fitting bespoke shutters because they advertised in the *Daily Telegraph*. They will certainly be appreciative if you give their name. There have been no break-ins since they were installed.

Money spent on ginger crinkles and Branston Pickle shocks me. Neither is made in Grimsby but I am instituting immediate enquires in my household to see who could possibly be responsible for introducing such dangerous substances. I have not so far traced empty containers of either. Whisky and Gin are another matter. I drink neither. I will check to see if my wife is an alcoholic and take appropriate action.

The sofas came with the flat twenty years ago. Since great holes had appeared in the covers, which were stained with

Branston Pickle, whisky, and gin, I decided that they would be detrimental to my career plans which at that stage involved inviting Neil Kinnock, Roy Hattersley, and Peter Mandelson round for drinks and bananas to impress them with my potential. We therefore had them reupholstered (the sofas that is, not Kinnock and Hattersley) which is surely more sensible, environmentally friendly, and a damn sight less expensive than buying new ones. You should consider me for a conservation award. The work was done in Yorkshire because everything is cheaper and better there, from lobotomies to French polishing. The covers are still available if the *Telegraph* would like to have them for its offices. They may be a little tatty for Buckingham Palace Road, but could show the spirit of sacrifice we all need in these austere times.

I'm sorry you don't see any justification for these claims. You should consider whether to communicate that view and your reasons to the Metropolitan police or Norman Baker.

Please use this reply in full. I'm sorry I can't comment further as I'm off to a seminar on 'Cleaning and Maintaining your Moat'.

Deputy editor Tony Gallagher and Chris Evans were so impressed by Mitchell's sense of humour, which drew a round of applause from those in the bunker, that they decided to take Mitchell up on his offer of printing the response in full the next day. It later became a hit on the internet when it was also posted in full on the *Telegraph*'s website.

As another momentous day in the bunker drew to a

close, Richard Oliver, the *Telegraph*'s production chief, who began each evening's work by announcing in gung-ho tones, 'Let's get this show on the road,' was putting the finishing touches to perhaps the strongest front page the team had yet produced. 'MP who claimed £16,000 for mortgage that did not exist,' shouted the headline, accompanied by a vast photograph of Elliot Morley.

William Lewis, who had arrived back in the office from Milan late in the afternoon to oversee the Morley story, looked over Oliver's shoulder. 'Cracking stuff,' the editor said. 'I should go away more often!'

Part of the bunker's routine was for Oliver to print off proof copies of each page of the next day's paper so that the reporters could check the stories before they went to press. At 10 p.m., after Watt had signed off her copy of the front page, she headed for the bar of the Thistle to unwind, and began to dwell on the events of the day. She was well aware that her article would at best destroy Morley's career and at worst put him in gaol. Watt took out her BlackBerry and emailed her best friend, a serving member of the armed forces who was in Afghanistan at the time. 'Miss you,' she said. 'Have been working on horrible story today and the MP has gone completely to pieces. I think he is in really serious trouble. It is v sad actually.'

Watt's friend emailed straight back. 'Remember – no one made him break the rules,' she wrote. 'He should know what is right and wrong.'

Watt's friend was to be married shortly, and the regular communication between the pair over the details of the wedding helped restore some sense of normality to the reporter's world. The next day, in between discussions about sash colours and marquees, Watt's friend wrote a couple of serious lines recalling the previous night's exchange. 'It may be hard for the families of those that are getting caught now but you may just have created the circumstances that lead to a different type of politician for the next decade.'

By then Morley had been suspended from the Labour Party. He went on the defensive, blaming his phantom mortgage claim on 'sloppy accounting' and saying he had not realized he had paid off his mortgage (prompting many observers to comment that he must be the first homeowner in the world to pay off their mortgage without realizing it). In the following weeks, he would announce his decision not to stand as a Labour MP at the next election and repay almost £40,000 for his mortgage overclaims, which had involved far more than the £16,000 uncovered by the *Telegraph*. In the weeks that followed, Morley's claims would also come under the investigation of the Metropolitan Police.

The Resignations Begin

Thursday, 14 May

'I hope you don't mind me asking, but are you an MP?'

CHAPTER 17

IN WESTMINSTER, SPECULATION about who would be next in the *Telegraph*'s spotlight was reaching fever pitch and generating a plethora of rumours, some of which were wildly off the mark. Many of the rumours were fed by political blogs – internet gossip sites which follow the machinations of Parliament and politicians on an hourly basis.

One such rumour doing the rounds on Thursday, 14 May was that the *Telegraph* was about to focus on the expenses claims made by husband-and-wife MPs. According to one version of events, Ed Balls and Yvette Cooper, Labour's 'golden couple' who both had high-profile ministerial jobs, had successfully taken out an injunction to prevent the *Telegraph* revealing any details of their expenses (they hadn't). Another suggestion was that the *Telegraph* had uncovered several examples of married MPs 'double-dipping' – meaning they had each claimed for a different address on expenses, enabling them to subsidize two houses with taxpayers' money. In fact, the *Telegraph* had done some preliminary checks on married MPs, but it had not found any widespread evidence of 'double-dipping' and was not intending to run stories on married MPs imminently.

Not that the married MPs were to know that. As the parliamentary rumour mill amplified the story, the couples became increasingly jittery. Among them were Andrew MacKay and Julie Kirkbride, Conservative MPs for Bracknell, in Berkshire, and Bromsgrove, in Worcestershire, respectively. Alone among husband-and-wife MPs, they had indeed been guilty of double-dipping. MacKay had claimed a second-home allowance for the couple's home in London, while Kirkbride had claimed for a flat in her constituency. In total, the pair had received well over £100,000 in taxpayer-funded expenses, and they were now worrying that their claims were about to feature on the front page of the next day's *Daily Telegraph*.

MacKay was in a particularly awkward position, as he was a senior parliamentary adviser to David Cameron, a member of the Tory leader's inner circle. Cameron had followed up his brutal response to the expenses claims of his Shadow Cabinet earlier in the week by attacking Gordon Brown at Prime Minister's Questions on Wednesday and accusing him of having a 'tin ear' over the public's anger. With his boss leading the moral charge against dubious expenses claims, MacKay was dreading a call from the *Telegraph*.

Part of MacKay's daily routine was to attend strategy meetings with Cameron and his top team at nine fifteen every morning, and that Thursday would be no different, apart from the fact that Cameron was otherwise engaged that day and William Hague, the shadow foreign secretary, was standing in for him by chairing the meeting.

The Conservatives, in common with the other political parties, were desperate to get ahead of the expenses story and demonstrate that they were in control of the situation, and the strategy meetings had started to resemble emergency planning meetings where responses to different scenarios involving MPs' expenses could be discussed. The rumour about 'double-dipping' featuring in the next day's *Telegraph* had reached Conservative high command, so Hague asked MacKay what the phrase meant. Without giving any in- dication of his inner turmoil, Mackay calmly explained to Hague that some married MPs had apparently been claiming expenses on two different properties at the same time. He made no mention of the fact that he and his wife had done exactly that. But as MacKay returned to his office after the meeting, the burden of the secret he was carrying was begin- ning to eat away at him. He was facing a simple choice: either come clean and tell Cameron straight away about his expenses claims, or wait until the *Telegraph* did it for him. Either way, MacKay was rapidly coming to the conclusion that his ambition of becoming a minister in a David Cameron government was over.

Earlier in the week, MacKay had told his local paper in Bracknell that he had nothing to fear from the *Telegraph*'s expenses investigation. 'I have checked through all my expenses claims over the past four years and there is nothing that stands out – I am confident there is nothing unreasonable in there at all,' he said. The conversation about double-dipping had made him think again. Within minutes of coming out of the meeting, he had picked up the phone to Cameron to explain what he and his wife had done. Cameron decided the couple's claims were 'unacceptable'. MacKay didn't need to be told what to do; he immediately tendered his resignation from his position as Cameron's adviser. In doing so, MacKay became the first MP to resign from any job as a result of the expenses row, even though his claims had not featured in the *Daily Telegraph*.

Back in the bunker, there was a certain amount of bemusement at the fact that the first casualty of the investigation was someone who had not been in the paper, while other MPs, who had been guilty of equally questionable claims, were still in their posts.

'Well,' said Chris Evans. 'I suppose this means we're going to have to do the couples tomorrow!'

Although the investigation team had made some preliminary checks on the expenses of married couples, they had not yet been looked at in detail, as there had been so many other stories to get out of the way first.

Ed Balls and Yvette Cooper, whose expenses claims had been the subject of such frenzied speculation among parliamentary gossips, failed to live up to the rumour mill's hype. Although Cooper had flipped the designation of her second home from her constituency home in Castleford, West Yorkshire, to the couple's London home after her husband joined her in Parliament in 2005, the couple had, on the whole, been scrupulous in splitting the bills for their London home 50/50. The *Telegraph* published a straightforward story about their flipping, which managed to enrage both the bloggers (who claimed the *Telegraph* had let Balls and

Cooper off the hook) and the two MPs (who complained vociferously that they had been treated unduly harshly and had not flipped their homes).

The *Telegraph* also looked again at the claims of Alan and Ann Keen, Labour MPs for adjacent constituencies in west London, who had been dubbed 'Mr and Mrs Expenses' by the press after a whole string of previous stories about their claims. The couple had bought a £500,000 flat within walking distance of Parliament, and claimed back the mortgage interest after nominating it as their second home, even though their 'main' home in Brentford was less than 10 miles away, just a 30-minute commute from Westminster. Incredibly, their claims were within the parliamentary rules because their constituencies were both classed as being in outer London, making them eligible to claim for a second home.

Peter and Iris Robinson, Democratic Unionist MPs who represented constituencies in Northern Ireland, had claimed a total of £159,208 in allowances between 2004 and 2008 for a Thames-side flat, including £30,525 for food alone. In 2007/8 the couple, who were paid separate wages and expenses for their second jobs as members of the Northern Ireland Assembly, had received between them a total of £571,939 in salaries and expenses in 2007/8 from their jobs in Westminster and Northern Ireland.

The final parliamentary couple were the Tory MPs Sir Nicholas and Lady Ann Winterton, who had claimed more than £80,000 in rent for a small London flat which was owned by a trust controlled by their children. The arrangement had been criticized by the Parliamentary Commissioner for Standards the previous year, when it had received widespread media coverage.

MacKay's decision to resign, together with the announcement later that day of Elliot Morley's suspension from the Labour Party, saw the bunker's 'wall of glory' turned into a rogue's gallery. Hazel Blears, with her £13,000 cheque, already adorned the magnetic wall, and now she was to be joined by portraits of MacKay and Morley. Over the coming days, more MPs would step down or announce their decisions to retire, and as the number of portraits grew, the wall began to resemble an evidence board from a television cop show. Matthew Bayley was particularly pleased with the result. 'Excellent. It's just like *The Wire*!' he said as he admired the overall effect. Bayley, in common with half the newsroom, had become addicted to watching boxed DVD sets of the US drama said to be President Obama's favourite television programme. It featured a Baltimore Police Department 'detail' whose detectives pinned up pictures of suspects and copies of documents on a board as they made connections between members of a major drug ring. As Bayley warmed to the theme, the reporters in the bunker became 'the detail' and anyone who failed would be threatened with returning to 'the rotation' – cop-speak for working rostered shifts.

Back in the real world, real policemen were still considering the complaint from the Speaker about the leaking of the MPs' expenses. William Lewis still harboured concerns that the authorities would find a way to 'close down' the investigation, in his words, either through the police or through the courts. His decision to publish the expenses claims of so many MPs in such a short space of time was driven in part by his belief that the newspaper should get as much material in the public domain as quickly as it could in case of an attempt to shut down the operation.

But the middle of May would provide another of the many watershed moments in the investigation. It was at this point that Lewis received information from a highly placed source that the Metropolitan Police Commissioner, Sir Paul Stephenson, had decided not to launch an investigation into the leak. Furthermore, the source also told Lewis that Sir Paul was considering investigating the MPs themselves. The news came as an enormous relief, and gave the editor renewed confidence as he pressed on with the campaign.

More than 200 miles away, a dramatic indication of the public mood was about to be played out on national television. The BBC was about to broadcast the first *Question Time* since the *Telegraph* had started publishing its revelations about MPs' expenses, and the venue was to be a technical college in Grimsby. Among the guests who had been invited on to the panel was Benedict Brogan, the *Daily Telegraph*'s recently recruited political commentator. As the Andrew MacKay saga was developing in London, Brogan was on a train to Lincolnshire, having decided to get to Grimsby early so he could sample the mood on the streets.

Grimsby had been the busiest fishing port in the world as recently as the 1950s and remained proudly working-class, employing thousands of people in food-processing factories, in its container port and at the nearby chemical works in Immingham. There could hardly have been a worse place for a group of politicians to have to face a live studio audience to explain, in the middle of a recession, why they and their colleagues had been throwing around taxpayers' money on fripperies like silk cushions and plasma TVs.

Brogan was first to arrive in the makeshift green room at the college, and sat transfixed as he watched television footage of motorists driving past Elliot Morley's house in nearby Scunthorpe, beeping their horns and shaking their fists.

'Ah, the Antichrist,' said a voice behind him. It was Sir Menzies Campbell, the 68-year-old former Liberal Democrat leader, who had arrived with the shadow work and pensions secretary Theresa May. Although the urbane Sir Menzies was as friendly as ever towards Brogan, he had clearly been bruised by the disclosures about his expenses revealed in the previous day's *Telegraph*. The evening's other panellists, the Labour minister Margaret Beckett, whose claims had featured on day one of the *Telegraph*'s expenses files, and Steve Easterbrook, chief executive of McDonald's UK, followed shortly afterwards.

The awkward small talk in the green room was interrupted by a producer, who told the guests: 'Just to let you know, all of the questions submitted by the audience tonight were about expenses. There weren't any questions about anything else, which has never happened before, so the whole programme will be about expenses.' It was clearly going to be a long night for the MPs.

The show's presenter and chairman, David Dimbleby, was first into the tightly packed auditorium, a few minutes before filming was due to begin. In keeping with his usual practice, he introduced each of the panellists to the audience in turn, inviting them to walk on to the stage and take their seat so that the panel would be seated and ready to go when the cameras started filming.

'Please welcome our first guest, the minister of state for housing and planning, Margaret Beckett.'

'Boo!!!' shouted the audience, with an unmistakable air of menace.

Theresa May received the same treatment; then it was the turn of Sir Menzies (commonly known as Ming), one of the most respected MPs in Parliament. 'Boo!!!' came the response from the audience, whose anger only seemed to be increasing.

Sir Menzies looked crestfallen as he made his way across the stage, and Brogan, still off-stage, turned to a producer and raised his eyebrows. The producer was starting to look worried.

'They've booed Ming!' she gasped. 'They never boo Ming!'

Finally it was Brogan's turn to be introduced – and this time there were cheers and applause from the audience. Brogan felt a blush rising from his collar.

If the MPs on the panel, or any of those watching on television at home, had any remaining doubts about the level of public fury over the expenses scandal, they were finally put to bed by the unbroken hostility of the audience throughout the hour-long show. As Beckett, Campbell and May tried to placate the audience, they were repeatedly heckled and barracked with shouts of 'Resign!' and 'You think you're above the law!' and 'You think you're better than us!' Brogan was so alarmed by what he was seeing that he began to worry that the audience, by now taking on the air of a lynch mob, might rush the stage, and producers later told him they had considered calling in security guards for the first time in the show's history. For the BBC the show was a ratings triumph, attracting a peak of four million viewers – the highest audience for seven years (aside from a general election special in 2005).

For the watching MPs, it represented a watershed moment: they could no longer credibly argue that the expenses story was anything other than a full-scale disaster for the political class. It was becoming clear that Andrew MacKay and Elliot Morley would be the first of many casualties. Within hours, one of those casualties would be a government minister.

The Justice Minister, his House and 'Osama bin Laden'

Friday, 15 May

'I'm going to cancel the papers if you go through the roof every morning'

CHAPTER 18

THE QUESTIONABLE EXPENSES claims of Shahid Malik, a junior justice minister, were originally pencilled in to be covered by the *Telegraph* on day two of the investigation, along with those of other ministers including Phil Woolas and Ben Bradshaw. Had the *Telegraph* stuck to its original plan, Malik's claims might have been lost in the mix, in the same way that Jack Straw, Alistair Darling and others had been able to rely on 'safety in numbers' at that point in the proceedings. In the first few days of the investigation, too, ministers could count on the Prime Minister for his support, as Gordon Brown viewed the entire story as a right-wing conspiracy and was in no mood to satisfy the public's cries for heads to roll.

But the *Telegraph* had held back from publishing Malik's expenses claims, because the more Robert Winnett had looked into them, the more complicated they had become. Like that of Elliot Morley, Shahid Malik's case would require a considerable amount of further investigation before the *Telegraph* could be sure it had got to the bottom of the story. It was Malik's great misfortune that, by the time the *Telegraph* was ready to publish his claims a week into the investigation, he could no longer use the fig-leaf of other ministers' spivvy behaviour, and the Prime Minister was no longer minded to turn a blind eye.

The expenses claims of Elliot Morley had been 'a game changer' for Gordon Brown: according to one source close to the Prime Minister, 'it was at that point that he decided there would have to be swift sanctions against anyone who broke the rules'. And Brown wouldn't have to wait long to show the public that he was, after all, willing to flex his muscles.

Shahid Malik was considered a parliamentary high-flier and had made history by becoming the first Muslim to be appointed a government minister. Despite having been elected as the Labour MP for Dewsbury as recently as 2005, Malik had been brought into the government in 2007 by Gordon Brown as a junior minister for international development. In October 2008 he was promoted to Jack Straw's Ministry of Justice, where one of his briefs was over-seeing the implementation of the deeply unpopular proposed national identity card scheme (which was all but abandoned by Labour in the summer of 2009).

But as Winnett read through Malik's expenses claims, he sensed that the MP's rise through the political ranks might be about to come to an end.

All the reporters working on the expenses files had noticed almost straight away that they gave a clear indication of the personality and character of the MP behind the claims. Some were disorganized, polite and apologetic, while others appeared more ruthless and aggressive in their deal-ings with the staff of the parliamentary fees office. Malik's claims were firmly in the latter category. Within months of becoming an MP in May 2005, he had begun testing the limits of the expenses system.

The MP was claiming expenses under the ACA for a property in south London that he had owned since 2001. It had only cost him £85,000 – but the taxpayer would soon have spent almost as much as that on the property. Between 2005 and 2008 he had claimed the maximum allowable amount for the house, £66,827 over the three years, and in 2006/7 his total expenses, including office and staffing allowances, had come to £185,421 (not including his salary), making him the most expensive MP of all that year.

In his first year in Parliament, Malik spent hundreds of pounds on new kitchen equipment, a microwave, dishwasher, rug, bathroom sink and other items. He even had claims for an iPod and portable DVD player rejected in December 2005. He then approached the fees office to ask whether he was allowed to buy a new television. They informed him that televisions were among the items for which MPs could claim – so he promptly spent more than £2,500 on a 40-inch flat-screen TV and home cinema system. To his fury, the parliamentary authorities refused to pay the full cost of the purchase after informing him that it was 'luxurious' and 'excessive'. There then followed an extraordinary series of exchanges with the fees office, in which he demanded that they should pay up. In one letter he said, 'from a natural justice perspective I feel a justifiable exception would be the fairest manner to deal with the current situation'. However, the fees office held firm and ultimately only paid him just over £1,000 towards the total cost. His response was to demand from the fees office a list of the maximum amounts that could be spent on other items on the 'John Lewis list'. They also declined this request.

Undeterred, Malik continued his spending spree over the next two years with the purchase of more rugs, another microwave, a new bathroom, fireplace, lamps and other items. The taxpayer was also to pay more than £700 for a 'massage chair' for the MP. He would later defend the purchase on the basis that he had back pain.

As Winnett scrolled through page after page of Malik's shopping receipts, he realized that he had found one of the most enthusiastic users of the expenses system. His claims were all the more surprising given that he was a newly elected MP who appeared highly ambitious. Why had he been so reckless?

Leaving aside Malik's extravagant spending on household goods, Winnett had a nagging doubt over another facet of the minister's expenses. He was claiming that his London house, where he lived with his wife, was his 'second home'. However, there was no trace in the files of another property. All his bills were sent either to the London address or to his office at the House of Commons. In the hundred pages of claims, the only non-London address was on a bill sent to his parents' home in Burnley – about 30 miles away from Malik's Dewsbury constituency. This was so unusual that Winnett decided to hold the Malik article back for further investigation.

To find out whether Malik had a home in Dewsbury,

Nigel Bunyan, the *Daily Telegraph*'s Manchester district reporter, was dispatched to the West Yorkshire town. Bunyan soon discovered that the MP rented a property in part of a converted barn complex on the outskirts of Dewsbury owned by Tahir Zaman, known as 'Terry' – a local businessman who might charitably be described as 'colourful'. Zaman, who spent much of his time in Dubai, owned a number of properties in the Yorkshire town and had previously pleaded guilty to letting out a property that was uninhabitable to a family of five (he claimed they were sitting tenants when he bought the property), a criminal offence for which he was fined £450 and charged £200 costs. In 2004 he had announced plans to invest £15 million in the area, only to be formally declared bankrupt three years later (though the decision was annulled after three months). Zaman lived in the main property on the barn complex. He also rented Malik his constituency office, which was funded by the taxpayer through the parliamentary office expenses system. It was an odd set-up, to say the least.

Bunyan went to Malik's 'main home' in the rented property, where there was no answer and not much to see apart from a rusty wok on the window sill and a dirty plate in the sink. Next door, at Zaman's house, the businessman was out, but his wife was at home.

'He [Malik] is a good friend and neighbour,' Mrs Zaman told Bunyan. 'He comes here just at the weekends. He was here this weekend just gone. He rang my little boy up because it was his birthday. Usually he comes here alone. He's always getting involved with local issues and he's always in the local paper.' Mrs Zaman also told the reporter that the house was normally occupied in the week by one of Malik's constituency workers. The situation was getting murkier – this was supposedly the MP's 'main' home.

Bunyan reported his findings to Winnett and Rayner.

'Sounds pretty dubious,' said Winnett. 'Wonder how much rent he's paying Zaman?'

The most obvious way to find that out was to ask Zaman himself, but first Winnett felt he would like to know more about the landlord. The task of looking into Zaman's background was given to Caroline Gammell, who had been asked to join the bunker team as its first new member since the stories had first started to appear.

Gammell had joined the *Telegraph* in August 2007 at around the same time as Winnett and Rayner, having previously been chief reporter at the Press Association, where she had covered the Bali bombings and the Indian Ocean tsunami and had twice been to Afghanistan to report on the war. Her other claim to fame was that, during a previous 'career' as a schoolgirl cricketer, she had appeared in the cricketing almanac Wisden as the most economical bowler of either sex at the country's independent schools.

One of the *Telegraph*'s most versatile reporters, Gammell had been in Germany chasing leads on another story when the results of the expenses investigation first began appearing in the paper, and had cursed her luck when she saw that she was missing out on a 'big one'. When Matthew Bayley asked her to get involved a week later she couldn't get to the bunker fast enough, though the smell of decomposing takeaways when she walked in quickly disabused her of any notion that she was about to get involved in anything glamorous.

Gammell began by speaking to local newspaper reporters in Dewsbury, and found they were entirely familiar with Zaman. It wasn't long before she had a mobile phone number for him, and not much longer before Winnett, after attaching a digital voice recorder to his phone, was dialling it.

A cheery voice answered, slightly to Winnett's surprise. 'Is that Mr Zaman?' the reporter asked.

'Speaking,' he replied.

'This is Robert Winnett at the *Daily Telegraph*.'

'Lovely. Have I won the lottery?' he joked, before launching into a lengthy account of his conviction as a 'slum landlord' several years previously.

Winnett began to ask him about the various properties that he rented to Malik. Zaman described in detail how the office was rented at normal commercial rates and had been independently valued.

Then came the key question from the reporter. 'It's a flat he's [Malik] got, next door, that's owned by you too?' Winnett asked.

'If it's a flat or if it's not a flat, it's his personal house. I don't really want to say,' Zaman said.

'You own that as well?' Winnett asked.

'Yes.'

'How much rent does he pay on that?'

'You'll have to ask him. I tell you what, he's not paying

me what the independent valuation said he should be paying me.'

'On the flat?'

'Because we got the independent valuation again for this house. This property's worth, if I were to sell it, maybe £400,000. I'm not even getting a yield of 5 per cent.'

'What's your yield on it then? We don't want to accuse you of profiting from this. So if he's paying you less than the market value rent . . .'

'He is definitely paying well under the market value rent,' Zaman said.

'So, what? £100 a week?' asked Winnett.

'It's even less,' came the response.

'Less than £100 a week?'

'I think so, yeah. Put it this way. Where he's living, I'm renting the next-door half the size of his property, they pay me more rent than what he's paying me.'

Winnett sat back in his chair, amazed at what the businessman had just admitted. A government minister, representing the Justice Department no less, had claimed that his 'main' home was a cheap flat provided by a friend who said he was renting it at well below the market rate. Meanwhile, he had gone to town spending taxpayers' money on the 'second' home he owned in London.

Not only did Malik appear to have abused the second-home allowance by claiming for what looked like his marital home in London, but his opaque rental arrangements with Zaman might also be in breach of another rule-book, the Ministerial Code of Conduct, which banned ministers from any financial arrangement which risked putting them under an obligation to someone.

Winnett turned to Chris Evans. 'The guy's just admitted Malik pays below market rent for the property in Dewsbury,' he said.

'Sounds like a splash. Better get writing,' Evans replied.

Earlier in the day, Winnett had also sent a series of questions to Malik. The MP had phoned back to say that he was too busy to answer them but would endeavour to do so 'over the weekend'. The reporter explained that it was important for the minister to find time to answer the queries as the newspaper was planning to publish a story the following day.

Late in the afternoon an email arrived in Winnett's inbox with the minister's answers to the questions. It was signed off: 'cheers Shahid'.

The MP confirmed that Dewsbury was his 'home'. 'I spend half a week in Dewsbury and I obviously have to be in Parliament and need somewhere to sleep from Monday night to Wednesday night. Overall I spent the majority of my time in Dewsbury because although I spent half the week in London when Parliament is in session I spent most of recess at my main home in Dewsbury.'

That's about as clear as mud, Winnett thought.

Malik strongly defended his claims but added that he regarded the present system as 'flawed' and in need of 'major reform'.

It was almost 6 p.m. and Winnett had yet to write a single word. The deadline was less than three hours away.

For such a complicated story, it was going to be tight. Moments later, an email arrived from executive editor Mark Skipworth asking to see a copy of the story. Winnett only had three paragraphs on screen.

By seven thirty the story was starting to take shape, and by eight fifteen, with input from Evans, Winnett was ready to press the button. It began:

> The controversial expenses claims of Britain's highest claiming MP – Justice Minister Shahid Malik – can today be disclosed by the *Daily Telegraph*.
>
> Mr Malik has claimed more than £20,000 a year from the taxpayer for his 'second' home – a house in south London. He put pressure on the Fees Office to pay controversial claims for expenses, including a home-cinema system, deemed to be a 'luxury' items by officials.
>
> However, it can be disclosed that his nominated 'main' home is, in fact, a constituency property he rents for less than £5,200 from a landlord with a questionable past.

A few minutes later, Lewis called Winnett in to his office. He was sitting at a table in the corner with a printout of the story which was covered in black marks.

'I don't think it's quite there,' he said. 'I'm not quite sure what we are trying to say. Can we give it another go?'

Winnett could feel his blood pressure rising as he returned to the bunker. There were only thirty minutes to go until deadline. Winnett and Evans called up the story and began again.

'The controversial way in which Justice Minister Shahid Malik was able to run up the highest expenses claim of any MP can be disclosed today by the *Daily Telegraph*.'

'Better, much better,' Evans said under his breath. Richard Oliver, the production chief, was now pacing around the bunker. 'We really need the splash guys, we're going to be late.'

At 8.55 p.m. the story was finally ready to leave Winnett's computer screen. Senior production journalist Keith Hoggins called it up on his own screen, where he was immediately surrounded by Winnett, Evans, Tony Gallagher and Gordon Rayner, all of whom felt there were still tweaks to be made. The unflappable Hoggins was the coolest head in the room as he made last-minute corrections with four different people's fingers pointed at words or sentences they wanted him to change.

Half an hour later the story had been laid out on the front page, checked by the lawyer, proofread and sent to the printers. The headline read: 'The justice minister, his home and the convicted landlord'. On one side of the page was a picture of Malik, on the other was a bearded, smiling Zaman.

Winnett had another sleepless night with the stress of the last few hours still weighing heavily on his mind. He was unsure how the Malik story was going to be received. It was the most complicated investigation into any minister the team had yet published – the sort of thing which might have taken weeks when he had worked on the *Sunday Times* – and he kept going over and over the facts in his head, with that 'did I lock the front door?' feeling in his stomach.

The following morning, Winnett switched on Sky News as he gulped down a cup of tea. He was about to leave for the office when he heard the presenter announce they were going 'live' to Dewsbury to speak to Malik in his home. 'Oh God,' Winnett thought. 'Here we go.'

What followed was surely one of the most extraordinary interviews given by a politician in recent decades. It was certainly compulsive viewing.

Malik was sitting at a table in what appeared to be his kitchen, drinking tea from an England mug. As Winnett had suspected he might do, Malik's opening gambit was to accuse the *Telegraph* of racism.

'It makes good copy to put a picture of me and someone who looks like Osama bin Laden on the front page,' Malik said. 'I don't believe my claims were out of the core. This is not dodgy stuff, this is right in the centre. This isn't helicopters, it's not tennis courts, it's not swimming pools, it's not horse manure. It's very much at the core of the rules.

'The Green Book is our Bible. MPs talked about it, we asked what the limits were. They were not able to give us the advice that we needed.

'I can't do my job if my main home is not Dewsbury. I'm proud of the fact that I'm the first MP for Dewsbury since the war to live in Dewsbury.'

The interviewer then asked: 'How much time do you spend here?'

'I've absolutely nothing to hide. I've nothing to be ashamed of. The majority of my time is here in Dewsbury. Monday night, Tuesday night, Wednesday night in London.

On Thursday I'm in my constituency. Friday, Saturday and Sunday. In the recess I spend the majority of my time here.

'Whether I spend £10,000 or £5,000 or £1 doesn't really matter. You can't choose which your main home is. For me my main home is here. I'm confident that what I've done is absolutely right.'

'Does anyone else live here?'

'Who lives here has nothing to do with anyone. There is nothing from the public purse that is linked to my Dewsbury home. We are being demonized. It's got to stop.

'If you prick me, I bleed. If I prick you, you bleed. People like you and others will feel in the future, "Maybe we went a bit too far, maybe we've tarnished the good guys."

'I think the *Telegraph* in the long term will have done a service to democracy, but I don't know whether we'll have any democracy worth saving after this bloodfest.'

He was then asked whether his job as a minister was safe – a question he dismissed as 'silly'.

'Of course my job as a minister will be intact. There is no question of me not continuing in my role. I hope I won't be proved wrong.'

The interview was turning into a rant from Malik. He had also said: 'I think this is a bit of a non-story, to be honest. I'm going one million per cent by the book. It's a non-story in the sense that I could have been one of five hundred MPs. I don't know why the *Telegraph* focused on me.

'Of course I feel that my reputation is tarnished, but my integrity is intact. I'm not in it to make money, I'm here to make a difference.'

Then came the most bizarre exchange. The Sky interviewer asked: 'Can I ask why an £800 massage chair is so important to you?'

Malik replied: 'You see, I'd have more respect for you if you were honest about the figures. You know full well it is £730.'

Back in Downing Street, the Prime Minister's watching advisers were agog. They had read the *Telegraph*'s story when it landed on the website at 10 p.m. the previous evening. 'The alarm bells had started ringing immediately,' one of those present later said.

In the Cabinet Office at 7 a.m. Sir Gus O'Donnell, the Cabinet Secretary and the most powerful civil servant in the land, was starting to immerse himself in the Malik case.

Sir Gus was a clear-headed and highly respected Whitehall veteran. He had been around John Major's unravelling government as the Prime Minister's press secretary, so he knew what a crisis looked like. By 8 a.m. he had spoken to the Prime Minister and given his initial thoughts on Malik's position. They were not positive. O'Donnell was concerned about the implications of Malik's rental agreement on the Ministerial Code of Conduct. The code stipulates that ministers must disclose to the senior official in their department any financial arrangement which could put them under an obligation to someone. No such arrangement had been registered by Malik.

By mid-morning, Jack Straw had also spoken to Malik, as had the permanent secretary at the Ministry of Justice. Again, the prognosis was not good.

Just before 11 a.m. on Friday, 15 May, Downing Street announced that Malik was to be investigated by the independent adviser on the ministerial code. Barely two hours after he had dismissed the *Telegraph*'s investigation as 'a nonstory', Malik announced he would be stepping down from his ministerial post while the investigation was carried out. Once again, the bunker team had apparently been vindicated, at least for the time being.

Such was the unstoppable momentum which the expenses investigation had gathered, however, that there was no time for anyone to rest on their laurels. The following day was Saturday, the *Telegraph*'s biggest-selling edition in any week, and a new batch of MPs were already being investigated by the team.

After the immense pressure of the Malik investigation, the veteran Labour MP Sir Gerald Kaufman was to provide some welcome comic relief. Kaufman's claims had first been examined the previous week by Gordon Rayner, who had been looking forward to writing about them for days.

Rayner had barely been able to contain his glee on the day he first looked through Kaufman's expense receipts.

'Have a guess how much Gerald Kaufman claimed for a television,' he asked the reporters in the bunker.

'Two grand?'

'No.'

'Two and a half?'

'No. Eight thousand, eight hundred and sixty-five pounds.' Cue gasps of disbelief.

Sir Gerald had bought a 40-inch Bang & Olufsen LCD

television for £8,865 and tried to claim for it in 2006. The fees office told him it fell into the category of 'luxurious furnishings' and paid him only £750. And there was much, much more. The Manchester Gorton MP, a former environment minister, had also charged the taxpayer £1,851 for what he described as a 'second-hand rug' on his claim form. It turned out he had bought it from an antiques centre in New York. His other claims included £220 for a pair of crystal grapefruit bowls and £225 for a rollerball pen. In one exchange with the fees office, regarding £28,834 of work on the kitchen and bathroom at his London flat, he had said the work needed to be done because he was 'living in a slum', even though his second home, off Regent's Park, was in one of the most expensive areas of the capital. He had also claimed £1,262 for a gas bill that was £1,055 in credit.

When Rayner contacted Sir Gerald, he admitted that the claim for the TV was 'a bit daft', insisted his flat had needed work because it was 'neglected' and said he would pay back the money for the rug if he was asked to.

Like so many other MPs, however, Sir Gerald found that the story continued to run in his local newspaper, and more than a fortnight later he agreed to give an interview to the *Manchester Evening News* in which he came up with perhaps the most bizarre attempt at an excuse in the entire history of excuses.

'I live very modestly. I don't have much in the way of luxuries,' he began, before addressing the subject of why he tried to claim £8,865 for a TV.

'I'd self-diagnosed myself with obsessive compulsive

disorder and I'd bought a new television set. Then I decided to have a bigger one. I thought to myself, "Well, you can claim for a TV, so why not claim for it?"

'Because I've got this self-diagnosed OCD, I do things according to rules that I've created.'

On the subject of the grapefruit bowls, he said: 'As part of my OCD, I have the same breakfast when I'm at home both in London and Manchester every day. Half a grapefruit, a bowl of muesli with semi-skimmed milk and a cup of coffee with a Rich Tea biscuit. That's breakfast. A cleaner broke one of the dishes, so I went and got a replacement.'

Readers of the *Manchester Evening News* were incredulous. One correspondent wrote: 'Sir Gerald blames "self-diagnosed obsessive compulsive disorder (O.C.D.)" for his behaviour. I have worked in the NHS for nearly 20 years and my opinion is that he suffers from self-diagnosed G.R.E.E.D.!'

While Rayner was chuckling to himself over Sir Gerald's expenses claims, Jon Swaine was about to make a breakthrough on a story which appeared to involve another 'phantom mortgage'.

Swaine, originally from Chelmsford in Essex, had joined the *Telegraph* as a graduate trainee in 2007, and from his very first day it had been clear he was going places. Spending six months on a local newspaper and six months with the Press Association as part of his training on the *Telegraph* scheme, he was a frighteningly quick learner who could not only rapidly turn around well-written, accurate stories but was also fully fluent in emerging web-based reporting techniques including blogging and Twitter. As one of the paper's newer recruits, he often had to work early shifts, starting at 6 a.m., to make sure the *Telegraph*'s website was bang up to date in time for the morning rush hour; so he was the only member of the team for whom the 8 a.m. starts in the bunker represented a lie-in.

For Swaine, still only twenty-four, the expenses story represented a chance to prove that he was not only bright but also capable of pulling his weight in a major investigation, and he repaid the faith of Bayley and Evans by quietly getting on with the job in hand, producing a string of excellent stories as the investigation progressed.

'The Swaine', as the other bunker reporters called him, had become highly suspicious when he had checked the expenses claims of David Chaytor, a little-known backbench Labour MP representing Bury North. Chaytor appeared to be the most frequent flipper in Parliament. His files showed that he had changed his designated second home six times in five years. One of his flips was to a property where his son was registered as the occupant, where he paid off thousands of pounds' worth of bills. Swaine prepared a letter for Chaytor asking him to explain why he had made claims for this property along with a number of other questionable expenses. While waiting for the MP's response, he started to delve more deeply into the various properties for which Chaytor had claimed.

Using Land Registry records, Swaine established that a London flat on which the MP had claimed £13,000 in mortgage interest in 2005 and 2006 was not currently mortgaged.

But had it been mortgaged at the time he made the claims? As Watt had done with Elliot Morley, Swaine asked the Land Registry office in Birkenhead to check the history of the mortgage, and was told that Chaytor had paid off his Yorkshire Building Society loan in January 2004, the year before he started claiming expenses for the mortgage.

'Are you absolutely sure?' Swaine asked the official.

'I've no doubt about it, Jon – we received an application to end the mortgage on the seventh of January, 2004, and there don't appear to have been any others since,' she said. Swaine asked her to fax over the document.

It didn't arrive.

Panic began to mount. Swaine called to check she had sent it – she had. He asked her to send the document again – she did. Still it didn't arrive. With the deadline looming, Swaine began to fear that the official had accidentally sent it to the news desk of another newspaper, or made up the whole thing as a 'Friday joke' after getting fed up with doing so many checks for the bunker team during the week.

Eventually Swaine found another fax machine in the main newsroom, gave the Land Registry the number, and then stood guard beside it, waiting. After what seemed like hours, the document eventually came through. It showed that Chaytor was indeed another 'phantom mortgage' claimer – the second in a week.

The rush was now on for Swaine to put a series of follow-up questions to Chaytor. He wrote a second, more serious, letter to the MP, asking whether he might have broken the law. The wording was identical to that of the letter that had been sent to Morley. He then called Chaytor's constituency secretary, to whom he had spoken when sending the first letter. 'I've got another letter for Mr Chaytor, this time with some very serious allegations,' he said. She explained that the MP was on a 'fact-finding' trip to America with a parliamentary committee to study education policy. An hour later, the secretary replied:

> Thank you for your two emails, which I confirm have reached David Chaytor's inbox. However, as he is away on a Select Committee visit abroad, and has had technical problems all week in accessing his inbox, I do not know whether he has yet received them personally. I am trying to contact him to let him know you have written and would like a response.

After another two and a half agonizing hours, Swaine still hadn't received a reply. He telephoned the secretary again, called Chaytor's mobile phone and even called Mrs Chaytor (who worked in the MP's Westminster office). Chaytor had switched off his phone and his wife was sounding incredibly stressed.

Just before 5 p.m. Swaine asked the secretary for her mobile number, in case she had to leave the office. 'I don't think that's going to be happening tonight,' she said. Swaine was encouraged.

At 5 p.m. precisely, Chaytor made contact with Swaine for the first time. 'As you know I am abroad on a Select Committee visit at the moment, and have been all week,' he said in an email. 'Because of this I have been unable to go through the documents properly. Because of this I am taking legal advice and therefore am unable to give a statement at this time. I will respond as soon as possible.'

After consulting Arthur Wynn Davies, Swaine replied:

As is widely accepted, our investigation concerns matters of enormous public interest. Given that each Member of Parliament is accountable for expenses claimed from public funds you are plainly under a duty to respond to legitimate questions raised with you as a matter of public interest and concern. This matter is urgent.

While we note what you say about being currently abroad, we cannot see any reason for your not being able to answer the relatively straightforward questions put to you in my earlier email.

Just eight minutes later, the MP sent back a long and detailed response.

Swaine crouched forward as he eagerly read Chaytor's email. As he got halfway down the screen, he collapsed back into his chair and breathed out heavily. Holding his outstretched arm towards the computer, he turned to Winnett.

'He's admitted it,' said a mightily relieved Swaine.

The reporters gathered round his screen, giving Swaine morale-boosting slaps on the shoulder as they read Chaytor's response.

'In respect of mortgage interest payments, there has been an unforgivable error in my accounting procedures for which I apologise unreservedly,' he had written.

Arthur Wynn Davies came into the bunker. 'He's coughed to it,' Winnett told him.

'Bloody hell – he must have had it ready all along,' said Wynn Davies.

Winnett passed the news on to the editor.

'He's the first one to actually just admit it and apologize, right?' said Lewis.

'Yep,' replied Winnett.

Winnett and Swaine started work on a story which would be headlined: 'The MP and the phantom £13,000 mortgage'. It was the first time the phrase 'phantom mortgage' would appear in print.

As the finishing touches were put to the story, Chaytor was heading for an airport in Washington DC to catch a flight back to Britain to face the Labour Party. Television crews would be waiting for him at his various properties the following day. Like Morley, he would be suspended from the Parliamentary Labour Party and would decide to pay back the money and announce he would not be standing at the next election. And, like Morley, his claims would become the subject of a police investigation.

Apart from stories about Chaytor and Kaufman, that Saturday's *Daily Telegraph* also contained stories about the expenses claims of another eight MPs – a measure of just how much was going on in the bunker on any one day. The paper also contained a new feature of the expenses investigation: the 'saints'. Readers had made it clear that as well as finding out which MPs had been up to no good, they wanted to know which members had been scrupulously honest. By the time the investigation had finished, the *Telegraph* had published the names and details of fifty 'saints' who had done all they could to minimize their burden on the public purse. They included Vince Cable, the Lib Dem Treasury spokesman, who was one of seven Lib Dem MPs representing outer London constituencies who had chosen not to claim the ACA despite being eligible to claim it. The Conservative MP Ann Widdecombe claimed just £858 of her second-home allowance in 2007/8 (for occasional hotel stays), having decided against buying a second home in London and opting instead to commute from her constituency home 42 miles away in Maidstone. Labour's 'saints' included the likes of Martin Salter, the Reading West MP, who claimed nothing at all under the second-home allowance, choosing to commute the 50 miles from his Berkshire constituency rather than buying a flat in London at taxpayers' expense.

The saints also included some of Parliament's wealthiest MPs: Geoffrey Robinson, the millionaire former paymaster general and Labour MP for Coventry North West, claimed nothing at all on his ACA, despite owning more than one property. True, he was wealthy enough not to need help from the taxpayer; but that hadn't prevented other wealthy MPs, such as Michael Ancram, from claiming thousands from the public purse.

The bunker team had written to about twenty MPs on that Friday alone, and the reporters were starting to feel the pace. Before they could go home for the evening, however, they were summoned into the editor's office for one last duty of the week: sharing a trolley-load of champagne bought by the proprietors and handed round by chief executive Murdoch MacLennan.

MacLennan was generous in his praise for the efforts of the team, describing the expenses investigation as one of the biggest scoops in Fleet Street history. But with the investigation only a week old, there were plenty more twists and turns to come.

A Very British Revolution

Tuesday, 19 May

'As soon as I saw what I'd
been up to, I knew the
Speaker had to go'

CHAPTER 19

FOR CHRIS EVANS, the *Daily Telegraph*'s head of news, the first two weeks of the expenses investigation had been even more nerve-racking than they had been for the rest of the team. Evans's wife was pregnant with the couple's second baby, which was due on 1 May – just two days after the *Telegraph* first obtained the expenses disk. Chris had resigned himself to the likelihood that he would miss the biggest story he might ever be involved with. Although he could never admit it to his wife, he had been secretly relieved when the baby became overdue and he had been able to steer the expenses investigation through its crucial first few days.

Coincidentally, Matthew Bayley, the news editor, was in a similar predicament. His wife was also expecting the couple's second child, due three weeks after Evans's baby, and each of them would share a joke every time their mobile phones rang without it being a call to rush to the hospital.

By day seven of the publication campaign, however, Mrs Evans could wait no longer. With the baby two weeks overdue, the birth would have to be induced; and so, as the suspension of Shahid Malik unfolded, the *Telegraph* news executive was pacing around a waiting room at University

College Hospital in central London, following events on his BlackBerry and sending regular 'thoughts' via email to Winnett and Bayley. The other parents-to-be on the ward were speaking of little other than MPs' expenses, but Evans decided not to disclose his key role in the story of the moment.

Julie Evans finally gave birth to a daughter, Sophie, at 11.15 p.m. on Friday, 15 May. For the next week, Evans's only chances to keep abreast of the growing parliamentary scandal he had helped trigger came during snatched moments in front of rolling news channels when his new daughter was asleep.

Over the weekend, pressure built on Michael Martin, the Speaker, following his disastrous handling of the expenses scandal the previous week. Sunday is the day when politicians traditionally head to the television studios to give lengthy live interviews to the likes of Andrew Marr and Adam Boulton. On Sunday, 17 May, the interviews were dominated by one subject – Speaker Martin's future.

Despite coming under criticism following his hectoring of MPs including Kate Hoey and Norman Baker in the Commons chamber, Martin had refused to back down. The respected Labour MP David Winnick had told Martin that his behaviour had been 'inappropriate' and his refusal to apologize 'inadequate', to which a bullish Martin retorted: 'If it's not adequate, then you know what you must do.' The Speaker, who was in overall charge of the allowances system, should have been the man to whom MPs looked for a solution. Instead, his belligerent behaviour over the previous week had meant he had become part of the problem.

That Sunday Nick Clegg, the leader of the Liberal Democrats, broke with the convention that party leaders do not criticize the Speaker and said that 'the Speaker must go'. On the Labour side Charles Clarke, the former home secretary, became one of the first senior figures to break cover, saying Martin's behaviour had been 'utterly deplorable' and he was 'not the right man to oversee the necessary reform of the members' allowance system'. For the Conservatives William Hague, David Cameron's deputy, said the situation was at 'crisis point'. Meanwhile Douglas Carswell, a little-known Tory backbencher, had begun gathering signatures for a motion of no confidence in the Speaker, which had been backed by a small number of MPs from all three main parties and had generated considerable coverage in the media.

On Sunday afternoon Gordon Brown and Martin had a private meeting during which the Prime Minister is under-stood to have assured the Speaker that the government would not allow a motion of no confidence in Martin to be debated. It was a crucial show of support, but one which was to be short-lived.

The following day pressure on the Speaker intensified with a new set of revelations in the *Daily Telegraph*. Jon Swaine had uncovered a peculiar deal involving a Labour MP, Ben Chapman, who had paid off part of his mortgage but was given permission by the fees office to continue making 'inflated' claims as if he were still paying interest for the entire loan. The arrangement – apparently sanctioned by the Speaker's own officials in the fees office but then stopped when spotted by another official in 2004 – beggared belief.

It quickly became obvious that the Prime Minister's patience was running out. Now, instead of backing Martin, a spokesman for Gordon Brown would say only that the Speaker's future depended on 'the will of Parliament'. Suddenly, Martin could see that his safety net of prime ministerial support had been whipped away from beneath him, just as he was starting to lose his grip on his lofty position.

Meanwhile, another key figure in the expenses scandal was also feeling the heat. John Wick had been 'outed' by the *Wall Street Journal* as the middleman who had passed the expenses information on to the *Telegraph*, and as a result he was under siege. The *Wall Street Journal* is a sister paper of *The Times*, and Wick suspected that his name might have been leaked by someone at the paper to which he had originally offered the material. Throughout Saturday, 16 May Henry Gewanter – who was fielding calls for Wick – had been swamped with calls from the *Sunday Times*, the *News of the World* and the *Mail on Sunday*. One newspaper offered Gewanter £50,000 just for Wick to speak to them on the telephone. The offer was politely declined following a frantic round of phone calls between Winnett, Wick and Gewanter.

The following day, the *Mail on Sunday* printed what is known on Fleet Street as a 'hatchet job' on Wick, calling into question his financial status and business history. Much of the article was based on conversations with people which Wick would later say had been taken out of context. To an extent it was inevitable that once Wick's identity was known rival newspapers would attack the *Telegraph* through him, but the *Mail on Sunday* was read with derision by senior executives at the *Telegraph* who thought that the newspaper had gone overboard on the basis of relatively meagre information. Wick was angry and was advised to take legal action, but Winnett was concerned that the situation could get out of hand if not handled carefully. He and consulting editor Rhidian Wynn Davies arranged to meet Wick and Gewanter for lunch the following day at Brown's in Mayfair.

As Winnett and Wynn Davies got out of the taxi outside the hotel, Wick and Gewanter were coming down the street. Wick was suntanned and smiling after his enforced exile in southern Spain; Gewanter, in stark contrast, looked a nervous wreck. His tie was at half-mast and he was smoking a cigarette as if it was going to be his last.

The foursome ordered a round of champagne and toasted the success of the story before beginning their three-course meal. Winnett explained that he and William Lewis had received reliable information suggesting the police would not be carrying out an investigation into the source of the leak of the expenses data. He proposed that, once the police had formally announced that the *Telegraph* would not be investigated, Wick strike back by going public with his reasons for blowing the whistle. It would be a brave thing to do – once out in the public domain, Wick would be exposed to intense scrutiny – but Wick felt he had an important story to tell.

As the meal progressed, Gewanter became more and

more excitable. He repeatedly stressed that Parliament as a whole needed to change, with a revolution if necessary, and that the Liberal Democrats should seize power. The stress of the previous few weeks was beginning to take its toll on the PR man, and at one point he was shouting so loudly that other diners in the restaurant began to stare. Wick, Winnett and Wynn Davies, who had been hoping to keep a low profile, were not impressed, and Wick suggested that Gewanter might want to 'calm down' in the bathroom. Fifteen minutes later he returned and apologized. However, Winnett and Wynn Davies were concerned about his state of mind. A loose cannon could be very damaging to the investigation.

Just after 3 p.m. Winnett received a text message saying that Michael Martin would shortly be making a statement in the House of Commons. He quickly paid the bill and hurried back to the office.

A few miles away, William Lewis was enjoying a rather different sort of afternoon. He was at the Chelsea Flower Show opening the *Daily Telegraph*'s show garden – a minimalist creation from a Swedish designer which would later be awarded the top prize of 'best show garden'. To Lewis's great amusement, as he was shown around the garden, he saw that it had a moat.

Lewis approached his annual appearance at the Chelsea Flower Show with trepidation. The opening day was traditionally attended by members of the royal family, and the previous year he had been asked by the Duchess of Cornwall whether or not he knew anything about gardening.

He had had to admit to her that his knowledge was rather lacking. This year, the opening of the show was one of his first 'public' appearances following weeks of early mornings and late nights in the office working on the expenses investigation. He was concerned that the high-profile guests, many of whom had regular contact with MPs who had featured in the *Telegraph*, might give him a wide berth.

His day got even more complicated when he received a call on his mobile phone from a member of staff whom he had mentored for several years.

'I've been meaning to tell you,' the staff member said, 'I'm resigning.'

Lewis was furious, but before he could say much in reply he had to end the call as several royal courtiers approached to tell him that the Queen wished to visit the garden.

'She's definitely coming here and she's going to spend a lot of time here,' said one courtier. Lewis was taken aback. Surely this wasn't royal endorsement?

Moments later he was welcoming the Queen to the garden. Another member of the royal family said they had been 'following [the story] very carefully', before asking whether the *Telegraph*'s enquiries might spread to cover the rest of the public sector.

One of the next guests was Lord Mandelson, who had publicly attacked the expenses investigation on the first day of publication. The Labour peer was now in a more playful mood, however. He gently slapped Lewis on the cheek and said: 'Who's been a naughty boy then?!'

Throughout the afternoon the *Telegraph* garden was

packed with famous faces, and everyone wanted to hear more details from Lewis about the expenses story. The visitors included Sir Cliff Richard, Cilla Black, senior members of the intelligence community, and the City businessman and Conservative Party treasurer Michael Spencer.

In the rather less glamorous surroundings of the *Telegraph* bunker, the reporters were gathered around a computer screen waiting for Michael Martin to address Parliament.

A hush descended on the Commons chamber – and on the bunker – as the Speaker rose to his feet.

'I would like to make a statement on Members' allowances,' he began. 'We all know that it is the tradition of this House that the Speaker speaks to the whole House, but in doing so please allow me to say to the men and women of the United Kingdom that we have let you down very badly indeed. We must all accept blame and, to the extent that I have contributed to the situation, I am profoundly sorry. Now, each and every Member, including myself, must work hard to regain your trust.'

'Blimey, this is a bit of a turn-up for the books,' said Rosa Prince, voicing the thoughts of the bunker team. But the drama had barely started.

The response from the MPs was brutal, merciless and utterly compelling. The reporters watched transfixed as the man who had been so defiant and aggressive in the face of criticism crumpled in front of their eyes. By the time his colleagues had finished with him, he was stuttering, confused and broken.

Backbenchers landed blow after blow on the Speaker's vanishing authority as they repeatedly demanded the chance to debate a motion of no confidence in him the following day.

David Winnick, the Labour MP who had confronted him several days earlier, suggested that the Speaker 'give indication of your intention to retire'. Douglas Carswell demanded to know when the House would get the chance to elect 'a new Speaker with the moral authority . . . [to] lift this House out of the mire', and Sir Patrick Cormack, a Tory MP since 1970, compared the situation to the 1940 'Norway debate' which led to the resignation of the Prime Minister, when Neville Chamberlain was urged: 'In the name of God, go!'

Martin said he would not allow a vote on the no confidence motion, but when asked why not he was unable to answer, having to consult his clerk before trying, and failing, to enunciate what he had been told. By the time he sat down, all the fight had been knocked out of him.

In front of a live television audience, and in the space of just fifteen minutes, Martin was reduced to a man worthy more of pity than respect.

The reporters in the bunker turned and looked at each other. They didn't need to say anything; all of them were thinking the same thing. Michael Martin was a man for whom they had no sympathy, but seeing him crushed in front of their eyes still came as a shock.

Outside the Commons, MPs lined up to give their thoughts to Sky News and the BBC News Channel. The sound of knives being sharpened came across loud and clear. One MP described Martin as 'a dead Speaker walking'. The Lib Dem Norman Baker said he had signed 'his political death warrant' with his performance and gave him 'less than a week'.

'So what happens now?' Rayner asked, turning to Winnett and Prince.

'He's gotta go,' mused Winnett. But the question was, how? No one really seemed to know if there was any mechanism by which the Speaker could be removed from office; in the absence of a written constitution such matters were governed by convention, and the convention was that Speakers were never challenged. But the consensus was that if Douglas Carswell got his wish for a no confidence vote, and the vote went against Martin, the Speaker would have to resign. As yet, however, Carswell had only fifteen signatures on his petition – nowhere near enough to force a vote.

It seemed that Martin's future was entirely in the hands of Gordon Brown. The two men had been close for decades, having both emerged from the 'tribal' world of Scottish Labour politics, but such was the public anger at MPs' expenses claims, personified by Martin himself, that unless the Speaker stood aside there was a very real chance that the Prime Minister's own position could be threatened. Downing Street's support for Martin had already become equivocal following the statement that morning that his position depended on 'the will of Parliament', and the reception the Speaker had received during proceedings that afternoon had, effectively, made his position untenable. Now Martin retreated to his office in Speaker's House, his grand residence in Parliament, where he held a private meeting with Gordon Brown. By the time the Prime Minister left, Martin was in no doubt that his career was finished.

He spent Monday night on the phone, talking to friends and confidants about what to do next. Sir Stuart Bell, one of his closest friends, later said: 'We were looking, those who were friends of Michael Martin, to arrange a graceful exit.' Martin went to bed well after midnight, by which time he was well aware that a 'graceful' exit was no longer available to him.

The next day's newspapers were full of speculation about how long Martin could cling on to his job, but even so the bunker team were stunned when reports started to circulate at ten thirty on Tuesday morning that Martin had decided to resign and would be making a statement to Parliament that afternoon. Within moments the Press Association had put out a newsflash confirming Martin's intention to resign. Tony Gallagher rushed into the editor's office to break the news to William Lewis and the pair shook hands to mark the momentous news.

'Crikey,' said Christopher Hope in the bunker. 'I can't believe it.'

'It's all getting a bit serious, isn't it?' Rayner reflected. It certainly was. Until now, the most tangible effect of the *Telegraph*'s investigation had been to end the careers of a handful of backbench MPs and force some more high-profile ones to pay back money. Martin's resignation wasn't just a step change in the investigation, it was history being made.

No other Speaker had been forced from office for 314 years. The last Speaker to suffer such a fate had been Sir John Trevor, appointed to the post by King James II and expelled from Parliament in 1695 after accepting a bribe of 1,000 guineas from the City of London to help get a new piece of legislation through the Commons. Since then, Britain had been to war with Louis XIV of France and Napoleon; it had colonized, and then lost, America; it had fought two world wars and built (and given back) one of the biggest empires in history – all without the need to dispense with any of the thirty-five Speakers who had held the post in that period.

At eleven o'clock, when William Lewis convened the daily leader conference – the meeting at which leader writers and columnists meet to discuss with the editor the content of the next day's comment pages – not everyone was aware that Martin was going to resign. Lewis began the meeting by making sure all those present were up to date with developments, and as he informed those present of Martin's impending resignation, leader writer Phil Johnston's face dropped with astonishment. Turning to Lewis, Johnston perfectly summed up the atmosphere in the room as he repeated Michael Caine's famous line from *The Italian Job*. 'Blimey, Will. We were only supposed to blow the bloody doors off.'

Lewis, in common with everyone working on the story, felt that Martin's resignation was the pivotal moment in the investigation. Until then, there had been a sense that the *Telegraph* was rolling a boulder up a hill, slowly gaining ground with each passing day, but all the time aware that there was a risk of being crushed at any moment. With Martin's imminent departure, it was as if the team had reached the summit, and the boulder was suddenly careering down the other side, out of control and liable to smash anything in its path.

For all the talk there had been of an exit strategy, the *Telegraph* no longer had the ability to close the story down. It had taken on a momentum of its own, and there was nothing Lewis, or anyone else, could do to stop it.

Martin was due to make a statement to the Commons at 2.30 p.m., but before that there was another important piece of business taking place in Parliament. Sir Paul Stephenson, the Commissioner of the Metropolitan Police, was giving evidence to the Home Affairs Select Committee, a routine appointment during which he was also expected to be asked by MPs for a progress report on the investigation into the leak of the expenses data. But no such question was forthcoming; so, as he left the committee room, Britain's most senior policeman was asked by a *Telegraph* reporter whether the newspaper was still being investigated. He said that Scotland Yard would shortly be issuing a statement.

At 1 p.m. the statement from Sir Paul arrived. It read:

We have concluded that in all the circumstances and based on all the information, we do not believe a police investigation to be appropriate.

The Metropolitan Police believe that the public interest

defence would be likely to prove a significant hurdle in securing a prosecution. An assistant commissioner has written to Malcolm Jack [the Clerk of the House of Commons] informing him that we have decided not to investigate the matters referred to us regarding alleged leaks to the *Daily Telegraph*. Consideration was given to the likelihood of a prosecution and whether a prosecution would be appropriate given other potential sanctions that might be available.

The newspaper was in the clear.

Winnett phoned Wick to tell him the good news. And, on a day when everything seemed to be boding well for the *Telegraph* team, Douglas Hogg announced he would be standing down at the next general election. His comments reflected a contrition that had been absent the previous week.

'I entirely understand the public anger that has erupted over expenses,' he said. 'The current system is deeply flawed; we parliamentarians have got it wrong and I apologize for that failure which is both collective and personal.'

Parliamentary wags suggested he had been 'demoated'.

Outside Parliament, College Green was becoming home to the biggest collection of broadcasting hardware since the day Tony Blair had left office. The main news channels sent their news anchors to broadcast live from Westminster, including Kay Burley, Sky News's top anchorwoman, and the BBC's Jon Sopel, who abandoned a planned day off to get stuck into the story. Andrew Porter, Benedict Brogan and

Andrew Pierce were out in force on behalf of the *Telegraph*, passing between the various broadcasters who were forming hastily arranged panels of MPs and commentators of different political persuasions.

With few MPs willing to support Martin over his stance on expenses it was left to an ex-MP, George Foulkes, to try to defend the indefensible. Lord Foulkes was still spoiling for a fight and persisted in asking Porter about where the *Telegraph* had got the story. 'That's not the issue,' Porter kept saying. Foulkes then turned on Porter and Sopel, apparently accusing them of sectarianism in questioning the conduct of the Speaker. He seemed reluctant to turn his attention to the one thing the viewers wanted to know about: the thoughts of Speaker Martin. By the end of the exchange, Foulkes and Porter were glaring at each other daggers drawn.

Porter finished the interview and dashed inside, making his way to the press gallery of the House of Commons to hear Martin's statement. The press gallery, which overhangs the Commons chamber, is furnished with tightly packed benches with small desks. The *Telegraph* has two dedicated desks right at the front of the gallery, where the reporters sit just 20 feet from the party leaders. Andrew Gimson, the *Telegraph*'s parliamentary sketch writer, usually takes one of the seats, and Porter squeezed in next to him.

Dozens of journalists were crowding around the door to the press gallery, trying to get in, but there was such a crush that many of them did not make it in time to hear Martin's extremely brief statement. Each day's parliamentary business begins with prayers, and journalists are only allowed in after prayers are over. Martin was to make his statement immediately after prayers, so that dozens of reporters were still jostling to get through the door when he rose to his feet.

'Since I came to this House thirty years ago, I have always felt that the House is at its best when it is united,' he said. 'In order that unity can be maintained, I have decided that I will relinquish the office of Speaker on Sunday, June 21. This will allow the House to proceed to elect a new Speaker on Monday, June 22.

'That is all I have to say on this matter.'

To mark the historic occasion Martin had been able to muster fewer than eighty words, which took him just thirty-three seconds to deliver.

Somewhat disingenuously, Brown, Cameron, Clegg and other MPs then paid glowing tributes to the Speaker they had spent the previous few days trying to remove.

The reporters in the bunker watched in total silence as Martin made his announcement. Minutes later, the Speaker's face was added to the portrait gallery on the wall. Lewis walked into the room after watching Martin's statement and made a brief statement of his own.

'I just wanted to say: respect,' he said, leaving as quickly as he had arrived.

Michael Martin's departure had not only been historic in a constitutional sense; it had made history in a far more fundamental, and far more important, way. The British public, appalled by the behaviour of the politicians who represented them, had stood together and told the political class: 'Enough.' And, for once, the politicians had found that they had no option but to listen. Instead of merely paying lip service to the wishes of the electorate, MPs who had abused the public's trust for years were seeing real change happening in front of their eyes. Never again would they be able to treat the Commons like a gentlemen's club, where they set their own rules and bent them to suit their whim. If the Speaker could lose his job as a result of the public outcry, no one in Parliament could assume that they were guaranteed to keep their job.

It had been, in the words of the *Telegraph*'s front-page headline the next day, a very British revolution.

The Duck House
Discovery

Wednesday, 20 May

'Do you think we could fit
a plasma TV in there?'

CHAPTER 20

AFTER THE DISCOVERY of Douglas Hogg's expenses claim for his moat, the investigation team – and, presumably, the public – assumed that the saga could not get any more surreal. But, as the team carried on ploughing through the expenses records of backbench MPs, reporter Nick Allen was about to discover a claim so ludicrous it would make even the moat seem relatively sober.

'What the bloody hell is a floating duck island?!' Allen called out across the bunker.

The other reporters jumped up from their chairs and crowded round Allen's screen. No one knew the answer to his question, but it sounded like this was something which was not to be missed.

Allen had been looking through the expenses claims of Sir Peter Viggers, a wealthy Tory MP who represented the constituency of Gosport in Hampshire. Like so many other Tory grandees, he had claimed thousands of pounds for his gardening bills, including nearly £500 for 28 tonnes of manure and a £213 electrician's bill which included fixing lights on a 'fountain' and 'hanging lights on Christmas tree'. Like Douglas Hogg, Sir Peter had an arrangement with the fees office which involved submitting a breakdown of the annual costs of running his grand constituency home, which ran to more than £30,000, and asking the fees office to pay him the maximum yearly allowance (which in 2007/8 was £23,083).

In the 2006/7 financial year Sir Peter had submitted a handwritten list of his spending, which came to £33,747.19 and included 'pond feature, £1,645'. Allen was, naturally, curious to find out exactly what this pond feature was, and discovered that among the receipts which Sir Peter had submitted to back up his claim was an invoice for a 'floating duck island'. It specified that the item was a 'Stockholm' model and that the 'price includes three anchor blocks, duck house and island'.

'Let's see if there's a picture,' said Allen, grinning as he typed 'Stockholm duck island' into Google. The bunker was filled with gales of laughter as a picture of the duck house popped up on his screen. The subject of Sir Peter's expenses claim turned out to be a miniature stately home for his feathered friends, complete with windows and a tiled roof and topped with an ornate cupola. Painted yellow, with green window frames, it stood proudly on a wooden pontoon, with a little drawbridge for the ducks to walk up.

'That's the most ridiculous thing I've ever seen!' said Caroline Gammell.

The website of the firm which made the 5-foot-high structure said it was based on an eighteenth-century Swedish construction which was now in the Stockholm Museum of Buildings. Other available duck-house designs included a castle with turrets and a flagpole, and a reproduction of a Gothic banqueting house in Cornwall. Sir Peter's expenses claim was, quite simply, beyond parody, and for the bunker team it was an absolute gift.

'See if it's on Google Earth,' suggested Rayner; so Allen put the address of Sir Peter's house into the search engine and found an aerial view. 'There it is!' Rayner pointed. Sure enough, there, in a garden pond which resembled a mini-Serpentine, was the unmistakable shape of the Stockholm duck house.

'Brilliant!' laughed Hope. 'You can see it from space!'

The only drawback with the story was that the fees office had written 'not allowed' next to the 'pond feature' on Sir Peter's claim, suggesting he had not been paid specifically for the duck island; but, as with Douglas Hogg, the inclusion of the item on his expenses claims demonstrated how out of touch he was with the average taxpayer.

Allen prepared a letter for Sir Peter, a member of Parliament's Treasury Select Committee, who was in Washington DC preparing for a meeting with representatives of the International Monetary Fund. His brief response defended the claim:

'The claims I made were in accordance with the rules, and were all approved by the fees office. Since then the situation has changed and we must all take account of that. My expenses are being examined by David Cameron's scrutiny panel and I await any recommendations they may make.'

David Cameron, when told about the duck house, was

incandescent. After a brief conversation with his party leader, Sir Peter announced that he would not be standing at the next election. He later expressed his 'shame' at what he said had been a 'ridiculous' attempt to claim for the island.

When the story appeared in the *Telegraph* the next day, the duck house instantly became the iconic image of the whole expenses story. Pictures of it were shown to disbelieving audiences around the world, and it featured in numerous cartoons – including one by the *Telegraph*'s Matt, which depicted one duck asking another: 'Do you think we could fit a plasma TV in there?' The public didn't know whether to laugh or cry. BBC Radio Five Live began its news headlines with the sound of ducks quacking, while on Radio Four Evan Davis, one of the presenters of the *Today* programme, memorably 'corpsed' as he tried to read the duck house story during a review of the papers, collapsing into such a fit of giggles that his co-presenter had to take over.

The story even sparked an intense debate among bird enthusiasts as to whether the duck house was fit for purpose. Sir Peter admitted that his ducks had 'never liked' their plush retreat, and he declared it a waste of money. Bas Clarke, who kept eight hundred wildfowl on his land in Lincolnshire, said the Stockholm model was 'not suitable for ducks', pronouncing the doorway 'far too big' for birds, which felt more secure squeezing through small gaps. Not so, retorted Ivor Ingall, the retired army officer who had designed it. He said that in his experience 'ducks vote with their feet' and that in his own pond in Farnham, Surrey, no fewer than fourteen ducklings had hatched in his duck house during the spring.

There was, however, one final question about the duck house: where was it? Sir Peter had sold his house in Hampshire in 2008 (after the Google Earth picture had been captured) and the island was no longer in the pond. When the *Telegraph* paid a visit to the house in an attempt to track down the celebrated structure, there were other reminders of the former owner's presence – including a well cover monogrammed with his initials in gold letters – but no duck island. Sir Peter eventually said the island was 'in storage' and announced that he would donate it to a charity auction.

Sir Peter may have claimed for the most ridiculous object of all, but the prize for the most ridiculous rant from an MP went to another Tory grandee whose claims had been exposed by Nick Allen a few days earlier – Anthony Steen.

The MP for Totnes, in Devon, who is the father of the television presenter Xanthe Steen, had featured in the *Telegraph* on the day that Chaytor's phantom mortgage appeared on the front page. Yet another wealthy Conservative who had spent thousands of pounds of the public's money maintaining a large constituency home, Steen had registered claims for the £1.5 million country estate including bills for a woodland expert to inspect '500 trees' as well as tagging shrubs and assessing whether there was a need for 'additional guarding' against rabbits. Over the course of four years he had claimed a total of £87,729. Once again, David Cameron was not impressed, and Steen later announced he would be stepping down at the next election, saying: 'I've had a very good innings, there's no bitterness, no anger, but as the saying goes, all political careers end in tears.'

Within hours of making that statement, however, the barrister had changed his mind: it turned out he was bitter and angry after all. In an interview with the BBC, he let rip with his true thoughts about the *Telegraph*'s investigation and the public's reaction to it.

'I think I behaved, if I may say so, impeccably,' he said. 'I have done nothing criminal, that's the most awful thing, and do you know what it is about? Jealousy.

'I have got a very, very large house. Some people say it looks like Balmoral, but it's a merchant house of the nineteenth century. It's not particularly attractive, it just does me nicely and it's got room to actually plant a few trees. As far as I'm concerned as of this day I don't know what the fuss is about.

'What right does the public have to interfere with my private life? None. It was this wretched government which introduced the Freedom of Information Act and this government which has insisted on things that have caught me on the wrong foot which, if I had been cleverer, it wouldn't have done.

'Do you know what this reminds me of? An episode of *Coronation Street*. Do you know what Members are doing? They are waiting by their phones between three and four o'clock in the afternoon, because that's the time the Prime Minister used to ring you if you were going to get a job, and now it's a question of whether the *Daily Telegraph* are going to ring you, because that's the time they ring you. Is it the Prime Minister? No. It's the *Daily Telegraph*. They just know this is a kangaroo court going on.'

David Cameron couldn't believe his ears when he heard the interview on *The World At One*. As soon as he could track down Steen, he gave him a piece of his mind and threatened to isolate him from the party. He then spoke on the radio himself, saying: 'I gave him a very clear instruction after that interview – one more squeak like that and he will have the whip taken away from him so fast his feet won't touch the ground.'

Steen put out a statement in which he apologized 'unreservedly' for his comments. 'I am sorry that in the heat of the moment I said inappropriate things that weren't as measured as I would have liked.'

Steen's hot-blooded outburst should have served as a cautionary tale for every other MP, but it didn't – not, at least, in the case of Sir John Butterfill, who had designated a small flat in his Bournemouth constituency as his 'main' home while claiming expenses on a £1.2 million country retreat in Surrey, which he said was his 'second' home (except when he came to sell it, of course, when it became his 'primary residence' for tax purposes). Sir John, another Tory grandee, had submitted claims which included £17,000 for a staff annexe where his housekeeper and his gardener lived. When he realized his expenses claims were about to be published in the *Telegraph* he wasted no time in appearing on *Newsnight*, before the paper had even hit the streets, to denounce the story in what turned into car-crash television. Becoming tongue-tied under interrogation from Kirsty Wark, Sir John made the fatal error of referring to his two old retainers as 'servants': 'The one mistake I made was that in claiming interest on the home, I didn't separate from that the value of the servants', er, the staff, wing.'

Studio guest John Strafford, of the Conservative Campaign for Democracy, watched Sir John's performance open-mouthed, and, when asked for his reaction, memorably said that the MP was 'toast'. Sir John had already told his Conservative Association months earlier that he intended to stand down at the next election, so in this instance there was no need for Cameron to intervene.

The edition of the *Daily Telegraph* which featured Sir Peter Viggers' duck house on the front page also focused on a third MP with an apparent phantom mortgage – the Conservative whip Bill Wiggin. The MP for Leominster in Herefordshire, who had been a contemporary of David Cameron at Eton, had received more than £11,000 in expenses for mortgage interest payments on his 'second home' in his Herefordshire constituency, even though it had no mortgage. When Martin Beckford challenged Wiggin over his expenses claims, the MP said that he had simply claimed for the wrong address: he had meant to claim for the mortgage on his London home, but had accidentally filled in his constituency address instead (on no fewer than twenty-three forms).

For the first time since his 'John Wayne moment', Cameron decided to contest the *Telegraph*'s version of events. After speaking to Wiggin, Cameron was convinced that the MP had made an innocent – albeit stupid – mistake, and did not fall into the same category as Elliot Morley or David Chaytor. Andy Coulson, the Tories' head of communications, made calls to Andrew Porter, to Benedict Brogan and to Robert Winnett, trying to argue that Wiggin should not be given the same prominence as Morley and Chaytor.

William Lewis discussed the story with Winnett and Tony Gallagher. Gallagher felt it would be wrong to treat Wiggin differently from others with similarly questionable claims when his expenses forms clearly showed he had claimed mortgage interest for a property which had no mortgage. It should be up to the public to decide whether Wiggin's defence of ignorance stood up to scrutiny. Wiggin's picture would appear on the front page, together with a photograph of a duck to illustrate Sir Peter Viggers' expenses claims.

Coulson took the news in his stride, as did many of the MPs who stood to lose the most. James Purnell, the work and pensions secretary, was also to feature in the same edition as Wiggin, as Holly Watt had confirmed that both he and Geoff Hoon had avoided paying capital gains tax when they sold properties. Purnell, who had billed the taxpayer for advice from an accountant on whether he needed to pay tax on the profit from the sale, phoned Andrew Porter after he had received a letter from the *Telegraph*.

'Is it the splash?' the MP wanted to know.

'It's on the front,' said Porter, though he said it was not expected to be the splash. Purnell, who rarely complained at what was written about him in the press, initially made little attempt to throw his weight around, and appeared simply to accept that he would have to face the public fallout.

However, he would later make strong representations over the article.

Earlier the same evening, Porter had encountered a rather less sanguine figure in the form of Alastair Campbell, the former spin doctor widely regarded as the second most powerful man in Britain during the time he worked for Tony Blair. Porter had been invited to a Downing Street drinks party for Alison Blackshaw, a civil servant who had for years been an events organizer in No. 10.

'So, are you lot happy now?' Campbell asked Porter sarcastically.

'Are you happy that these MPs have been at it for years?' Porter replied. Campbell admitted he wasn't, and changed the subject before making his way down the famous staircase in No. 10. Porter thought to himself that if Alastair Campbell didn't have the stomach to defend the MPs' behaviour then the *Telegraph* was clearly doing something right.

On the other side of the room, Benedict Brogan was being buttonholed by Michael Dugher, the press aide who had been given the job of defending the Prime Minister's own expenses claims. Dugher was reasonably good-humoured, but still smarting at the way the *Telegraph* had started its coverage, saying the newspaper had 'stitched [Labour] up' and given the Tories 'a three-day head start'. It was an accusation that Labour politicians would trot out repeatedly over the coming weeks and months.

In the meantime, Parliament needed to turn its collective attention to the small matter of finding a new Speaker to replace Michael Martin. MPs who wanted the job had already started to throw their hats into the ring, so Matthew Bayley asked Gordon Rayner to prepare stories on the expenses claims of all of the potential candidates.

Three of the bookies' early favourites, Sir Menzies Campbell, Sir Alan Haselhurst and David Davis, had already appeared in the paper: Sir Menzies for the £10,000 spent on redecorating his flat, Sir Alan for £12,000 of gardening bills, and Davis for his £5,700 portico and thousands of pounds' worth of gardening and furniture bills. The Labour back-bencher Frank Field, who had been a minister in Tony Blair's first government and was now considering running for Speaker, had appeared as one of the 'saints' because he was one of the 200 lowest-claiming MPs despite having a con-stituency 220 miles from Westminster. The only MP who had already openly declared an intention to stand for the post, the veteran Lib Dem Sir Alan Beith, was found to have claimed £117,000 in second-home allowances over the course of seven years while his wife, Baroness Maddock, claimed £60,000 in House of Lords expenses for overnight stays at the same address. The couple responded by saying each of them had claimed only half of what they were entitled to, which they believed was 'within the letter and the spirit of the rules'. Another early front-runner, Sir George Young, the Old Etonian Conservative MP known as the 'bicycling baronet', had relatively straightforward expenses claims; although he had claimed the maximum second-home allowance for each of the previous two years, almost all of it had gone on mortgage interest.

That left Rayner with just one other candidate for the

Speaker's job to investigate – the Conservative backbencher John Bercow. At forty-six, Bercow was not only the youngest of the Speakership candidates but also the most unlikely. Despite being a Tory, Bercow had virtually no supporters on the Conservative benches, where he was seen as something of a traitor. He had started his political career on the far right, calling for 'assisted repatriation' of immigrants in his twenties and professing his admiration for Enoch Powell. After entering Parliament in 1997 he had gradually moved towards the centre of politics and had twice been given frontbench posts, only to fall out with the two party leaders who promoted him, Iain Duncan Smith and Michael Howard.

After returning to the back benches, Bercow had repeatedly criticized party leaders, and following his marriage in 2002 to the Labour-supporting Sally Illman (a woman so much taller than him that they tended to pose for pictures sitting down) he had veered so far towards the left that many of his colleagues thought he was about to 'cross the floor' and defect to Labour. One senior Conservative dryly noted: 'The problem with John Bercow is that he discovered sex and New Labour at the same time.' He had even accepted a request from Gordon Brown to carry out a review of children's educational needs, which was seen by Bercow's critics as little more than a declaration of his intent to swap sides.

The only reason Bercow was being talked about at all as a potential Speaker was that, after two Labour Speakers, there was huge pressure on the government to let another party have a turn and, as a left-leaning Tory disliked by his own party, Bercow represented the least bad option in the eyes of some Labour MPs. It was the worst possible reason for someone to be in with a shot at one of the most important jobs in Westminster, and it made Bercow something of a 'joke' candidate in the opinion of many political observers.

Rayner expected Bercow's expenses to be pretty straightforward, particularly in the light of a letter Bercow had written to the Labour MP Martin Salter (shortly to become his campaign manager) in which he declared his intention to run for the post, saying: 'I am asking people to vote not for a Conservative but for a Speaker who has what it takes to restore trust in Parliament and politicians.' Clearly, anyone who believed they could restore the public's trust in politicians must have been supremely confident that their own expenses claims would not attract any adverse comment.

Not for the first time in his life, Rayner was to be reminded that making assumptions is a dangerous habit in journalism. As he scanned Bercow's expenses claims, he discovered that the MP had flipped his second-home designation from his constituency house to a £540,000 flat in London, and back again. Land Registry checks showed he had also bought and sold properties both in London and in his constituency in 2003. Had he paid capital gains tax on the sale of either property? Rayner sent an email to the MP to ask.

Seven hours later Bercow replied, but his answer was

frustratingly vague. He said that 'so far as I can remember' his constituency home was his nominated second home at the time of both sales, and his accountant had told him at the time there was 'no chargeable gain' on the profit from the sale. Rayner pressed him for more detail, and Bercow said he would seek 'written confirmation' from his accountant the next day.

On Thursday the *Telegraph* ran a page five story headlined 'Would-be Speaker is another "flipper"', but Rayner, and news editor Matthew Bayley, felt Bercow still had questions to answer on the issue of capital gains tax. So the following day Rayner chased up Bercow, sending him an email asking him to obtain the 'written confirmation' he had talked about. For nine and a half hours Bercow maintained a stony silence, much to Rayner's frustration.

'Anything from Bercow yet?' Bayley kept asking. Because it was a Friday, articles had to be ready earlier than usual so the presses could start rolling early enough to print the bulky Saturday edition. With plenty of other stories already taking shape, it was looking increasingly likely that the pursuit of Bercow would have to be carried over to the following week.

'It looks like Bercow's trying to avoid us,' Rayner reported back to Bayley. 'His staff say he's going to reply but they've been saying that for hours.'

Finally, at 7.21 p.m., by which time the next day's completed paper was ready to be printed, Rayner received an emailed reply from Bercow.

'Bollocks!' Rayner hissed. 'Bercow's replied. Can we still get it in?'

'We might be able to squeeze a few pars in,' replied Bayley. 'What's he say?'

Bercow admitted that, during the course of 2003, 'I did make changes in the designation of my main and second homes as a result of which capital gains tax was not payable.'

In other words, he had avoided paying CGT, perfectly legally, just as Hazel Blears had so controversially done.

Bercow went on to say that he had decided to pay £6,508.40 to HM Revenue & Customs, plus interest, in lieu of the CGT he might have paid if he had been required to do so by the taxman.

Rayner felt that admitting to flipping his homes and avoiding paying capital gains tax in the process would be curtains for Bercow's already slim chances of making it to the Speaker's chair, given his previous bluster about his ability to restore public trust. But he was frustrated that the MP's late response – which he saw as a deliberate ploy to run down the clock – meant that the story would be buried. Production chief Richard Oliver managed to find space on page seven for four paragraphs about Bercow's admission and his CGT payment, but Rayner was smarting over the fact that, in his eyes, he had been outwitted by the MP, whose story would have been given much greater prominence if he had replied earlier in the day, before the pages had been laid out.

'Bloody Bercow,' Rayner grumbled to Bayley as they left the office together an hour later. 'I suppose the only consolation is that everyone'll have forgotten who he is by this time next month.'

Keeping It in the Family

Friday, 22 May

'HAPPY NOW?'

Chapter 21

THREE WEEKS INTO the investigation, the reporters in the bunker were getting increasingly used to receiving letters and emails from readers who wanted to see their local MPs' expenses featured next in the pages of the *Daily Telegraph*, many of them making serious allegations about what the correspondent believed their MP had been up to. A lot of these letters amounted to no more than idle gossip and pub talk, but a few contained valuable nuggets of information from genuine insiders which made the reporters look anew at the expenses claims of certain Members who had, on the face of it, done nothing hugely interesting.

An email which arrived in reporter Gordon Rayner's inbox on Tuesday, 19 May fell squarely into the latter category. Concise and to the point, it began:

> I have recently been told that Dr Ian Gibson MP (Lab; Norwich North) is apparently quite frantic with worry that attention will be brought to bear upon his second home expenses claims, in case it is revealed that the London flat he bought in approximately 2000 (or possibly 2002) was seemingly primarily for the use of his daughter, Helen, who has

lived there with her artist boyfriend ever since, as far as I am aware.

The emailer, who wished to remain anonymous, then provided other information about Dr Gibson which left Rayner in little doubt that the correspondent had a genuine working knowledge of the MP's financial affairs.

'This looks good,' he told Winnett, whose head bobbed up from his computer screen to make eye contact with the reporter opposite him. 'Do you know an Ian Gibson?'

'Yeah, Labour MP?'

'According to this, he's used his expenses to buy a flat for his daughter.'

Rayner was already working on a lengthy feature about the downfall of Speaker Martin, so Holly Watt offered to look into Gibson's property deals. As she delved into his expenses claims, Watt soon discovered that the west London flat on which Gibson had been claiming expenses had indeed been shared between the MP, his daughter and another man. However, in 2008 the flat was apparently sold by Gibson to his daughter and her boyfriend for £162,000.

'Seems rather cheap for a nice flat in that part of London,' said Watt. A quick check of Land Registry records and a couple of phone calls to local estate agents quickly established that similar flats in the same area were selling for around twice that amount at the relevant time. Gibson had claimed almost £80,000 from the taxpayer to help pay the mortgage interest on the flat before selling it on to his daughter for half its market value. It was one of the most clear-cut cases of what the *Telegraph* team had dubbed 'keeping it in the family' – MPs using the parliamentary expenses system to give their children or other relatives a leg-up on the property ladder.

And that wasn't all. Earlier that week, Gibson had trumpeted the fact that he had voluntarily published his expenses online on his own website; but large swathes of the documents had been blacked out – including anything which would disclose the financial deal involving his daughter. It was an ominous sign of the widespread cover-up to come.

When contacted by the *Telegraph*, Gibson was among the most open and frank over his arrangements of any of the MPs the paper had approached. He freely admitted that he spent only three nights a week at the address and that it was his daughter's 'main home'. He then said that he would discuss standing down with his local Labour Party.

His subsequent treatment by the Labour Party served as a perfect illustration of the seemingly arbitrary way in which MPs were punished for their misdemeanours. Before he had a chance to consider his future, Gibson was referred to Labour's version of the 'star chamber' and told he would not be allowed to stand as a Labour candidate at the next election. In effect, he had been fired by the Labour Party. The party was well within its rights to discipline the MP, but many observers wondered why Gibson's expenses claims were any worse than those of Hazel Blears, Alistair Darling or other prominent figures who had escaped censure. Many of Gibson's supporters in Norwich – where he had been a popular MP – believed he had been harshly disciplined because he was a long-standing opponent of the Prime Minister, having been one of only a handful of Labour MPs who had refused to endorse Brown's campaign to become the party's leader.

While every other MP who had announced the end of their career had decided they would not stand again at the next general election, Gibson took the honourable decision to stand down straight away. In doing so, he would not only save the taxpayer the cost of employing him for another year, but also waived the right to a large redundancy payment, worth a year's salary (paid to all outgoing MPs at a general election). Many voters in Norwich applauded Gibson's principled stand, but it was the worst possible news for Gordon Brown. It meant there would have to be a by-election – the first since the expenses story had broken. When the election eventually came around in July, it was a disaster for Labour. The party lost the seat to the Conservatives and saw its share of the vote slump from more than 40 per cent in 2005 to just 18 per cent. Many local Labour activists refused to campaign on behalf of Chris Ostrowski, the candidate the party had lined up to replace Gibson. And then, in the days before the poll, Ostrowski caught swine flu, sparking jokes about MPs, pigs and troughs. Bizarrely, however, Nick Clegg and the Liberal Democrats failed to capitalize on the scandal; indeed, their showing in the polls had actually dipped slightly, despite their MPs avoiding the worst of the controversy.

If Gibson had been stabbed in the back by his Labour

bosses, other MPs seemed intent on killing off their careers without the help of anyone else. Chief among them was Nadine Dorries, a relatively obscure Conservative MP who had previously clashed with reporter Martin Beckford after she provided inconsistent answers over the location of her 'main' home. On the day Ian Gibson's expenses claims were published, Dorries, the MP for Mid Bedfordshire, made a spectacularly ill-judged attempt to garner public sympathy just as the public's anger with MPs was reaching its peak.

Addressing listeners to the *Today* programme, Dorries said: 'People are seriously beginning to crack. The last day in Parliament this week was, I would say, completely unbearable. I have never been in an atmosphere or environment like it, when people walk around with terror in their eyes and people are genuinely concerned, asking: "Have you seen so and so? Are they in their office? They've not been seen for days."

'There's a really serious concern that this has got to a point now which is almost unbearable for any human being to deal with.'

Her self-pitying comments enraged listeners, who bombarded the BBC with hostile emails. One said: 'I listened with incredulity to the bleating of Nadine Dorries on how MPs are near to cracking because they have milked the system. I'm near to cracking, working forty hours a week and looking after a disabled husband.'

Dorries' comments were backed up by a posting on her blog, where she laid the blame for MPs' despair squarely at the feet of those nasty *Telegraph* journalists who had dared to tell the public what their money was being spent on. 'The technique deployed by the *Telegraph*, picking off a few MPs each day, emailing at 12, giving five hours notice to reply . . . is amounting to a form of torture and may have serious consequences,' she wrote.

> MPs are human beings like everyone else. They have families too. McCarthyite witch hunts belong to the past, not the present. As do archaic, cowardly, methods of pay. If MPs are guilty, so are those who knew the system was in place, including the *Telegraph* journalists who have now decided for their own political reasons to expose the system, in a way which profits the *Telegraph*, for their own reasons.

The blog was read with a mixture of bemusement and shock by senior Conservative Party officials. David Cameron moved to distance himself from his backbench colleague, letting it be known through aides that he regarded Dorries' comments as 'barmy'. The Conservative leader then added: 'Of course MPs are concerned about what is happening but, frankly, MPs ought to be concerned about what their constituents think and ought to be worrying about the people who put us where we are.' It was a withering rebuke for Dorries.

Bizarrely, the Church of England also appeared determined to ignore public opinion and defend MPs. Dr Rowan Williams, the Archbishop of Canterbury, wrote a piece for *The Times* in which he criticized the 'witch-hunt' of MPs.

'Many will now be wondering whether the point has not

been adequately made,' the Archbishop wrote. 'The continuing systematic humiliation of politicians itself threatens to carry a heavy price in terms of our ability to salvage some confidence in our democracy.'

The comments led to a furious – and virtually entirely negative – response from readers of *The Times*, many of whom had begun reading the *Telegraph* during the expenses scandal.

Following the announcement by the Metropolitan Police that it would not be investigating the leak of MPs' expenses to the *Daily Telegraph*, the newspaper was about to pull off yet another surprise. John Wick had agreed to 'out' himself by talking publicly for the first time about his role in the leak and the reasons behind the decision to give the material to a newspaper. It was a high-risk, but calculated, gamble. Although the police had ruled out a criminal investigation, the admission by Wick that he was involved would put him in the public eye and possibly drag him into lengthy parliamentary inquiries. However, with other newspapers still pursuing him and increasingly anxious that his reputation was being sullied, Wick decided to push ahead. He also decided to give a short television interview with Telegraph TV, an internet-based channel designed to complement the newspaper, which could be released to broadcasters. The interview was recorded on Thursday, 21 May, when Wick and his partner Tania visited the *Telegraph*'s headquarters. They had been given a private guided tour of the open-plan office, their identities known only to a handful of people at the newspaper.

In his article – headlined 'I am proud to have played my part in exposing this scandal' – Wick explained the decision to hand the information to the *Telegraph*:

> As a former military man, I have been in some pretty tricky situations . . . I took legal advice. It appeared that there were some very grey areas and it could be that the police would want to investigate if I was identified as the person who orchestrated the release of the information. My military training had, however, prepared me for far worse than a police cell – and the public interest in this information being published was clear and compelling.

He concluded: 'I have played my part in history. It is now for others to decide on the best way to move forward and punish those who have been exposed.'

During his television interview – conducted by Guy Ruddle, the *Telegraph*'s head of visuals – Wick was asked what it was like watching as the scandal that he had triggered unfolded. 'The biggest problem was not knowing how violent the writhing of the snake was going to be,' he replied. The clip was to be played on television channels throughout the world.

The team who had produced the video brought an edited version of the interview to show Lewis on a laptop in his office. He was delighted by the composure of the whistle-blower. 'Very *Telegraph*,' he said approvingly. Wick, meanwhile, was preparing to leave his home again for the second time in a month. He had decided to lie low in a sedate

Sussex town for the weekend after being warned that his interview would be likely to spark a renewed spate of media interest. But at the last moment, the carefully laid plan to release the interview almost fell apart.

It had been decided that *Telegraph* PR Fiona Macdonald would release the tape to all the broadcasters at 9 p.m. – on the strict understanding that they would not use it before 10 p.m. It was the Friday evening before the Whitsun bank holiday weekend and the broadcasters were running low on staff – particularly after such a taxing week covering Parliament. Reeta Chakrabarti, the BBC's main political correspondent that night, was on her way to Bracknell to cover the meeting between Andrew MacKay and his constituents. (MacKay was to be given an extremely tough time. After emerging from the meeting he attempted to say that he had been warmly received, only to be contradicted and confronted by others who had been present. The following day, he announced he would be standing down from Parliament at the next election.) However, as Chakrabarti was travelling to Bracknell she received the call from Macdonald. 'We are going to have some video footage for you tonight,' the *Telegraph*'s PR woman said. 'It is of the whistleblower behind the expenses scandal.' There was a long silence at the other end of the phone, as the BBC correspondent realized that her carefully planned evening was about to be blown apart.

The call played havoc with the BBC's plans for the ten o'clock evening bulletin. The editor of BBC News phoned and Chakrabarti was on the line to Macdonald almost constantly over the course of the next hour. The *Telegraph* was intending to place the interview footage on a secure part of the newspaper's website which broadcasters could log into – but a few minutes after the scheduled release time of 9 p.m. both the BBC and Sky News said they were unable to access the footage on the site. Sensing imminent disaster with the deadline for the ten o'clock news rapidly approaching, Macdonald ordered a taxi and was preparing to deliver a computer memory stick containing the interview to the broadcasters' Westminster studios – only to receive another call from the broadcasters to say they had finally managed to access the material, with just minutes to spare.

The interview with Wick led that evening's news programmes, but the whistleblower himself missed his moment of fame – owing to technical problems of his own at the B&B he had chosen for the night.

In the Thistle Hotel's Harvard Bar, meanwhile, Robert Winnett had been joined by Arthur Wynn Davies for a drink after work. Wynn Davies, fiercely proud of his Welsh roots, was delighted to discover that the hotel guests in the bar included a coach party from north Wales. Unable to resist the opportunity of speaking in Welsh to them, the lawyer hurried over to introduce himself, while Winnett chatted to some of the other reporters who had joined them.

Ten minutes later, Winnett was bemused to see Wynn Davies frantically beckoning him across. He was talking to a sheep farmer from Wales who wanted to talk to one of the reporters who had been directly involved in the expenses scandal. To Winnett's intense embarrassment, Wynn Davies theatrically announced – both in Welsh and in English – that Winnett was the reporter behind the expenses scoop, prompting the coach party to stand up and applaud.

'It has been brilliant, absolutely brilliant,' the garrulous sheep farmer said to Winnett. 'I've never bought the *Telegraph* before but now it sells out at the local newsagent. We can't get enough of it – what these MPs have been up to is a bloody scandal.'

'Great, thanks,' Winnett replied nervously. 'You don't think we should start to wind everything down yet then?'

'Absolutely not!' the farmer spluttered in surprise. 'It's our money and I want to know how every last penny is being spent. Keep going, and good luck to you,' the farmer added, giving Winnett a rather hefty slap on the back which propelled him back towards the bar.

A New Front

Sunday, 24 May

CHAPTER 22

THE FALLOUT FROM the *Daily Telegraph*'s disclosures about the Cabinet's expenses on the first day of the investigation had caused such resentment in Downing Street that more than two weeks later the newspaper's entire working relationship with No. 10 remained under threat. In particular, the Prime Minister and his aides had been furious that they had been contacted only at 1 p.m. on that first Thursday afternoon, giving them, they believed, too little time to react to such an explosive story. The *Telegraph* team was unrepentant, believing that ministers had had plenty of time to respond, and citing the fact that two other newspapers had been tipped off about the *Telegraph*'s enquiries that day as proof that caution was entirely justified to protect the integrity of the scoop.

Now the *Telegraph* was preparing to reopen the Cabinet's expenses files and was braced for further fury to be directed at them from Downing Street. It was a crucial decision and one that needed to be handled with great delicacy.

Christopher Hope had spent several days trawling through the ministers' office expenses – which in some cases ran to several hundred pages for each year – looking for stories buried among the receipts for staples, headed paper and envelopes. It was laborious work, but Hope was quickly rewarded when he started looking through the office expenses claims of the Chancellor, Alistair Darling. Here he discovered an invoice for £763.75 from an accountant who had provided 'taxation advice' and prepared and submitted the Chancellor's self-assessment tax return for him.

'Darling's claimed for an accountant to do his tax return,' Hope announced triumphantly to the bunker. 'That's bloody outrageous!'

Self-assessment tax returns, brought in by the Labour government, had become a bane for millions of taxpayers who had to spend endless hours trying to decipher the lengthy forms and would often be reduced to a state of despair in the process. The fact that the politician in charge of the tax system had had to get an accountant to fill in his forms for him was the height of hypocrisy, and would severely dent the Chancellor's credibility. For him to have arranged for long-suffering taxpayers to foot the bill for his accountant put the top hat on it. Hope confidently – and correctly – predicted that the story would cause uproar.

Nor was Darling the only minister to have enlisted the help of an accountant, courtesy of the taxpayer. Eight other members of the Cabinet, including Hazel Blears, Geoff Hoon and Jacqui Smith, had done the same thing. A leading accountant consulted by the *Telegraph* described the arrangement as 'scandalous', pointing out that ordinary members of the public were not allowed to claim back the cost of hiring an accountant to fill in their self-assessment forms as a legitimate business expense.

For the first two and a half weeks of the expenses investigation, the *Telegraph* team had concentrated on the second-home allowance, but this was only part of the story of MPs' expenses. Their office expenses claims represented a whole new front in the development of the story.

Just as the investigation team had discovered a whole range of scams which the MPs had used to take advantage of the second-home allowance, Hope discovered that some of them had been every bit as creative when it came to their office expenses claims. Some appeared to have subsidized the cost of running their main home by having an office in their house, enabling them to claim for phone calls and utility bills, including heating. They were also able to claim up to £250 every month for 'petty cash' without providing receipts, and, not surprisingly, some MPs took full advantage. In addition, the wide scope of the category 'office equipment' allowed many MPs to claim large sums for digital cameras, camcorders and iPod accessories. Jacqui Smith, the home secretary, had billed the taxpayer for three digital cameras and a camcorder over the course of three years, saying she needed them to take pictures used in constituency material. She had also claimed £240 for an Apple iPhone for her husband Richard Timney (already in the spotlight for his porn films), who worked as her office manager. James Purnell, the work and pensions secretary, claimed £247 for a set of 3,000 fridge magnets. Purnell and his fellow ministers John Hutton and Douglas Alexander had also claimed hundreds of pounds to promote themselves on pitch-side advertisements at football and rugby matches.

It was the issue of tax, however, which would cause the biggest rumpus. Hope, who had spent virtually the whole week trawling through the maddeningly complex office expenses claims, took a deep breath as he prepared to send out emailed letters to twenty ministers – virtually the entire Cabinet – asking probing questions about their finances. Only a few weeks earlier, it would have been unheard-of for a newspaper to 'front up' the entire Cabinet with such serious allegations in the space of a day; but the expenses investigation had torn up the rule-book, and now it was not just a single newspaper, but a single reporter who was doing just that.

The normally exuberant Hope was starting to show the strain, becoming unusually quiet and sitting at one point with his head in his hands.

'Are you all right, Chris?' Winnett asked him.

'Yes, thanks, Rob,' Hope replied, managing a smile, though the truth was he had butterflies in his stomach as he contemplated the gravity of the task ahead.

By 1.04 p.m. that Sunday, Hope had sent off all of the emails. Gordon Brown's press aide Michael Dugher said he would try to make sure that ministers replied promptly. But the ministers themselves were rather less positive. Many were incensed at having to deal with a fresh set of enquiries from the *Telegraph* when they were in the middle of a bank holiday weekend. Some were even more angry when Hope, double-checking their expenses claims during the course of the afternoon, found more questionable items and emailed supplementary questions.

'Why are you coming back to people at 4 p.m. with new lines of enquiry?' an exasperated Dugher emailed Hope. 'This is not on.'

Hope replied: 'Sorry. These were basic factual points and I wanted to cover all the bases and details.'

Most ministers had sent staff to their offices to check through their expenses claims, a huge amount of work which was particularly soul-destroying when the rest of the country was making the most of the superb May weather. One of the last to reply was Alistair Darling, who sent his answers at 6.59 p.m., via his special adviser. On the key point, he said: 'Like many MPs, I employed an accountant to prepare tax returns for each of the years in question to ensure that the correct amount of tax was paid in respect of my office costs.'

Hope breathed a sigh of relief. The Chancellor had been caught red-handed. However, his reply had been slightly disingenuous, as he had also claimed for personal tax advice. Arthur Wynn Davies was particularly vexed by the latest revelations. 'The readers will absolutely hate this,' he fumed. 'This really is the last straw.'

Within the hour another attention-grabbing front page had been drawn up, under the headline: 'How you paid to fill out the Chancellor's tax return.'

As Hope drove home that night, shattered after one of the most testing days of his career, he tuned in to Radio Five Live and discovered that the MPs' accountancy bills were already the subject of a heated phone-in, chaired by a host who read out the *Telegraph*'s story with genuine incredulity in his voice. Arthur Wynn Davies had been spot-on about the public's reaction; listeners were beside themselves with disgust at the thought that their taxes had paid for ministers to have their wretched self-assessment forms filled in for them (not to mention the issue of whether the accountants had also helpfully told them how to avoid paying capital gains tax). Among the callers was Mike Warburton, one of the country's leading tax experts and a senior partner at the accountancy firm Grant Thornton, who had patiently explained the tax implications of the MPs' claims to the *Telegraph* team, and had been as cross as anyone else about what they had been able to get away with.

As well as opening a new chapter in the investigation, the story about the Cabinet's office expenses prompted a temporary breakdown in communications between the government and the *Telegraph*. Many ministers were unhappy with what they saw as the niggardly amount of space given in the paper to the lengthy responses they had compiled on Sunday afternoon, and Downing Street decided to employ a new tactic. From then on, any ministers who were asked questions about their expenses by the *Telegraph* would first speak to their local paper, then release a statement to the Press Association shortly before 8 p.m. No. 10 hoped the *Telegraph* would be embarrassed into ending the investigation if rival media organizations were given the story at the same time. Downing Street aides described the new strategy as 'low level harassment of *Telegraph* journalists'.

Needless to say, it didn't work. Other journalists, unfamiliar with the background, could usually not fathom what the statements referred to, and the tactic often served simply to add to the fevered excitement over what would be uncovered in the following day's *Telegraph*.

On Tuesday, 26 May the *Telegraph* revealed that Dennis Bates, the husband of the Labour MP and former foreign office minister Meg Munn, had been paid more than £5,000 via parliamentary expenses to give personal tax advice to at least five ministers, including David Miliband, the foreign secretary. Bates had even been paid out of the public purse to give tax advice to his own wife.

The taxman was taking an increasing interest in the *Telegraph*'s disclosures, and the following day, Wednesday, the newspaper reported that dozens of MPs could face an investigation by HM Revenue & Customs over their claims for accountancy bills. In a highly unusual move, a spokesman for HMRC told the *Telegraph* that MPs were not exempt from tax laws and should have paid tax on their expenses claims for accountants.

'It's a general principle of tax law that accountancy fees incurred in connection with the completion of a personal tax return are not deductible,' the spokesman said. 'This is because the costs of complying with the law are not an allowable expense against tax. This rule applies across the board.'

Wednesday, 27 May saw yet another bold new phase in the expenses investigation. William Lewis had decided that the only logical, and fair, way eventually to bring the investigation to a conclusion would be to feature the expenses claims of all 646 MPs in the *Telegraph*. The bunker team took the news in their stride – with around 200 MPs already covered, it become increasingly obvious that every MP would have to be written about in the end. So on day twenty of the investigation, the *Telegraph* featured the first part of an A to Z of the MPs who had not yet been covered (and whose claims did not merit a major story) with sixty MPs covered in a double-page spread.

While the tax affairs of government ministers had enraged many members of the public, it was MPs' second-home claims which continued to cause the most problems with constituents. Following the resignation of the Speaker, people power was ending the careers of an increasing number of MPs. Some, like Sir Peter Viggers, the duck house man, had gone swiftly; others clung on, only to suffer a slow, agonizing demise. One of these was Julie Kirkbride, the Tory MP for Bromsgrove whose husband, Andrew MacKay, had earlier announced his decision to step down as an MP at the next election, following his earlier resignation as an aide to David Cameron over the couple's 'double-dipping'.

MacKay's decision to quit politics altogether had been interpreted as a last-ditch attempt to save his wife's career, but two weeks after their his'n'hers expenses claims for two separate houses had been exposed, Kirkbride's constituents were making it increasingly clear that she, too, was surplus to requirements. Local activists had started a 'Julie Must Go' campaign, collecting five thousand signatures calling for her head. As the days wore on, more and more stories about her expenses appeared both in the *Telegraph* and in her local paper: she had paid her sister to work as her secretary, even though she lived 125 miles away from either the constituency or Westminster; she had claimed £540 for a flattering set of photographs of herself posing in front of bales of hay; and she had used taxpayers' money to fund a £50,000 extension to her second home so that her brother did not have to share a bedroom with her son.

On Thursday, 28 May, Kirkbride had been due to conduct a walkabout in her constituency, but when she woke up that morning to yet more revelations about her expenses in the *Telegraph* she realized the game was up. What had made the *Telegraph*'s persistence particularly galling for her was that before she had become an MP she had been a political correspondent on the paper; having left in 1996, she still knew many of the longer-serving staff.

Kirkbride, who was staying in Plymouth at the time, rang David Cameron to tell him she had decided to step down at the next election. Cameron was at the Said Business School in Oxford when he took the call, being interviewed, appropriately enough, by the *Telegraph*'s William Lewis and Andrew Porter. Cameron, who had agreed to grant the *Telegraph* his first newspaper interview since the expenses story had broken, had been passionately expressing his view that MPs who claimed for 'phantom' mortgages should face fraud charges when he had to excuse himself to take the call from Kirkbride. Together with his communications chief Andy Coulson, who had accompanied him to Oxford, Cameron walked outside into a courtyard, where he spoke on the phone for five minutes before returning to Lewis and Porter.

The Tory leader told the two journalists about the latest resignation, and the strained expression on his face left them in little doubt that Cameron was finding it difficult seeing so many of his MPs falling by the wayside. Lewis and Porter agreed to abide by an embargo on the news of Kirkbride's resignation until it had been announced via the Press Association, and Cameron carried on with the interview, saying he was 'ashamed' of the Tory MPs who had claimed for swimming pools, duck houses and moats.

Kirkbride wasn't the first MP to quit that day as a result of the irresistible pressure of people power. Precisely one minute before her resignation was announced, Margaret Moran too finally bowed to the inevitable after being hauled over the coals for three solid weeks by her constituents in Luton over her £22,500 claim for dry rot at her husband's home in Southampton. Moran had shown remarkable stubbornness in refusing to quit after the public airing of her own wrongdoing, but ran for the hills when she was faced with an altogether more formidable foe: Esther Rantzen. The consumer champion and TV presenter fancied her chances of toppling Moran by standing against her in a general election, and began charming the voters of Luton, who became hugely excited at the prospect of having an MP they'd actually heard of. Moran threw in the towel, saying the controversy had caused her 'great stress' and affected her health, while claiming for the umpteenth time that she had done nothing wrong. The contempt of her constituents was summed up by one of them who took a can of red paint to her constituency office and, with a nod to Esther Rantzen, daubed the words 'That's Life' on the door.

Esther Rantzen's overtures towards the voters of Luton started something of a trend, with a whole host of well-known names considering taking a tilt at vulnerable expenses claimants. They included the author Robert Harris, who was eyeing up Alan Duncan's seat; the consumer journalist Lynn Faulds Wood; and David Van Day, the former singer with Dollar, who hatched an unlikely plot to oust the Tory maverick Nadine Dorries. Even the *Daily Telegraph*'s own Simon Heffer threatened to enter the fray, warning his own local MP, Sir Alan Haselhurst, that if he didn't pay back £12,000 worth of gardening claims for his country house in Essex he would have 'The Heff' to deal with come the next general election.

The voters, meanwhile, had had enough of the endless talk of reforming 'the system'. They wanted to reform the MPs themselves – by getting rid of them. Six out of ten voters questioned in a YouGov poll for the *Daily Telegraph* said they wanted an early general election. The electorate knew Gordon Brown was presiding over a lame duck parliament which was likely to remain in a state of paralysis for almost a year, until Brown was finally forced to go to the polls by the expiry of the five-year maximum term.

The opinion polls certainly weren't encouraging him to go earlier. As the expenses investigation entered its fourth week, Gordon Brown's approval rating was down to 17 per cent, making him even more unpopular than Michael Foot, who led Labour to a disastrous general election defeat in 1983. Politicians, of course, always dismiss opinion polls as meaningless when they contain bad news, but on this occasion Brown couldn't bat away the numbers so easily. Ominously for Labour, the country was just days away from getting a chance to deliver its verdict on Labour's performance by voting in the European and local council elections. Thursday, 4 June would be election day, but for Gordon Brown it was looking increasingly like Doomsday.

The most alarming number to come out of the opinion polls was one which placed Labour virtually neck and neck with the Lib Dems and the UK Independence Party (UKIP) in a three-way tie for a distant second place behind the Tories in the Euro elections. That meant there was a very real prospect that the governing party could come fourth. The polls also suggested Labour councillors would become virtually extinct across swathes of England by the time the votes were counted.

For the first time since the expenses story had first broken, there were dark murmurings that the Prime Minister's own position might not be safe. When he was interviewed on Andrew Marr's television show on Sunday, 31 May, he faced questioning about whether he would stand down if senior Labour figures told him the party would be better off without him. He said he would not. At the time, the question was more an attempt to make mischief than a serious suggestion that Brown's time might be up, but within a matter of days events would take such a sudden and unpredictable turn that Brown would be in the fight of his political life.

The first week in June would begin, as the previous week had begun, with a front-page story in the *Daily Telegraph* about Alistair Darling's expenses. The bunker team had decided to go through the Cabinet's second-home expenses claims for a second time, conscious that they had been checked at such speed the first time around that things might have been missed. The team had also gained a huge amount of experience in the intervening weeks and had become aware of yet more scams to look out for. Holly Watt, tasked with going through Alistair Darling's second-home allowance claims, discovered that Darling had claimed expenses for a flat that he let to tenants while he was also claiming living allowances for his grace and favour home in Downing Street. In July 2007, ten days after he became Chancellor, he had submitted a £1,004 invoice for a service charge on his south London flat. It covered the six-month period to the end of December 2007; but Darling had, in the meantime, switched the designation of his second home to Downing Street, where he was also making claims.

Holly Watt set out the allegations about Darling's expenses in an email to the Chancellor's special adviser, Catherine MacLeod, at three o'clock on Sunday afternoon. By now Darling's forbearance was starting to wear thin. Instead of resorting to the usual 'all within the rules' explanation, Darling went on the attack, authorizing MacLeod to brief broadcasters that the *Telegraph* was intending to print a story which was 'wrong'. At 9.30 p.m. MacLeod sent Watt a formal reply, denying that the Chancellor had claimed the allowance for his private flat while designating Downing Street as his second home. At 11 p.m. that same night a 'spokesman for the Chancellor' denied any breach of the rules in an official announcement.

But Watt, and the *Telegraph*, were sure of the story.

'Darling billed us for two homes at the same time,' pronounced the front page the next day.

Gordon Brown began Monday morning by backing his Chancellor, telling listeners of the *Today* programme: 'I don't think there is any substance in these allegations.' Among those listening was Holly Watt, who began to feel sick as she lay in bed listening to the Prime Minister's denials. Surely the Downing Street press operation would have checked Darling's version of events before allowing the Prime Minister to deny the *Telegraph*'s story to millions of listeners?

By the time she got into work, Watt was feeling so nervous that if she had been asked her own name she would have checked before answering. Winnett was already at his desk when she arrived, and welcomed her with a smile – but both were privately thinking how catastrophic it would be for the *Telegraph* to have to correct a front-page story at this point.

News editor Matthew Bayley was also in the bunker. 'You're sure your maths is better than the Chancellor's?' Bayley asked before she sat down.

Watt was close to panicking. 'Yes, absolutely,' she said, but it was only when she checked the figures for a fifth time that she felt completely able to relax.

At around the same time Darling returned to his office,

double-checked his claims, and realized that the *Telegraph* knew more about his expenses than he did. At 10 a.m. he performed the perfect U-turn, announcing he would be repaying £350 to the taxpayer to avoid 'ambiguity' (he later had to admit he had got even that sum wrong and would actually be repaying £668).

The Chancellor, just like his expenses claims, was all over the place. Brown was furious. Less than two hours after he had publicly backed his fellow Scot, he was being made to look a fool. He had supported Darling over his home flipping, and over his accountancy bills, but now the Prime Minister's patience had finally run out. In an interview with Sky News at 2 p.m., he said that 'where a mistake was pointed out to him, and I think it was inadvertent, he acted immediately'. It was what Brown didn't say, however, that appeared to seal Darling's fate. Asked three times if Darling would still be Chancellor in ten days' time, Brown refused to back his friend. On three occasions he spoke of Darling's job in the past tense, saying: 'Alistair Darling has been a great Chancellor.'

Darling's punishment, in traditional New Labour style, was to be wheeled out in front of a succession of television cameras to say that he wanted to apologize 'unreservedly' for his actions. Not for the first time, the bunker team watched transfixed as a politician was forced to appear on live TV to admit the *Telegraph* had got its facts right and they were in the wrong. Darling looked like a man who had given up the ghost. Asked if he was about to lose his job, he replied: 'It's up to the Prime Minister. He's got to decide the team he wants to be the next government. Gordon and I work very, very closely together, but at the end of the day it's his call.'

'God. He looks like he's given up,' said Rosa Prince. 'Where's all this going to end up?'

One thing seemed certain: Darling was finished as Chancellor. Parliamentary journalists were being briefed that Gordon Brown's closest ally, the schools secretary and former Treasury adviser Ed Balls, was being lined up to replace him, with Baroness Vadera, another former member of Brown's Treasury team, playing a prominent role by his side.

The subject of Darling's future dominated the next day's headlines, relegating to the inside pages the news of the previous day's Air France tragedy, in which five Britons had been among 228 lives lost when Flight 447 crashed into the Atlantic en route from Rio de Janeiro to Paris.

With the European and local elections looming, and Alistair Darling's career seemingly over, Westminster was preparing itself for what was clearly going to be the biggest test of Gordon Brown's premiership.

Brown on the Brink

Thursday, 4 June

'Is there still a Labour party?'

CHAPTER 23

LESS THAN TWO HOURS after Alistair Darling made his humiliating apology on live television, Labour MPs made their way to the second-floor committee corridor of the Houses of Parliament, overlooking the River Thames, and gathered in Committee Room 15 for what promised to be one of the most fraught gatherings since Labour had come to power more than twelve years previously.

Members had returned to Westminster following a week's break in their constituencies, where they had become all too aware of the depth of public anger over their expenses claims. Many had hoped that by removing the Speaker they might have lanced the boil, but they had quickly discovered that fury was still raging on the doorsteps. There was a growing realization that huge numbers of Labour MPs would be for the chop at the next general election, and now, instead of just blaming the *Daily Telegraph* for their perilous position, the politicians were pointing their fingers at the hopeless response of the party's leaders, and in particular at Gordon Brown.

Many Labour MPs felt that Brown was still failing to grasp the magnitude of the events unfolding around him.

On Monday morning, at the time he was, briefly, defending Alistair Darling, he had revealed during an interview on GMTV that he had found time over the weekend to ring Simon Cowell, the omnipresent music industry Svengali, to enquire about the well-being of Susan Boyle, the *Britain's Got Talent* runner-up whose eccentric behaviour in the show's final had led to concerns for her state of mind. Many observers were staggered that the PM had had time to worry about such trivia when he was under such pressure.

The Parliamentary Labour Party meets every week on a Monday evening when the Commons is sitting. The meetings, which are held behind closed doors, are often brief, anodyne affairs. Not this time. The 150-plus MPs crowding into the room wanted their chance to put the Prime Minister on the spot. They also hoped their leader might calm their nerves with a morale-boosting speech as they prepared for what was certain to be a difficult week with the European and local council elections just days away.

They were to be sorely disappointed. Brown didn't turn up. Instead, it was his deputy Harriet Harman who once again had to step into the breach. Harman urged the back-benchers to have 'iron in their souls', telling them: 'We can get through this,' though 'it is going to be tough,' but her bracing words had little effect. Barry Sheerman, who was later to become one of Brown's chief critics, complained about the way Michael Martin had been driven out of the Speaker's chair, saying it was a sign of how the Labour leadership had failed to stand up for MPs during the expenses scandal. David Hamilton, the MP for Midlothian, accused ministers of 'making policy on the hoof'. Ian Davidson, the Glasgow South West MP, drew hoots of laughter when he mischievously, and ironically, suggested: 'This is not the time to panic.' Dennis Skinner, the veteran left-wing MP known as 'the beast of Bolsover', shouted a lot.

One of the most pressing questions debated by the MPs was whether they should voluntarily publish their expenses claims, to spike the *Telegraph*'s guns, or do everything they could to keep them secret. The majority were against publication, particularly so close to the elections. Virtually all those present were expecting the party to be annihilated at the polls, and many of them, particularly those who had prospered under Tony Blair, had had enough. As they left the meeting, some were already preparing to turn their backs on Parliament for good.

The following morning, Patricia Hewitt, a former health secretary, unexpectedly announced that she would be stepping down at the next election, diplomatically citing a desire to spend more time with her family as her reason. The decision came as a surprise to many Westminster-watchers, but before they had time to digest the news Beverley Hughes, the children's minister, announced she, too, would be quitting Parliament at the next election, and would step aside from her government position when the next reshuffle came. Then Tom Watson, a Cabinet Office minister and one of Brown's key allies, said he would be leaving the front bench. His resignation drew gasps in Westminster, as Watson had been one of the key players in the 'coup' to replace Tony Blair with Gordon Brown and had only recently joined the government. But Watson, it seemed, had seen the writing on the wall. With Labour living on borrowed time, he was said to have become disillusioned with politics, and he, too, wanted to spend more time with his family.

Now came the biggest shock. The 24-hour news channels began reporting that Jacqui Smith, the home secretary, had told the Prime Minister she wished to leave government and return to the back benches. All of a sudden, the public could see that Labour's ship was sinking, and its once-loyal crew were rushing to jump overboard before they were dragged down with it. In Downing Street, Gordon Brown's aides convinced themselves that a coordinated attempt to undermine the Prime Minister had been launched. Spin doctors hit the phones to tell journalists that Smith had told Brown several months previously that she wished to leave the government at the next reshuffle. If that were so, the obvious question was: why had news of her decision leaked now? It had not come from Smith herself, so who had it come from? Was there a traitor in the Cabinet who had opportunistically told the broadcasters about the home secretary's plans in order to fan the flames?

Suspicion quickly fell on 'friends' of Hazel Blears, the communities secretary, who had already become a loose cannon on the deck following her criticism of the Prime Minister's YouTube performance. She was one of the few people who was both in a position to know of Smith's secret decision and sufficiently disloyal to make it public knowledge.

Smith later backed the Prime Minister, saying he 'can

and should' stay on as leader of the Labour Party, and that he still had her 'utmost respect'. It did little to steady the ship, however, as a reshuffle was now inevitable. Cabinet ministers began to jockey for position, eyeing up each other's jobs. Lord Mandelson, the increasingly influential business secretary, was reported to covet a move to foreign secretary. David Miliband was touted as a possible home secretary to replace Smith. The schools secretary Ed Balls, Brown's closest colleague, was openly being talked about as the next Chancellor, as the Prime Minister prepared to make Alistair Darling walk the plank.

But as the evening wore on, it became increasingly clear that Brown was facing a mutiny. David Miliband said publicly that he had no intention of leaving the foreign office. It was rumoured that he had even persuaded Hillary Clinton, the US Secretary of State, to call Brown and urge him to keep the young Blairite in his post. Worse still, Alistair Darling started to dig his heels in. Emboldened by the day's dramatic resignations, and seeing the Prime Minister's authority waning by the hour, Darling defiantly faced down his leader, telling him he was not prepared to go quietly.

What a mess. Harriet Harman (who else?) dutifully gave the broadcasters a target to aim at that evening as she tried to persuade the public Brown was still in control. 'It is not the wheels falling off the government,' she was forced to say in one interview that evening, but the ground seemed to be opening up beneath Brown's feet. For the first time, the country began to get a real sense that the Prime Minister could be just days away from being forced from office.

Although few people knew it at the time, Brown held a private meeting that night with John Reid, the combative former home secretary, who has never been a man to mince his words. Officially, Reid was in Downing Street to have a conversation about football (an odd choice of topic by the Prime Minister, as his government collapsed around him). But reports would later suggest that Brown, in desperation, was pleading with Reid to return to his old job at the home office. One account of the conversation, later published in several newspapers, ran like this:

Brown: 'Will you be my home secretary?'

Reid: 'No.'

Brown: 'You have to support me.'

Reid: 'No, I don't. I have to support my country and my party, and that means you have to stand down.'

Although Reid later described the transcript as 'inaccurate', he pointedly failed to deny the substance of the reports.

A few miles further west, a rather different sort of drama was taking place. Matthew Bayley's wife Liz had warned him that morning that she felt as though the birth of the couple's second child might be imminent, but Bayley, knowing that details of the last of the 646 MPs' expenses were to be published that day, decided to risk going in to work anyway. After writing up that day's newslist, which included Jacqui Smith's resignation, he dashed home and took his wife to hospital: baby Nye was born at five thirty that evening.

Gordon Rayner was woken at 6 a.m. the following day

by his radio alarm clock switching on to the headlines on the *Today* programme. Never at his best in the mornings, Rayner had found the early starts in the bunker tough going, with a 50-mile commute to London every day from his home in rural Berkshire, where he lived with his partner and three children. But on this occasion he was wide awake within seconds, scarcely able to believe what he was hearing. The programme was reporting that the *Guardian*, New Labour's most slavishly loyal ally in the media, had printed a front-page editorial calling on the Prime Minister to resign.

'Did you hear that?!' Rayner said, as he shook his slumbering partner, Julie. 'Brown's finished! He can't carry on now, surely?'

After a hasty breakfast, Rayner set off for the office, stopping off at a petrol station to pick up a copy of the *Guardian*. The newspaper contained a devastating full-page attack on Brown which tore into not only his political failings but also faults in his character.

'The Prime Minister demands the right to carry on, even as the Cabinet implodes around him,' it said.

The Home Secretary, the Chancellor, and perhaps even the Foreign Secretary may go, and Labour faces its worst defeat in history on Thursday, but the Prime Minister does not recognise his direct responsibility for the mayhem.

The truth is that there is no vision from him, no plan, no argument for the future and no support. The public sees it. His party sees it. The Cabinet must see it too, although they are not yet bold enough to say so . . .

Flaws in his character that drove his party close to revolt last summer now dominate again. He is not obviously able to lead. He blames others for failures and allows them insufficient credit for successes, as the current dismembering of Alistair Darling's reputation shows . . .

His timidity in the face of the expenses crisis has been painful. The blunt reality is that, even if he set out a grand programme of reform now, his association with it would doom its prospects . . . Labour has a year left before an election; its current leader would waste it. It is time to cut him loose.

As character assassinations go, it wasn't so much a sniper's bullet as a cruise missile programmed to explode on the Prime Minister's breakfast table.

'Seen the *Guardian*?' Rayner breathlessly asked the other reporters as he arrived in the bunker.

'Yeah,' said Rosa Prince. 'It couldn't be worse for Brown.'

'I'm starting to think he might go, you know,' Rayner replied.

'It's unbelievable,' Christopher Hope said, shaking his head. 'This whole thing might just end up bringing down the Prime Minister.'

There was still plenty of work to be done, with more expenses stories to be written, but the bunker team found it hard to concentrate during the course of the day, with one eye always straying to the television news for any further signs that Brown might be about to go.

By now, the Prime Minister's plight was starting to draw

comparisons with a Shakespearean tragedy, though Julius Caesar never had to deal with anyone quite so poisonous as Hazel Blears. Few doubted she had been the source of the 'Jacqui Smith quits' leak, but now, not content with stabbing her boss in the back, on Wednesday Blears got up and decided to stab him in the front for good measure.

At 9.30 a.m. she held a blistering meeting with Brown at No. 10, during which Brown expressed his displeasure over her expenses claims. Blears responded by telling her boss she was going to quit the Cabinet for 'personal reasons'. At 10 a.m., less than twenty-four hours before polling stations opened for the European and local council elections, Blears went public with the announcement.

She timed it to have the maximum possible impact. Brown was due at the dispatch box in Parliament just two hours later to face David Cameron at Prime Minister's Questions. Instead of preparing for the broadside he would inevitably be getting from the opposition leader, Brown watched with horror as news channels carried Blears's resignation letter, in which she offered no praise or support for Brown but instead talked of the need for Labour to 'reconnect with the British people'. It said:

> Today I have told the Prime Minister that I am resigning from the Government.
>
> My politics have always been rooted in the belief that ordinary people are capable of extraordinary things given the right support and encouragement.
>
> The role of a progressive government should be to pass

power to the people. I've never sought high office for the sake of it, or for what I can gain, but for what I can achieve for the people I represent and serve.

In this next phase of my political life, I am redoubling my efforts to speak up for the people of Salford as their member of parliament. I am returning to the grassroots, where I began, to political activism, to the cut and thrust of political debate.

Most of all, I want to help the Labour party to reconnect with the British people, to remind them that our values are their values, that their hopes and dreams are ours too.

I am glad to be going home to the people who matter the most to me – the people of Salford.

Finally, there's an important set of elections tomorrow. My message is simple: get out and vote Labour.

Having delivered this statement, the tiny MP then strutted out of her office wearing a brooch inscribed with the words 'rocking the boat'. No one could accuse her of being subtle.

Some of Westminster's most respected commentators began to write the Prime Minister's political obituary. Chris Moncrieff, the Press Association's 77-year-old parliamentary reporter (who is such an institution after fifty years' service that he even has a bar named after him in Parliament), said he had 'never seen anything like this at all' and believed it was 'extremely doubtful that [Brown] can carry on'. He described him as 'a dead man' who 'can't even trust his own Cabinet colleagues'.

Blears had become the fourth female MP to announce

her resignation in the space of twenty-four hours, prompting fears in Downing Street that the Prime Minister was facing a mass walkout of senior Labour women, dubbed the WAGs (Women Against Gordon).

Brown had little time to brood on this latest act of treachery before he had to be in the Commons. Cameron seized the opportunity at Prime Minister's Questions to suggest that Brown's authority over the Cabinet had 'simply disappeared'; he accused the Prime Minister of being 'in denial' and challenged him to go to the country. Nick Clegg, the Liberal Democrat leader, suggested: 'The Prime Minister just doesn't get it . . . the country doesn't have a government. It has a void. Labour is finished.'

It was brutal stuff, but Cameron failed to land a knock-out blow on the Prime Minister. Downing Street aides thought this was proof that the Tory leader lacked the 'killer instinct', but many Conservative MPs were privately hoping that Brown would limp on as Prime Minister and speculated that Cameron might deliberately have gone easier than he might. The last thing they wanted was a new, more popular, Labour leader.

Brown returned to Downing Street after Prime Minister's Questions in a foul mood. And there was plenty more bad news to come. As he retired to his office that night, he was updated on the progress of an email being discussed by Labour backbenchers attempting to gather seventy-one signatures – the number needed, under Labour Party rules, to trigger a vote on a leadership election. The email, in the form of a letter to Brown, said:

Over the last 12 years in Government, and before, you have
made an enormous contribution to this country and to the
Labour Party and this is very widely acknowledged.

However, we are writing now because we believe that in the
current political circumstances you can best serve the
interests of the Labour Party by stepping down as Prime
Minister and so allowing the party to choose a new leader to
take us in to the next election.

The plan was that the letter would be published the day
after the local and European elections, provided that at least
fifty Labour MPs had agreed to sign it. Nick Brown, the chief
whip, suggested the plot had been organized by Alan
Milburn and Stephen Byers, two arch-Blairite former
ministers who had done their darnedest to block Brown's
unopposed takeover from Tony Blair two years earlier (only
to find they had no alternative candidate to put forward).
Nick Brown later had to apologize to the pair, admitting he
had no evidence that they were involved.

With each passing minute, Brown's chances of surviving
as Prime Minister appeared to be diminishing. Alan
Johnson, the health secretary, was installed by bookmakers
as 6–4 favourite to be the next Labour leader, with Harriet
Harman at 5–1 and David Miliband at 8–1. Lord Mandelson,
the calmest head in the gathering crisis, toured television
studios to plead with Labour MPs not to 'make it worse' for
the party by signing the email.

Brown went to bed on Wednesday night as Prime
Minister, but could he survive another day?

Thursday, 4 June was polling day in the European and local elections, a day which had for weeks been pencilled in as a crisis point. Brown would be left to gnaw on what was left of his stubby fingernails until 10 p.m., when the polling stations closed and exit polls would give him the first impression of just how bad a defeat his party had suffered. That was the moment when the knives would surely start coming out for Brown, and the Prime Minister and his aides began working on a survival plan.

It soon became apparent from local Labour activists that their voters were staying away from the polling stations in droves. The picture was pretty dismal, though not quite as bad as it could have been. The Liberal Democrats were not prospering either, and people were not defecting in large numbers to the Conservatives. The big winners appeared to be the smaller, minority parties that are not even represented in Westminster.

Unusually, the results from the elections would not be announced that evening. The local election votes for councils across England and Wales would be counted the following day. The counting for the European elections would be on Sunday, after polls across the entire continent had closed. This was a mixed blessing for Downing Street strategists. On the one hand, they had some breathing space to finesse the survival strategy; but on the other, the poor election results would be spread over three days. Would this lead to pressure building or subsiding?

Back at the *Telegraph*, another day of expenses coverage was being planned. Spurred on by the success of re-examining the expenses claims of Alistair Darling earlier in the week, the team had been studying Brown's claims once again.

The Prime Minister's expenses were a mess. Holly Watt and Gordon Rayner discovered that Brown, like Darling, had submitted bills for council tax, utilities and service charges for one property which covered a period when he was claiming on another. In particular, Brown had claimed for council tax and service charge bills for his London flat over a period when his second home was in Scotland, following his decision to flip second homes. He also submitted an estimated electricity bill for his home in Fife which partly covered a period when his London flat was his designated second home. In total, Brown appeared to have made claims totalling £512 for the 'wrong' properties.

During previous discussions with Downing Street over the handling of the newspaper's investigation, William Lewis had decided to offer one concession to Gordon Brown out of respect for the office of Prime Minister. Lewis had given Brown a promise that if the *Telegraph* intended to run any more stories about his expenses, Lewis would personally inform Downing Street staff himself, enabling Brown to deal with the editor directly. Now, honouring his earlier promise to the Prime Minister, Lewis called Brown's aide Michael Dugher to warn him that Rayner would be contacting him with some queries over the PM's expenses.

After the questions arrived asking about the apparent discrepancies in Brown's claims, Downing Street instructed the House of Commons fees office to conduct an urgent investigation into the Prime Minister's expenses claims. The fees office discovered that there had been some improper claims, albeit on a minor scale. Brown immediately agreed to repay money wrongly claimed, and at 7.48 p.m. Lewis received a lengthy statement explaining Brown's expenses.

However, on reading the response Lewis remained unconvinced of the seriousness of the Prime Minister's conduct and therefore the merit of the story. Although interesting, it was not the silver bullet that everyone had now come to expect from the *Telegraph*. With the deadline rapidly approaching, as a precaution the production team had prepared two versions of the next day's front page. But Lewis had already made up his mind and he rejected the version containing the Brown story. The editor called in Winnett to explain the decision.

'It just didn't feel quite right,' Lewis told him. 'The one thing any editor will tell you is that you've got to follow your instincts, and I'm just not sure about this one. Let's regroup tomorrow.'

In the event, the story was published later that week.

Meanwhile, within an hour the week's biggest bombshell of all was about to sweep every other story off the next day's front pages.

With half an hour to go until the polls closed, Brown was in the Downing Street 'war room' with Lord Mandelson and key advisers. A side room leading off it had been cordoned off since that morning with a 'no entry' sign on the door. Inside was a whiteboard which had on it the names of everyone in government. This was where the reshuffle was being planned. But at 9.30 p.m. the war room was disturbed by a call from the Downing Street switchboard. James Purnell was on the line. The work and pensions secretary wanted to inform the Prime Minister that he had decided to resign.

Both Brown and Mandelson were taken aback. Only the previous day, they had discussed promoting Purnell to schools secretary (replacing Ed Balls, who was pencilled in as the new Chancellor once Darling had been forced out), and he had given them cause to believe he was interested in the job. Each in turn now spoke to the young minister, who had himself been tipped as a future Prime Minister, to try to persuade him to change his mind. He replied that he had made his decision and would be sticking to it. Unbeknown to Brown and Mandelson, Purnell had already written his resignation letter and sent it to several newspapers which were being printed as they spoke.

As the call ended, both men were perplexed; then, at 9.53 p.m. Purnell's resignation letter arrived by email. The mood in the room quickly turned to anger as Brown and Mandelson read it. It said:

Dear Gordon,

We both love the Labour Party. I have worked for it for twenty years and you for far longer. We know we owe it everything and it owes us nothing.

I owe it to our Party to say what I believe, no matter how hard that may be. I now believe your continued leadership makes a Conservative victory more, not less, likely.

That would be disastrous for our country. This moment calls for stronger regulation, an active state, better public services, an open democracy. It calls for a government that measures itself by how it treats the poorest in society. Those are our values, not David Cameron's.

We therefore owe it to our country to give it a real choice. We need to show that we are prepared to fight to be a credible government and have the courage to offer an alternative future.

I am therefore calling on you to stand aside to give our party a fighting chance of winning.

The party was here long before us, and we want it to be here long after we have gone. We must do the right thing by it.

I am not seeking the leadership, nor acting with anyone else. My actions are my own considered view, nothing more. If the consensus is that you should continue, then I will support the government loyally from the backbenches. But I do believe that this question now needs to be put.

Thank you for giving me the privilege of serving,

Yours

James Purnell

Disastrously for Brown, Purnell had become the first Cabinet minister to call for him to go. And before the Prime Minister and Mandelson had had time to discuss the implications of the full-frontal attack in the letter, the BBC *Ten O'Clock News* began, and its main story was Purnell's resignation, including the damning letter which Brown had received only minutes earlier. It was the ultimate act of betrayal.

Television and radio stations cleared their schedules for a frenzy of speculation about Brown's future. Pundits and politicians were virtually unanimous in their predictions of the Prime Minister's demise. Mike Smithson, editor of the website politicalbetting.com, told BBC Radio Five Live he was offering odds of 5–1 against Brown surviving another two months. 'I think Gordon Brown is now dead,' he said. 'Once someone has put their head above the parapet others will follow and it's going to be a bloody ending.'

Winnett was in the Thistle Hotel next to the office, having a much-needed pint, when his BlackBerry buzzed in his pocket with a text message from Andrew Porter telling him the news. Production chief Richard Oliver was standing next to him as he read it.

'Shit. Purnell's resigned!' Winnett gasped. 'This is it. There's no way Brown can survive now. We'd better get back to the office.'

Winnett, Oliver and *Telegraph* design guru Himesh Patel downed their drinks and rushed back, with Winnett's BlackBerry constantly receiving texts and emails.

'Jesus! This is it, surely,' texted Rosa Prince.

'Got to be,' Winnett typed, as he walked across the *Telegraph*'s main newsroom, where he was quickly joined by Tony Gallagher, who had been halfway home when he heard the news and had promptly turned around and come back. Andrew Porter, still in Westminster, began writing a new splash, while political correspondent James

Kirkup started working up a profile piece on Purnell.

In Downing Street, Brown, Mandelson and Balls began hitting the phones. One of Mandelson's first calls was to David Miliband, one of the major potential leadership contenders. Word had reached Downing Street that Purnell had told Miliband of his intentions several hours before. The plans for a reshuffle were abandoned as Brown and his team set about finding out if Purnell's resignation was part of a coordinated coup attempt. If Miliband intended to follow his close friend out of the Cabinet, Brown could safely assume he was about to face a leadership challenge which he would be unable to survive.

To his immense relief, Brown was told that Miliband was not intending to resign. The foreign secretary was effectively promised he could keep his job in return for a pledge of loyalty to the Prime Minister. He agreed. But there were other potential leaders who still needed to be contacted. Panic began to set in when Brown, Mandelson and Balls could not get hold of Alan Johnson, the health secretary and bookies' favourite to be the next leader. His phone was switched off. He eventually called back and also pledged his loyalty.

By 1 a.m. a survival plan was largely in place. The reshuffle had been torn up, Darling and Jack Straw had been told they would keep their jobs, and it seemed the Prime Minister might just cling on. Brown went to bed for a few hours' sleep while Mandelson remained for a short while to make a couple more calls.

By 6.30 a.m. the Prime Minister was back in the 'war

room' to finish the reshuffle. The first visitor – before the cleaners had even arrived – was Harriet Harman, Labour's deputy leader, who was assured her position was secure. However, by the end of the day Mandelson would be installed as 'First Secretary of State', in effect Deputy Prime Minister. Then came the Chancellor, who had already told his wife Margaret that he would not accept another government job. Brown could not risk Darling going to the back benches. He too was safe. But Brown's plans for the rest of the Cabinet would soon have to be shredded on another day of shock resignations.

As the investigation team assembled in the bunker, there was only one topic of discussion: could Brown survive the day?

'I reckon he's finished,' Nick Allen said.

'What do you think?' Gammell asked Winnett. 'Are we going to end up bringing down the government?'

'If there's any more resignations I think that'll be it,' Winnett replied.

'It's history in the making, you know,' Prince mused. 'I just can't believe this is happening.'

Turning to the magnetic wall, by now covered with pictures of MPs who had resigned, Rayner said: 'We'd better get a picture of the Prime Minister printed off, just in case.'

Within an hour, the mood had changed again. David Miliband had been interviewed as he left his house, and had given his support to the Prime Minister. Perhaps, then, there was no organized coup after all, and Purnell had shot his bolt for nothing.

But then came news of another resignation. John

Hutton, the defence secretary, had decided he wanted to leave Parliament at the next election and was to step down from the Cabinet straight away. Although he issued a statement in support of Brown, the minister was known to be sceptical about the PM's abilities and his exit from government while British troops were heavily engaged in Afghanistan looked bad. As renewed talk of a coup swept Westminster, Brown tried to seize the initiative by carrying out the reshuffle he had sketched out only hours before. It didn't go according to plan. The steady stream of resignations was about to turn into a flood.

Geoff Hoon, another of the longest-serving Cabinet ministers, was one of the first into No. 10. The transport secretary had told the Prime Minister a year previously that he wanted an 'international role'. However, there were no vacancies. Hoon told Brown he too would be resigning, but he decided not to cause a stir. His friend Darling was safe and the prospect of becoming the next European Commissioner was still on the table. He resigned to the back benches and offered his support.

Margaret Beckett, the former foreign secretary who had rejoined the government as housing minister just months before, was disgruntled at not being offered a Cabinet position. She also decided to leave government (and later made an unsuccessful bid to become the next Speaker). However, she too did not go on the attack.

Paul Murphy, the Welsh secretary, and Tony McNulty, employment minister, also decided they wanted to return to the back benches.

At one stage, for those watching at home and in offices up and down the country, it seemed as though it was impossible even to pop to the loo without missing another ministerial resignation. By mid-afternoon, the number of ministers who had resigned since Tuesday of that week stood at ten. Crucially, however, none of those who resigned on reshuffle day had openly criticized the Prime Minister or called on him to stand down.

Brown and his team managed to put together a patched-up Cabinet, finding new faces to fill the vacancies left by those who wanted out. The Prime Minister decided it was time to face the media, and summoned reporters to Downing Street for a press conference to begin at 5 p.m.

As the journalists looked through a printed list of the new Cabinet, several noticed a glaring omission. Caroline Flint, the Europe minister often described as 'Parliament's most glamorous MP', was missing from the list. Had she simply been forgotten? Had she resigned? What was going on? Flint had been one of Brown's most steadfast supporters during the crisis, and had even rushed out to make a statement of support on live television the previous evening, criticizing Purnell's resignation.

In fact, even as the media were gathering outside No. 10 for the press conference, she was discussing her future with the Prime Minister. She had been expecting a major promotion as a reward for her loyalty. But Brown wanted her to remain as Europe minister, albeit with the offer of a full place in the Cabinet. Flint declined the offer and left, seething.

Minutes later, Brown arrived at the lectern in the

briefing room looking shaken. His voice trembled as he vowed to fight on.

'If I didn't think I was the right person to lead these challenges I would not be standing here,' he said to the assembled press. 'I have faith in doing my duty . . . I believe in never walking away in difficult times. I will not waver. I will not walk away. I will get on with the job.'

Outside the press conference, however, all hell was breaking loose. Flint had released a resignation letter, and it was the most incendiary yet.

'You have a two-tier government, your inner circle and then the remainder of Cabinet,' she wrote in the letter to Brown, which the Prime Minister had not yet seen. 'Several of the women attending Cabinet – myself included – have been treated by you as little more than female window dressing.'

Within moments, the BlackBerries of the reporters inside the press conference began vibrating.

'Why has Caroline Flint resigned and said you think women are window dressing?' demanded one reporter.

Brown staggered back a step, as if absorbing a physical blow, before insisting that there were still plenty of women in Cabinet.

'Besides, I am delighted to announce we have a very strong candidate for Europe minister: Glenys Kinnock,' he added.

Glenys Kinnock? The reporters in the press conference looked at each other, incredulous. Had they misheard? The wife of former Labour leader Neil Kinnock had spent the previous few years making a tidy living as an MEP, having never sat in Parliament. Had Brown just said he was parachuting her into the government?

'Are you telling us you cannot find a single candidate to be minister for Europe out of 350 MPs?' asked one reporter. He certainly was. And there were more surprises to come. Sir Alan Sugar, the star of the television show *The Apprentice*, was to be given a peerage and a post as 'enterprise tsar'. The news was greeted with disbelieving stares, followed by laughter.

It had been another disastrous day for the Prime Minister – but he had survived, against all odds, through a combination of sheer stubbornness and the Labour Party's utter inability to get rid of leaders.

'If this had been the Tories, Brown would have been gone three times over,' observed Holly Watt in the bunker. 'Thatcher was basically booted out on the strength of one critical speech from the back benches, never mind all this!'

Boris Johnson, the Mayor of London and *Telegraph* columnist, memorably likened Brown's would-be assassins to the inept criminal masterminds who try – and fail – to kill Inspector Clouseau at the end of the *Pink Panther* films.

The day's events proved to be a headline-writer's dream. 'Stiletto in the heart of Brown' was the *Telegraph*'s splash, reflecting on Caroline Flint's resignation, alongside pictures of her posing in high heels and scarlet lipstick for a magazine shoot.

Away from Westminster, the results from voting in thirty-four councils across England showed that the public had resoundingly rejected Labour. The Tories gained 233 councillors while Labour lost 273 seats and the Liberal Democrats 4. The Conservatives recorded 38 per cent of the national vote; Labour was beaten into third place with a historic low of 23 per cent of the vote.

Friday's dismal local council results were compounded on Sunday when the results of the European polls began to come in. Labour had been beaten into third place behind the UK Independence Party. It had failed to win the popular vote in Wales for the first time since 1918 and had been crushed by the SNP in Scotland. Most worrying was that the failure of Labour voters to turn out in the north had led to the BNP winning two seats in the European Parliament. It was the worst electoral showing for Labour in almost a century. Brown clearly wasn't out of the woods just yet.

Monday, 8 June saw another weekly meeting of the Parliamentary Labour Party. The gathering – back in Committee Room 15 – was now being seen as crunch time. After days of plotting, it was the moment when the rebels would have to either show their hand and demonstrate they had the support or else leave Brown to focus on his role as Prime Minister.

Brownites spent much of the day working the phones, cajoling waverers into weighing in behind the Prime Minister. MPs in marginal seats claimed they were being threatened with withdrawal of support for their re-election campaigns if they spoke out. Frank Field, a former minister, accused Brown's aides of 'terrorizing' Labour MPs into line. Jane Kennedy, a farming minister, refused to give an assurance that she would remain loyal to the Prime Minister and left her post, becoming the twelfth minister to leave the government in a week.

This time, Brown did turn up for the meeting. The room was so packed that several Cabinet ministers were struggling even to get through the door. The corridor outside the committee room was filled with journalists and the broadcasters were reporting live from outside the entrance to the Commons.

Brown stood up. 'I have my strengths and I have my weaknesses,' he said. 'There are some things I do well, some not so well. I have learned that you have to keep learning. You solve the problem not by walking away.

'I'm not making a plea for unity, I'm making an argument for unity.'

Labour MPs were surprised. For the first time that many could remember, Brown had shown humility.

Although a few spoke out against Brown, it became clear that the rebels had not managed to gather enough support for a leadership vote. They may have been 'bullied into submission', as the *Telegraph* put it the next day, but one way or another the Labour Party had failed to depose their leader. Gordon Brown was still Prime Minister.

A Sea of Black Ink

Thursday, 18 June

CHAPTER 24

FROM THE VERY first day the expenses scandal broke, MPs who felt they had nothing to hide had been clamouring for Parliament to bring forward the publication of the expenses documents as a way of pricking the *Telegraph*'s balloon. They believed that if the public and, more importantly, the media were swamped with information on all 646 MPs the story would blow itself out in a matter of days, rather than being controlled by the *Telegraph* and drawn out over what became several weeks.

Luckily for the *Telegraph*, the redacted versions of the expenses documents had still not been signed off by MPs, and so Parliament was left in a state of paralysis while officials tried to hurry the process along in order to bring forward online publication from the original target date of July.

Thursday, 18 June 2009 was eventually announced as the day the public would finally get their chance to see the expenses claims of every MP, and find out for themselves exactly what their local Members had been up to.

Although the *Telegraph*'s expenses investigation would have been going for almost six weeks by then, it would still be a crucial day both for Parliament and for the newspaper. If the House of Commons published detailed information about each MP's claims, the story could still rebound on the *Daily Telegraph* to some degree, as politicians would line up to renew their erroneous accusations that the newspaper had paid for what they claimed was 'stolen' information just so that it could 'jump the gun' by publishing the leaked files ahead of time. The *Telegraph*'s insistence that it had acted in the public interest by publishing material which would otherwise have been kept secret would also have been seriously undermined. On the other hand, if the material appeared in a heavily censored form, the newspaper would be vindicated.

The day would also prove a crucial test of whether the Commons had listened to the public anger over MPs' expenses by publishing more information than it had originally planned to release.

In the run-up to Parliament's publication day, the *Telegraph*'s coverage of the expenses story – which at its peak was taking up thirteen pages per day – had been wound right down, with the bunker team contributing no stories at all to the newspaper on some days. But behind the scenes the reporters, designers and sub-editors had been busier than ever, working flat out to produce a supplement on the expenses scandal under the guiding hand of group consultant editor Derek Bishton. *The Complete Expenses Files* was to be a 68-page magazine which would detail the claims made by every MP.

William Lewis stressed that he wanted the magazine to

be a treasure trove of fascinating details, modelled on the design of the *Sunday Times* Rich List. But whereas the annual Rich List took almost a year to compile, *The Complete Expenses Files* had to be put together in little over a fortnight. Lewis had initially set a publication date of 27 June – comfortably before the original parliamentary publication date – but when Parliament brought forward its own publication date to 18 June, Lewis responded by changing the magazine's publication date to 20 June, when it would be distributed free with the newspaper.

With a week less to prepare the supplement than had originally been expected, the bunker team worked later and later into the nights as they wrote new material on each MP and compiled new figures breaking down what they had spent on furniture, gardening, mortgages and other items. The magazine had to be finished by 12 June to make sure of its printing slot, and the bunker team worked until 3.30 a.m. that night to finish the job, before breaking out a warm bottle of white wine and some plastic cups from the water cooler for a weary celebration.

The Complete Expenses Files, published the following week, amounted to a Domesday Book of MPs' profligacy, and it proved to be a massive hit with a public who were still clamouring for information. The reporters' efforts would be rewarded with a sales increase of 150,000 – one of the biggest one-day rises in the *Telegraph*'s history, making that day's paper by far the biggest-selling issue of the whole investigation. By lunchtime, newsagents across the country had completely sold out of copies.

Sales were helped by Andrew Pierce's characteristically cheeky plugs for the supplement during a round of television interviews, in which he waved a copy of the magazine in front of millions of viewers. One TV producer tried to stop Pierce taking the magazine on set, so the indomitable reporter hid a copy down the back of his trousers before producing it with a flourish on camera.

Although the media coverage of MPs' expenses had diminished following Gordon Brown's reshuffle, the Westminster rumour mill was being cranked up to full power again with whispers that the *Telegraph* had held back a 'big story' for publication on the eve of the parliamentary disclosure.

'Please, just give us a hint of what you've got – have you kept back the affairs?' Winnett was asked by one caller from the upper echelons of the Conservative Party.

'Erm, not quite, but I think you'll enjoy what we have got,' came the hesitant reply.

In fact, the truth was that once again the rumour mongers were wide of the mark. The *Telegraph* had nothing spectacular up its sleeve at all. But, not for the first time, luck was about to shine on the newspaper and the prophecy would, in the end, be fulfilled.

Having put the magazine to bed, the bunker team had started going back through the expenses files to tie up any loose ends and chase any leads they hadn't previously had time to follow up. The team had hoped to come up with two or three front-page stories to run in the build-up to the official publication. By Tuesday evening, however, there was little sign of the major breakthrough required for Thursday's paper.

'Found anything good yet?' Chris Evans kept asking.

'We're working on it,' Winnett would reply.

Then, as Winnett was travelling home on Tuesday night, he received a text from Martin Beckford. 'Think I may have found something interesting, give me a call if you can.'

Winnett immediately did so, and Beckford, who had been going through the office expenses of junior ministers, explained that he had found a bill for accountancy advice for Kitty Ussher, the junior Treasury minister who had featured in the paper in the early days of the investigation after she tried to claim for having 'swirly' Artex removed from her ceiling.

Winnett was distinctly underwhelmed by Beckford's news. After all, the *Telegraph* had already devoted considerable coverage to the fact that several senior ministers, including the Chancellor, Alistair Darling, had claimed for advice from accountants. This sounded like more of the same – an OK story but not one which was likely to make the front page.

'Sounds all right,' said Winnett, trying not to communicate his disappointment to a reporter who had worked as hard as anyone over the previous weeks.

'Hang on, I haven't finished yet,' Beckford continued. The letter setting out the advice Ussher had received from her accountant was in the file. Beckford said: 'I'm not sure whether it means what I think it means. But this is what the letter says:

'"I am enclosing a declaration to vary your previous

main residence election for a period of one month to [Burnley home] and then back to [London home].

'"The effect of varying the election is that [Burnley home] will receive the final three years' main residence exemption and the gain will be completely exempt from capital gains tax provided [Burnley home] is sold before April 2007."'

'Bloody hell!' Winnett spluttered. 'She's flipped the designation of her main home for a month just so she can avoid capital gains tax. It's completely premeditated.'

Beckford had stumbled across one of the biggest scandals of the whole investigation. Ussher wasn't the first MP, or even the first minister, to be accused of avoiding capital gains tax, but whereas other ministers had been able to muddy the waters by saying they had been assured they were not liable for CGT, or that the issue had never even crossed their mind, here was proof positive that a government minister – and one who worked in the Treasury, no less – had knowingly and deliberately flipped the designation of her main home specifically for the purpose of avoiding paying CGT when she sold it. Although she hadn't broken any laws, Ussher had been guilty of what could only be described as sharp practice.

The following morning, checks with the Land Registry revealed that Ussher had sold the property in her Burnley constituency for a profit of more than £40,000. The tax flip had saved her between £9,750 and £16,800. She had also claimed for the cost of accountancy advice to fill in her personal tax return.

Beckford began to draft a formal letter to the minister, and at lunchtime he sent it.

Meanwhile, Jon Swaine had also uncovered an interesting new avenue of enquiry. He had been studying the office expenses claims of David Chaytor, the Labour MP who had made phantom mortgage claims and had already been forced to announce his resignation at the next election. He had found that Chaytor had made a series of payments to 'consultants' totalling thousands of pounds. On closer examination, it turned out that many of the 'consultants' were Labour Party activists in Chaytor's constituency.

There was also a series of intriguing invoices for work worth almost £5,000 from a 'Sarah Rastrick' – whose address was the same as that used by Sarah Chaytor, the MP's daughter. Swaine ordered a copy of Sarah Chaytor's birth certificate from a register office in Yorkshire, where she had been born, and when it arrived by special delivery the next day his suspicions were all but confirmed – Rastrick was one of Sarah Chaytor's middle names. She had been a graduate student in London when the payments were made.

Swaine rang Chaytor's office, and it was Chaytor himself who answered.

'Oh, hi,' Swaine said, 'it's Jon Swaine here from the *Daily Telegraph*.'

On the other end of the line, there was deadly silence for a couple of seconds, before Chaytor eventually replied: 'Hello.'

In response to Swaine's questions, Chaytor said that his daughter was working part-time in his office. She had, he said, 'thought to adopt a professional name for work purposes'. The arrangement looked odd, however, and Swaine began working on a story.

As Beckford waited for Ussher's response, the bunker team was summoned into the editor's office. It was the sixty-fifth birthday of chief lawyer Arthur Wynn Davies, who had put his retirement plans on hold indefinitely, particularly in the light of the expenses story. As the staff toasted Wynn Davies's 32-year career on Fleet Street – and chief executive Murdoch MacLennan presented him with the traditional gold watch – Wynn Davies enthusiastically eulogized the expenses investigation.

'I thought I'd seen it all,' he said. 'But I want to tell you all now that it's been a privilege to have worked with you all on what's been the greatest scoop in my time working in our business.'

By now it was 6 p.m., and there had still been no word from Ussher. Shortly after returning to the bunker, Beckford called her mobile phone. He could hear her two young children playing in the background as Ussher explained that she had been unable to get to her email because of her family duties. As father of a new baby himself, Beckford had some sympathy for the minister, but he stressed that the paper would be running a story about her the next day and the time for her to respond was short.

By the time another hour had passed the story had been laid out on the front page with a gap left for Ussher's reply. But now the minister had turned off her mobile phone. Beckford scrolled through her expenses files until he found a handwritten builders' invoice that showed her home phone number in Brixton and gave it a call. 'How did you—?' Ussher began, then broke off when the penny dropped. She said she had read the email and promised to send a response immediately but when Beckford called the landline again half an hour later, there was no answer. Beckford was becoming increasingly nervous that something was up. Was the minister going to try to scupper the story by denying it out of hand? Was she seeking an injunction?

'Don't worry,' Winnett reassured him: 'If she did have a reasonable explanation, she would have given us it by now.'

Head of news Chris Evans read through the story on his computer screen.

'Are we absolutely fine with this?' he asked Winnett.

'Yep. The letter in her file's crystal clear and she's had all day to respond,' Winnett replied. 'We know she's seen the email from us because Martin spoke to her.'

By 8.30 p.m. Richard Oliver was coming under pressure to send the pages to the printers. The story was written, the front page was ready, with the headline 'The minister and the £17,000 tax dodge', and Oliver started typing in a final paragraph saying the minister had failed to respond to the *Telegraph*'s requests for a comment.

Then Winnett's BlackBerry vibrated on his desk. He picked it up and scrolled through the email he had just received.

'Ussher's resigned,' he announced calmly.

'You're kidding,' Beckford responded.

'Nope. They're going to announce it any minute.'

Beckford puffed out his cheeks in relief, then began pacing the room to get rid of the nervous energy that had been building up all afternoon as he waited for the reply. The other reporters, apart from Winnett, had left for the evening, but within minutes Ussher's resignation statement had appeared on the Press Association newswire, and as the bunker team heard the news from radio and television reports they started calling and texting Beckford to congratulate him on his scoop.

At 8.46 p.m. Downing Street issued a formal statement announcing the resignation. The *Telegraph* was just minutes away from the deadline for the first edition. The headline was hastily rewritten to read: 'Treasury minister quits over £17,000 tax dodge'. It was the perfect way to reignite the public's interest in the expenses story on the day that Parliament prepared to release the information. And the rumour-mongers were able to say 'told you so' about the *Telegraph* having a big, agenda-setting story, though none of them knew how close they were to being wrong.

Every MP's expenses files were due to be published on the parliamentary website at 6.30 a.m. on Thursday, 18 June. Every national newspaper had teams of reporters at their desks by that time, ready to trawl through the data. The *Daily Mail* had even advertised for a team of students to help them out, while the *Guardian* invited its readers to help look through the files and point up anything of interest they noticed. The race was on to find anything the *Telegraph* had missed.

The bunker team were relatively confident that they had

not missed anything major, though there was a certain amount of apprehension as the day approached. Some of the best journalists in the business had, in the past, looked through books or documents which their newspapers had paid big money to set eyes on first, only to find when the material was put on general release that they had somehow missed the biggest story contained in them. The last thing any of the bunker reporters wanted was to be embarrassed by another newspaper finding a scoop buried in the expenses claims of one of the MPs they had ticked off the list weeks earlier.

As it turned out, they needn't have worried. As the reporters filed into the bunker at 7 a.m., each logged on to the Parliament's official website to look up the MPs they had been responsible for checking. Once they had done so, it wasn't fear which filled the room, but laughter.

'Every single page is almost entirely black,' Holly Watt said. 'They've made themselves look ridiculous. How could they have been so stupid!'

'Look at this,' said Jon Swaine, pointing at a sea of black ink on his computer screen with only a tiny letterbox-shaped rectangle of white in the middle. 'There's a phone bill here where they've blacked out everything except the total for the bill. You wouldn't even be able to tell it was a phone bill if you saw this.'

'They've taken out everything even vaguely interesting,' Rosa Prince added, gawping at the screen. 'We would hardly have got a single story out of this. The other papers are going to have a nightmare.'

It was abundantly clear that Parliament had learned nothing from the previous six weeks. An email from Lewis to Winnett at 7.52 a.m. summed it up: 'Cover up!'

As the investigations team trawled through the official files, they were amazed at just how much had been removed. The Firestorm disks, which contained the provisional re-dactions from the documents before they had been sent to the MPs for checking, had shown carefully drawn grey boxes over addresses, suppliers' names, bar codes, and a host of other details which had been deemed sensitive. But in the final versions great swathes of other information had been blacked out as well, leaving far more black than white on many of the pages.

Gone were the Ikea receipts submitted by the Prime Minister for his new kitchen. Nine pages from Gordon Brown's 2004/5 file had been removed altogether. The refer-ence to the Prime Minister's brother, to whom he had paid £6,500 towards the cost of a cleaner whose services they shared, had also been removed, as had the correspondence which revealed his dispute with the fees office over the 'Noah's animals' blind. Even the references to his claims for Sky TV, which had so enraged the TSO staff, had been expunged.

The most notorious expenses claims, including Douglas Hogg's letter about his moat and Sir Peter Viggers' duck island letter, had also been removed, as had Sir Gerald Kaufman's receipt for a rug from a New York antiques centre. Michael Martin, the Speaker, had blacked out the word 'chauffeur' from receipts he submitted. Although the name of the firm was included, the type of business had been inexplicably removed. Even the lawnmower maintenance bill submitted by Alan Duncan, the Shadow Leader of the Commons, was severely redacted, as was David Willetts's claim for having his light bulbs changed.

In fact, virtually none of the scams uncovered by the *Telegraph* would ever have come to light if there had not been a leak of the uncensored versions of the MPs' expenses. Because all the MPs' addresses had been removed, no one would have known about flipping, about phantom mortgages or about capital gains tax avoidance. The public would not have found out about MPs climbing the property ladder with the help of taxpayers' money, or how, like Jacqui Smith, they had claimed their 'second' home was their family residence while their 'main' home was someone's spare bedroom. Nor would we have been any the wiser about MPs who had given their children a helping hand by claiming for a property which was their children's main home, or by selling them a property at a discount. And Margaret Moran's £22,500 claim for dry rot at her house in Southampton would have seemed like essential maintenance at her constituency home.

Instead of providing newspapers with a batch of new revelations about MPs' expenses claims, the parliamentary authorities had given them a far better story by trying to pull off one of the biggest cover-ups in history.

For the *Telegraph*, it could hardly have been better. Where rival newspapers could only rage about the lack of information contained in the material released on the website, the *Telegraph* had the advantage of being able to show exactly what had been covered up by printing, side by side, original documents and the redacted versions.

Parliament's censorship had made a mockery of Gordon Brown's claim on 17 May, days after the first expenses stories were printed, that 'Transparency to the public is the foundation of properly policing this system.' One *Telegraph* reader, David Wright from Worcestershire, neatly commented that 'Gordon Brown is now so transparent I can see right through him.'

The public, predictably enough, were outraged at Parliament's pathetic attempt to pull the wool over their eyes and MPs themselves tried to distance themselves from the decision to redact so much material. David Cameron said: 'I think that people will be disappointed with the amount of information that is held back.' Vince Cable, the popular deputy leader of the Lib Dems, who had nothing to hide, said: 'The publication of the expenses in this format has only made people even more frustrated.'

As the day wore on, the blame game began. Some MPs tried to point the finger at parliamentary officials, saying they had asked for more information to be released, only for their requests to be rejected by Commons staff. Others said they were warned off publishing their own expenses in full, alleging that civil servants had told them they could face legal action under data protection legislation if they did so.

It was a farce. The following day's *Telegraph* devoted the entire front page to the story. 'Blackout: the great expenses cover-up' was the huge headline, with much of the front page taken up by one of Gordon Brown's phone bills, which had been so heavily censored that only his name and the amount owed were showing. Even the BT logo had been blacked out.

There was one more blunder to come on 18 June. In the afternoon, the House of Commons decided to publish a full list of all those MPs who had repaid money they had claimed on their expenses. In total, 183 MPs had repaid more than £470,000, mostly as a result of their claims being exposed in the *Telegraph*. The only problem was that the list was wrong. Not only did it 'name and shame' MPs who had not repaid any money at all, it also mysteriously included the name of someone who wasn't even an MP (and, as far as anyone could tell, didn't even exist). As a result the entire list had to be hastily withdrawn.

After six weeks of almost uninterrupted revelations about MPs' expenses, which Gordon Brown later described as 'the biggest parliamentary scandal for two centuries', 18 June marked the moment when the biggest gamble in the *Telegraph*'s history was finally vindicated beyond any doubt. In the weeks that followed, other stories would take over the headlines and the MPs would finally get the chance to draw breath by taking a long holiday during the summer recess. But they did so knowing that the public would not forget the extraordinary events of the summer of 2009, and knowing also that the issue would rear up again when they had to fight for their seats at the next general election.

As David Cameron put it in a speech to members of his party:

What the *Daily Telegraph* did – the simple act of providing information to the public – has triggered the biggest shake-up in our political system for years.

Information alone has been more powerful than years of traditional politics. Of course it has been a painful time for politics and for individual politicians – but let us be clear, it is without question a positive development for the country.

It is information – not a new law, not some regulation – just the provision of information that has enabled people to take on the political class, question them, demand answers, and get those answers. That's exactly as it should be.

Charges

June 2009 to April 2010

'This is your local MP . . .'

CHAPTER 25

THE PUBLICATION OF the censored expenses files by Parliament marked the moment when the *Telegraph's* marathon expenses investigation finally seemed to have run its course.

But one of the lessons the reporters had learned was that this had become a story they could no longer control, and over the next eight months the scandals and the resignations would just keep on coming.

By Monday 22 June, the Complete Expenses Files supplement had been published and the time had finally come for the bunker team to get back to their day jobs and leave the airless, cheerless room which had become their home from home.

That morning the team assembled for one last time, to clear up three months worth of mess, to take down the cuttings and pictures from the magnetic wall, and to shred anything at all which might be deemed sensitive.

'Has it really only been a few weeks?' asked Chris Hope as he heaved another pile of old newspapers into a recycling bin. 'I can hardly remember what life was like before we moved in here.'

Everyone in the room was having similar thoughts.

After the most intense and successful episode of their careers, the demobbed bunker reporters were all wondering just how long it would take to get their feet back on the ground.

The media industry rarely affords its employees time to wistfully look back on their past achievements, however. Every day brings new challenges and new stories, and editors are always more interested in your next story than your last one.

Nor is there any room for sentiment in a newspaper office. Within a few days the bunker was plain old Training Room 4 again, and at the start of 2010 its glass and steel walls were dismantled altogether so it could be absorbed by the marketing department as part of an office reorganization. Today there is nothing left to suggest it ever existed.

While most of the expenses team merely had to walk a few dozen steps from the bunker back to their normal desks in the newsroom, Robert Winnett had a rather more awkward transition to contemplate as he left the office and walked down Victoria towards the Houses of Parliament.

Thankful that his Commons pass had not been cancelled as a parting shot by the Speaker or one of his officers, Winnett managed to slip largely unnoticed through the panelled corridors leading to the press gallery. Many of the MPs who had proved the worst abusers of the expenses system had apparently gone into hiding and would not be seen until the autumn.

Journalists from rival newspapers were relieved to see Winnett return, as it signified that their nightmare few weeks of having to relentlessly follow up the *Telegraph*'s expenses stories had finally come to an end.

Rayner, meanwhile, quickly found himself back in the

swing of things when Michael Jackson died on 25 June. As he anchored the *Telegraph*'s coverage of the story from London, Nick Allen, the reporter who had found Sir Peter Viggers' claim for a duck house, flew to Los Angeles to cover the Jackson story on the ground.

For now, at least, it seemed that the expenses investigation was becoming old news.

But in a quiet room in an anonymous Westminster office block, a new episode in the expenses saga was only just beginning.

In May, at the height of the *Telegraph*'s revelations, the Commons authorities had drafted in a former civil servant called Sir Thomas Legg to carry out an independent audit of all MPs' expense claims over the preceding four years.

Sir Thomas had seemed a shrewd choice for the job. A former Royal Marine who had gone on to work in the Ministry of Justice, he had sat on various Parliamentary committees which had overseen parts of the expenses system.

Regarded as part of the establishment, he was seen by many MPs as a safe pair of hands who was unlikely to rock the boat too much. As the scandal unfolded, his involvement also gave members a convenient response when they defended their claims, as they could point to the fact that that they would all be scrutinized by Legg.

However, several Cabinet ministers who had previously come across Legg harboured concerns about the choice of the man appointed to lead the review and expressed their fears to Number 10. Having seen him at close quarters, they regarded him as a man who could not be pushed around, and who was well capable of causing trouble if he decided to. They were concerns which would later prove to be well-founded as Sir Thomas took to his new role with an unexpected vigour.

He began by drafting in a team of fifty-four people, including top accountants from PricewaterhouseCoopers and former government statisticians, and began the arduous task of trawling through each and every claim. Within a matter of days, if not weeks, Sir Thomas had come to the conclusion that hundreds of MPs had not just milked the system, they had broken the rules.

After studying the parliamentary Green Book, Sir Thomas pointed out to his staff that it quite clearly stated that claims were not to be excessive and must be entirely essential. So much for duck houses, plasma TVs and antique rugs, then.

One of his first, and most unpopular, decisions was to rule that dozens of the claims for cleaning and gardening were simply unjustifiable. He decided that any claim for more than £2,000 a year for cleaning and £1,000 for gardening was excessive and should be repaid. The introduction of the proportionate limits was a brave decision which led to many disgruntled MPs accusing him of unfairly moving the goalposts by introducing limits retrospectively.

Meanwhile, even cursory checks of the complicated Parliamentary forms by the team of accountants – who were used to dealing with far more straightforward expense claims in the private sector – found that many of the claims were simply wrong.

Electricity bills and invoices for repairs had been submitted and paid twice. Some MPs were claiming for both the capital and interest repayments on their mortgages, when the rules clearly stated that only interest could be reclaimed.

Others had so-called conflicted living arrangements in which they were paying money to relatives. The Legg team were shocked to discover that the MPs who had broken the rules as defined by Sir Thomas were in the majority.

Blissfully ignorant of the fresh scandal which was brewing in Sir Thomas's offices, many MPs were using the summer recess to get away from it all as they tried to put their most wretched spring behind them. Gordon Brown's wife Sarah forced him to take an extended break in the Lake District and Scotland, while David Cameron took his family to Cornwall, Brittany and Greece.

Alan Duncan, who had made some of the most notorious claims for the garden at his Rutland cottage, had his own unique way of trying to restore his public image by inviting a group of anti-expenses protestors to see him at the Commons.

One of them was Heydon Prowse, the leading light of an anarchic organization called Don't Panic, who had filmed himself planting a flower bed in the shape of a pound sign in Duncan's garden in May, as well as digging up a hidden treasure chest supposedly containing taxpayers' cash – in what became a huge hit on the internet.

For reasons best known to himself, Duncan decided to speak candidly with Prowse as he gave him a guided tour of the Commons, complaining that MPs were now treated like shit and forced to live on rations.

'I'm afraid the world has gone mad', the Tory MP concluded.

It was another catastrophic mistake by Duncan; inevitably Mr Prowse had secretly filmed the encounter and the recordings dominated the news for days. Duncan was soon sacked from the Conservative shadow cabinet by a furious David Cameron.

As MPs returned from their summer holidays and headed to the annual conferences, there was a clear need to confine the expenses scandal to the past and prepare for the forthcoming election with a flood of new policies and initiatives. At the Conservative conference in Manchester, MPs were banned from drinking champagne, for obvious reasons. One of the few MPs to defy the ban, and be pictured quaffing from a champagne flute, was the now infamous Alan Duncan.

In the bars and restaurants of the party conferences, MPs and ministers were confidently predicting that Legg would take well into 2010, possibly even after the election, to complete his audit. They were visibly relaxed at the thought of the extra time this afforded them before the scandal could rear its head again.

But they were very wrong. While the party conference season had been in full swing, Sir Thomas's team had been burning the midnight oil to enable them to present each and every MP with a letter when they returned to Parliament in the second week of October.

Each of the letters would set out his preliminary conclusions detailing how much he believed the individual MP should repay, or asking for more information to justify mortgage or other claims. A relatively small number of MPs were told their claims were acceptable.

On Friday, 9 October, just days before Parliament's return,

Downing Street got word that the Prime Minister was one of those to face a large repayment. Legg was to ask him to repay more than £12,000, one of the largest amounts of any MP. The repayment covered excessive cleaning bills and invoices for repairs which had been submitted twice. It was a major embarrassment for Brown, who had stridently defended his own claims during the first few days of the expenses scandal.

The following Monday, MPs waited for hours to receive their buff coloured A4 envelopes from Legg's team. The letters were to be delivered by hand to pigeonholes in the Members Lobby at the heart of Parliament, and politicians and their secretaries waited anxiously for them, mingling with tourists who had no idea of the drama surrounding them. Every time a new mail bag arrived there was a ripple of nervous excitement.

By mid-afternoon, a rumour was sweeping round that only those with surnames beginning with the letters A-C would receive their letters that day. Then there was word that all the letters were going out at 7p.m. Their nerves frayed, MPs told their secretaries they couldn't leave.

'The girls have been told to collect their envelopes, so they've been sitting there, not going to the loo, not drinking tea, not doing anything while they wait for the letters', one bemused Commons official said.

By the end of the day, more than three hundred MPs had received letters informing them that they were expected to make repayments which totalled more than £1 million. The expenses scandal was once again dominating the news.

Back at the *Telegraph*'s headquarters in Victoria, reporters had also received interesting information about several MPs and their expenses. Martin Beckford, Jon Swaine and Holly Watt were asked to trawl back through some of the newspaper's expenses files to check out the tip-offs that were being received.

David Wilshire, a controversial Conservative MP, was exposed for claiming more than £100,000 to pay a company he owned. He claimed the money under his office expenses at a rate of up to £3,250 a month.

When contacted by Swaine, Wilshire said the money was used to buy printing and other services he needed to function as an MP. He said he did not profit from the funds but it was not clear why he didn't simply buy the services directly and submit receipts for the work as other MPs do.

Within hours of the allegations being put to him, and following a frantic round of private meetings with senior Tory aides, it was announced that Wilshire would not be contesting the next election.

The case involving David Curry, another Conservative MP and former minister, was even more complicated. Curry had recently been made the new chairman of the Parliamentary Committee on Standards and Privileges, which disciplines MPs found to have broken the rules. His committee had been overwhelmed by complaints about MPs accused of breaking the expenses rules.

However, Rosa Prince learnt that a peculiar episode in Curry's personal life cast doubt on the validity of his second home expense claims.

Four years before the expenses scandal began, Curry had an affair with a local headmistress and used a cottage in his

Yorkshire constituency for his illicit meetings with the woman.

When the affair had been exposed, Curry and his wife temporarily separated. However, the pair were soon reconciled on the alleged agreement that Curry no longer stayed overnight in his Yorkshire property.

The *Telegraph* was informed that when he visited his constituency and needed to stay overnight, he checked in to the Skipton Travelodge hotel. However, he continued to claim for the cottage, an asset which had undoubtedly risen in value.

Holly Watt travelled to north Yorkshire to see what Curry was up to. Sure enough, she discovered him staying in the Skipton Travelodge on the evening of Thursday, 5 November. Watt arranged for a photographer to wait outside the hotel early the next morning to get a picture of him leaving.

'We've got him', Watt said when she phoned Winnett. 'Great,' he replied. 'Now go and talk to the neighbours.'

Householders living near Curry's taxpayer-funded second home told Watt they did not recall him staying there.

'I probably shouldn't say this but we never see him', said one close neighbour in the tiny North Yorkshire hamlet.

When confronted by the *Telegraph*, Curry insisted the cottage was his constituency home but said that he had been unable to stay there recently as much as he had in the past. He was unable to provide evidence showing when he had stayed there in recent years, much to the annoyance of Tory aides.

By early evening on the day before the story was published, Curry had announced that he was standing down as the head of the Standards Committee and referring himself to the committee for investigation.

The following day, his main home in Essex was besieged by reporters from other newspapers. He headed to Yorkshire, where he was happy to pose for the cameras preparing to stay overnight at his cottage.

His wife, Anne, said: 'It's his problem', when asked about the furore over his claims.

Curry joked: 'I'm not expecting to end up in the Tower of London', and said he had stayed at the property hundreds if not thousands of times.

Nor was the expenses scandal restricted to the House of Commons. Lord Hanningfield, a Tory peer, had claimed more than £100,000 for overnight allowances in London when it appeared he had been going home to Essex most of the time.

There were also new problems on the Government benches. Sion Simon, a Labour minister, was found to have been renting a flat from his sister, despite the practice being banned since April 2006.

In total, Simon claimed more than £40,000 in rent for the property in the exclusive Regent's Park area of central London. When asked about the claims, he apologized and said he had been unaware that the rules had changed. He announced he would repay more than £20,000, covering rental claims for the property since April 2006.

Within two months, he announced he would not be standing at the next general election.

By now dozens of MPs had announced they would not be contesting the next election, but for three MPs losing their job was the least of their worries.

Elliot Morley and David Chaytor were still the subject of

police investigations into their expense claims, and Scotland Yard had also begun taking an interest in the claims made by a third MP, Jim Devine.

Devine, the Labour MP for Livingston, was investigated over what appeared to be false invoices which he submitted to back up claims of almost £9,000 for cleaning and stationery during 2008 and 2009.

Lord Hanningfield and two other peers were also investigated by the police.

When they were questioned about their expense claims by detectives, both Morley and Chaytor declined to comment.

They said that the centuries-old convention of Parliamentary privilege meant that their cases were not a matter for the law courts but for Parliament. It was for Parliament to decide whether they had broken any rules, they said. The police chose to disagree.

On 23 November, the Metropolitan Police passed files on the MPs and the Lords claims to the Crown Prosecution Service, which would begin the lengthy process of deciding whether charges should be brought against any of the six.

In the meantime, the expenses story was about to be given a whole new impetus with the release of a whole new batch of MPs' expenses. Parliament had promised that it would, in future, publish MPs' expense claims once every quarter, and on 10 December the first such release would cover the 2008–09 financial year as well as the first three months of the 2009–10 financial year, information which was not contained on the leaked disk.

It meant a reunion for the bunker team (though not in

the late lamented bunker) and as the familiar faces arrived in the office shortly after breakfast they greeted each other like footballers returning for the first day of the season.

Only Nick Allen, now permanently based in Los Angeles for the *Telegraph*, was absent.

'I seem to remember it was Chris Hope's turn to get the teas in', said Rayner as Hope arrived. After a round of bad jokes, the reporters settled down at their computers in the newsroom and began what was likely to be a frantic day's work. This time the *Telegraph* had no advantage over other newspapers as these were unseen claims, meaning a race against every other media organization to uncover any outrageous claims.

It would also be the parliamentary authorities first opportunity to deliver on earlier promises that they would no longer censor the claim forms as blatantly as they had in June.

To the disappointment of the team, many of the pages were still covered by large black boxes, and it was still impossible to determine the addresses on which claims were being made.

It looked as though the main story the next day would be about how details were still being censored – and how MPs had virtually stopped claiming once the *Telegraph*'s disclosures had begun.

As the reporters gathered in the central hub of the newsroom shortly after 11a.m. to discuss with their news editors how the story would be divided up, the mood was distinctly downbeat.

This was nothing like the buzz and excitement of the

weeks in the bunker. But then Winnett's BlackBerry started vibrating urgently.

Grabbing it from his pocket, Winnett read the text message he had just received from a senior Conservative.

'Quentin Davies' claims might well be worth a look, have a look at page twelve', said the enigmatic text. Davies was a Labour minister who defected from the Tories in 2007 after Brown became Prime Minister and was therefore one of the most hated figures within Conservative circles.

The reporters hurried back to their desks and Rosa Prince quickly scrolled down to the page in question.

'Oh my God!' she shouted. 'Its a bell tower. He claimed for a bell tower.'

Watt quickly dug out Davies' details from the original *Telegraph* disk to get his address. After typing the name of his large country home into Google, she saw a picture of a stately home in Lincolnshire flash up on her screen.

'We've got another duck island!' Watt said as the reporters gathered around her computer. On one flank of Davies' country pile was what looked at first glance like a chimney, but which on closer inspection had an open arch part of the way down, and in the arch, a bell.

Davies, it seemed, had claimed for repairs to the bell tower, an appendage which few traditional Labour supporters have on their homes, and had subsequently withdrawn the claim in May 2009 after the expenses scandal first broke.

All of sudden, the *Telegraph* had its front-page story for the following day. Over a picture of the bell tower, the headline read: 'The last hurrah.'

All told, MPs had gone on a £10 million spending spree in the run up to the expenses system being exposed. Other claims disclosed in the new set of expenses included £16,000 spent on a new kitchen by disgraced former Treasury minister Kitty Ussher, and an £88,000 profit made by John Healey, the Housing Minister, on his taxpayer-funded second home.

While work was well underway to punish MPs for some of their past misdemeanours, the system for present and future expense claims had still not been fundamentally reformed. Despite the weeks of allegations, MPs were still free to claim mortgage interest, flip their claims between different properties, employ their wives and children and even go grocery shopping – all at the taxpayers' expense.

The man who had been given the job of ending the MPs' gravy train was Sir Christopher Kelly, another former civil servant, who summoned the country's media to a grand room overlooking the river Thames in the National Liberal Club on 4 November. The choice of location seemed overly grand for an announcement which would condemn MPs for their profligacy.

Sir Christopher's 144-page report proposed a root-and-branch overhaul of the entire system. He proposed that in future MPs could only rent second homes, not buy and claim mortgage interest at taxpayers' expense. All claims for food, cleaning, gardening, furniture and electronics would be banned. MPs would be forbidden from employing family members. In short, they would no longer be able to personally profit from the expenses system.

Many MPs were aghast at the scale of the proposed

reform. But the party leaders had little choice but to back the plan in full.

Brown said: 'People want to know that the system in future will be different. It will be open. It will be transparent. It will be fair. It will not be managed by MPs themselves but by an independent body that will take responsibility for it.

'That is why it is right to refer the Kelly report for action and implementation, not by ourselves, but by the Independent Parliamentary Standards Authority. That is the recommendation of the Kelly report and that is what we should do.'

Cameron also said it was important that the Kelly recommendations were accepted in full.

'By accepting this report, today should mark an important day, a day when we say that from now and into the future, MPs should not vote on our pay, our expenses, our pensions, our terms of service, our resettlement, or our expenses packages.

'Isn't that an essential part of restoring faith in Parliament, in politics and in this House of Commons, that all of us care about?'

Nick Clegg added: 'After a shameful year for this Parliament I agree that Sir Christopher Kelly's report finally gives us the opportunity to start restoring people's trust in the work of MPs here, and that is why it must be implemented in full without any further delay.'

Sir Christopher ended with a warning. He said: 'There is a risk that, as the impact of the revulsion caused by the *Daily*

Telegraph's revelations fades with time, some may be thinking of distancing themselves from their earlier expressed determination to implement our report in full. If so, that would, in my view, be an error. The damage that has been done by what has been revealed about past malpractice and about the culture that goes with it has been very considerable.

'I don't believe the trust in those who govern us will be restored unless those in authority show leadership and determination in putting the abuses of the past behind them, however uncomfortable that may be.'

As 2010 began, the expenses saga still hung over Parliament, with the twin threats from the Legg report and the police investigation still to be played out.

To the dismay of those MPs who had hoped the Legg report would be delayed until after the election, Sir Thomas announced that he would publish his findings in the first week of February.

Across 240 pages, the former mandarin detailed how he had ordered 390 MPs to repay just over £1.3 million. The biggest single repayment ordered was almost £65,000.

For the first time, the public was given a completely independent verdict on how MPs had behaved. The fact that well over half of MPs were deemed to have broken the rules was a fresh shock to an electorate which had, no doubt, been hoping that the scale of the MPs' greed had been exaggerated by the media.

If anything, Sir Thomas's verdict was even more damning than anything which had gone before.

'The saga of MPs' expenses and freedom of information has been traumatic and painful', Sir Thomas said. 'Public confidence has been damaged, and the scars will no doubt take time to heal.

'But there is a positive side. In responding, our national institutions, including a free press, an independent judiciary and – in the end – the executive government, political parties and above all the House of Commons itself, are showing that, when things do go wrong, we have together the will and the means to put matters right, heal and reform the systems and the culture, and move forward.'

Sir Thomas, however, proved to be simply the warm-up act for a far bigger bombshell which would be dropped the following day.

On 5 February Keir Starmer, the Director of Public Prosecutions, made a live televized announcement to disclose the Crown Prosecution Services decision in the cases of the three MPs and three Lords whose cases had been referred on by the police.

The decision had been an impeccably guarded secret; no newspapers or media organizations had received leaked information about whether anyone would be charged, so the *Telegraph* newsroom stood in silence to hear what he had to say.

Starmer's words drew gasps from the watching reporters; all three MPs were to be charged with multiple criminal offences. Lord Hanningfield would also face prosecution.

He said: 'In four cases, we have concluded that there is

sufficient evidence to bring criminal charges and that it is in the public interest to charge the individuals concerned. Accordingly, summonses in these cases have been obtained from the City of Westminster Magistrates Court and will now be served on the individuals in question.'

All four were to be charged with false accounting under section seventeen of the Theft Act 1968, which carries a maximum sentence of seven years' imprisonment.

Elliot Morley was accused of making mortgage claims of £30,000 'in excess of that to which he was entitled' and, for part of the period, when 'there was no longer a mortgage on that property'.

Chaytor was accused of 'dishonestly claiming' £1,950 for IT services and also claiming sums of £12,925 and £5,425 relating to rent on properties which he and his mother allegedly owned.

Devine was accused of 'dishonestly claiming' money for cleaning services and for stationery, using false invoices, and Lord Hanningfield was accused of dishonestly claiming 'for expenses to which he knew he was not entitled'.

All four said they would deny the allegations when they made their first court appearance on 11 March.

No date has yet been set for the men's trials, but a year after the *Telegraph*'s expenses investigation first began, the most dramatic twist in the tale may be yet to come.

Epilogue

March 2010

'*I think I'll push off
now as well . . .*'

ALMOST A YEAR after the start of the *Daily Telegraph*'s expenses investigation, it has brought about major changes in Parliament and altered forever the relationship between the governed and governing classes.

The 2010 general election will be remembered as the poll which led to the biggest clear out of incumbent MPs ever seen.

The new intake of MPs, from every political party, will have to re-establish the trust of the British public in the political class. Establishing MPs' worth and accountability will be a long and arduous process following the behaviour exposed in 2009.

The secretive ways of the House of Commons will have to be opened up to scrutiny in a new age of transparency. The gentleman's club aura of the hallowed buildings has been laid to rest as a result of the expenses scandal.

MPs were left in no doubt by the reaction to their behaviour that they are the servants of the people rather than a self-serving political elite which deigns to go to the country every four or five years.

The system of MPs expenses has already been reformed under duress from the voters. It is important that there is no back-sliding from the reforms and no chipping away at the new standards now falling into place which will prevent many of the previous abuses emerging and flourishing again.

Yet there have been worrying signs that MPs have not, so far, learned the art of humility in the face of the public backlash over their expenses. As the *Telegraph* said in June 2009 there is ample evidence that MPs still don't get it.

The resignation of Michael Martin as Speaker gave Parliament the chance to show that MPs of every party could put their tribal differences aside by choosing a candidate behind whom the entire House could unite. However, the more respected Parliamentarians – such as Frank Field, Sir George Young and Ann Widdecombe – were quickly passed over.

Instead, Labour used its parliamentary majority to elect John Bercow, not because he was whiter than white (he wasn't, having flipped his homes and avoided capital gains tax), not because he was universally popular (he was quite the reverse) but because Labour knew that installing John Bercow would infuriate the Tories who saw him as untrustworthy and suspected him of being a closet turncoat.

Unable to justify electing a third successive Labour Speaker (when tradition dictated they should alternate between parties) Labour MPs thought it a terrific wheeze to choose a Tory who was hated by his own party. In doing so, they dragged politics down to the level of the school play-ground and lowered themselves still further in the public's estimation.

A survey of MPs carried out in August 2009 by the

polling company BPRI also suggested that politicians have yet to accept responsibility for the expenses scandal. Asked who was most to blame for the erosion of the reputation of MPs, sixty-four per cent of them replied the press, while twenty per cent blamed the fees office. Only half said MPs themselves were to blame.

However, there are also encouraging signs that political parties are willing to change the way they do business. In August 2009, for example, the Conservatives experimented with a new way of selecting parliamentary candidates. Needing to find a replacement for Anthony 'you're-all-jealous' Steen when he steps down from his Totnes constituency, the Tories held a US-style primary, asking voters from all parties to choose a Conservative candidate who will go forward to fight the next election, rather than simply choosing a candidate from an internal short list. The winner, a local GP called Sarah Wollaston, beat two other candidates who, as local councillors, had previous experience of politics. By choosing a non-politician to fight for a parliamentary seat, the people of Totnes were reflecting a growing public desire to be represented by real people rather than political hacks. Similar contests have now been held to select Conservative candidates in several other seats and people from different walks of life who will add to the quality of political debate have been selected.

One undeniable achievement of the expenses story was that it got people talking about politics like never before, at a time when fewer and fewer people were engaging with the political process by using their right to vote.

As for the *Daily Telegraph* and the *Sunday Telegraph*, the expenses investigation led the front page of both titles for thirty-five consecutive days, an unprecedented record for a peacetime story. The success of the investigation, which helped to redefine the *Telegraph* titles in the eyes of the public, as well as selling more than a million extra newspapers, has led to something of a renaissance for investigative journalism, with newspaper editors more willing than at any time in the last decade to give their reporters the time and the resources to conduct complex research.

It also proved that news can still sell newspapers as well as drive online traffic. It was a brave decision to go with a story others in Fleet Street decided was too risky, but the decision was rewarded commercially and journalistically. The unique multi-media mixture of the story – combining paper, web and television – also demonstrated how big scoops are likely to be handled in the twenty-first century.

The ultimate praise for the *Telegraph*'s story came from rival journalists, many of whom privately told colleagues at the *Telegraph* that they didn't think their own newspapers would have been so even-handed, or prepared to cover every single MP, if they had got the disk. The traditional broadsheet format came into its own when displaying the questionable claims made by MPs. Industry experts described it as a triumph for design as well as journalism.

But what became of the moles who put their jobs on the line by leaking the material in the first place?

Throughout the *Telegraph*'s investigation, no-one at the

newspaper knew for certain where the leak had come from, or who had given the disk to John Wick.

It was only in early August 2009 that the authors of this book finally knew the source of the leak, and met one of those who had worked there and been involved in passing the disk to Wick.

The material in chapters two and three is based on interviews with the mole, who spoke to us on condition of anonymity and was pursued for months by the Parliamentary authorities.

So had it been worth it?

'I'm bloody glad we did it', he told us. 'There's no two ways about it. We saw what was happening, we saw that information, and you just couldn't keep that from people.

'Everyone in that room was of the same mind: this was our money and these were our employees, effectively, but no-one could hold them to account. Pretty much everyone working in that room was being paid a pittance to do their job. Meanwhile the MPs were being well paid and claiming a fortune on their expenses, yet what have they done for us in the last ten years?

'The people who were working on redacting the MPs' expenses were people who are proud to be British, and they were saddened by what they saw.

'Now that the *Daily Telegraph* has put this in the public domain, it has to bring about reform. That was why we leaked the information, because the British public deserves better.'

Appendix:
The Expenses Files

TOP TEN MOST
NOTORIOUS CLAIMS

1. **Elliot Morley** (Lab, Scunthorpe)
Elliot Morley claimed more than £16,000 for a mortgage
which had been paid off.

2. **David Chaytor** (Lab, Bury North)
David Chaytor was another MP who stands accused of
improperly claiming expenses for a property he owned outright, receiving almost £13,000 in all.

3. **Jim Devine** (Lab, Livingston)
Jim Devine is suspected of submitting false invoices to
claim £3,240 for cleaning services and £5,505 for stationery.

4. **Douglas Hogg** (Con, Sleaford and North Hykeham)
Douglas Hogg infamously included the £2,115 cost of
having his moat cleared in his expenses. The MP had come
to a special arrangement with the fees office under which
he provided a list of the costs of running his estate, which

were greatly in excess of the maximum second home allowance, and he was paid one twelfth of the maximum each month. The ten-page costs letter included the moat, piano tuning, £18,000 a year for a full-time gardener, £671 for a mole-catcher and around £200 a year for maintenance of an Aga oven.

5. **Margaret Moran** (Lab, Luton South)

Margaret Moran renovated three properties at the tax-payers' expense – including a £22,500 course of dry rot treatment at a seaside house a hundred miles from her constituency – by repeatedly 'flipping' her second home designation.

6. **Julie Kirkbride** (Con, Bromsgrove) and **Andrew MacKay** (Con, Bracknell)

As married MPs, Andrew MacKay and Julie Kirkbride were both entitled to claim additional costs allowance. However, the couple chose to designate different properties as their second homes. In 2007–08 Mr MacKay claimed £11,968 on a flat in Westminster. During the same period his wife claimed £13,377 on a flat in her constituency.

7. **Ben Chapman** (Lab, Wirral South)

Ben Chapman claimed about £15,000 of expenses for interest on part of his mortgage he had already repaid – but unlike other claimants for 'phantom mortgages' – he did so with permission from an official in the Commons fees office. He had complained that 'by paying off capital I am forgoing interest and investment opportunities elsewhere'.

8. **Sir Peter Viggers** (Con, Gosport)

Sir Peter became famous for trying to make perhaps the most ridiculous claim of all – that of £1,645 for a floating house for ducks on his pond. The 'Stockholm' duck house was based on the design of an eighteenth century building in Sweden and was almost 5ft tall. Sir Peter's claim was rejected by the fees office. He had however been paid more than £30,000 of taxpayers' money over a three-year period for 'gardening', including the cost of twenty-eight tons of manure.

9. **Shahid Malik** (Lab, Dewsbury)

The former justice minister has claimed the maximum available in second home expenses for his house in South London, despite having quite a modest mortgage. He owns his 'second' home in London, but rents his 'main' home in his constituency.

10. **Bill Wiggin** (Con, Leominster)

The opposition whip had formerly designated his second home as a house in Fulham, West London, worth at least £900,000. In April 2004 he and his wife spent £480,000 on a constituency property near Ledbury, Herefordshire. He changed his second home designation to the new property and began claiming mortgage interest payments totalling £11,514. But the couple owned the property outright. In December 2007 the fees office asked him about his living arrangements and he was allowed to change his second home designation back to his London house 'retrospectively'.

SOME OF THE
MORE LUDICROUS CLAIMS

Peter Ainsworth (Con, Surrey East)
Peter Ainsworth's claim for a £957 'pewter finish' radiator cover was rejected by the fees office.

Mark Hoban (Con, Fareham)
£35 on a toilet-roll holder, £100 for a shower rack, £79 for four silk cushions and £18 for a lavatory brush. He said: 'At the time, I believed these claims were within the spirit of the rules'.

David Jones (Con, Clwyd West)
£119 for a Corby trouser press.

Sir Gerald Kaufman (Lab, Manchester Gorton)
Claimed £8,865 for a Bang & Olufsen television. The claim was rejected, but the fees office did pay him £750 – the maximum allowable for a television under the second homes allowance.

George Howarth (Lab, Knowsley North and Sefton East)
Tried to claim £999 for a chest of drawers in his second home, telling the fees office that it was the only one that 'matched' the rest of his furniture.

David Wilshire (Con, Spelthorne)
Claimed a total of £6,000 towards redecorating his second home at some point in the future. He arranged to claim £66.66 a month for the 'share of renewal of carpets/curtains every ten years'.

Rosie Winterton (Lab, Doncaster Central)
Tried to claim for 'soundproofing' the bedroom of her London home. The £890 bill was rejected by the fees office.

Mike Penning (Con, Hemel Hempstead)
Claimed £2.99 for a stainless steel dog bowl. He told the *Daily Telegraph*: 'This was claimed for mistakenly, for which I apologize sincerely and will pay back.'

Natascha Engel (Lab, Derbyshire North East)
Claimed £117.50 for ten copies of a DVD of her maiden speech to Parliament. She has since said she will pay the money back.

Fraser Kemp (Lab, Houghton & Washington East)
Claimed for sixteen bed sheets in less than two months.

Austin Mitchell (Lab, Great Grimsby)
Claims included 67p for Ginger Crinkle biscuits and 68p for a jar of Branston Pickle.

Tim Yeo (Con, South Suffolk)
Claimed £905.95 for a pink Sony Vaio laptop in November 2007. When his claim was disclosed Mr Yeo responded: 'A laptop is a laptop whatever colour it is. This is a trivial point.'

Peter Luff (Con, Mid Worcestershire)
Claimed £17,000 on his parliamentary expenses for furniture, linen and electrical goods over four years. This included three lavatory seats, three food mixers, two microwaves and ten sets of bed linen.

Andrew Smith (Lab, Oxford East)
Claimed a 50p carrier bag from Ikea as part of the £34,000 of expenses he used to renovate his house.

Charles Kennedy (Lib Dem, Ross, Skye & Lochaber)
Claimed back £35.75 spent in the House of Commons gift shop on three boxes of mints and two cuddly toys.

David Heathcoat-Amory (Con, Wells)
Between 2004 and 2007 claimed a total of £388.80 for horse manure for the garden of his second home.

John Gummer (Con, Suffolk Coastal)
The tax payer was billed more than £100 a year to remove moles from John Gummer's estate, as part of more than £9,000 a year for gardening.

The Saints

The twenty-nine MPs who made no expenses claims

Adam Afriyie (Con, Windsor)
Lives twenty-seven miles from Westminster and has never made a claim under the additional costs allowance for a second home, commuting every day instead.

Richard Benyon (Con, Newbury)
A former soldier, Richard Benyon has not made a single claim since 2006.

Tom Brake (Lib Dem, Carshalton & Wallington)
An MP since 1997, Tom Brake chose not to claim any money under the second home allowance. In 2005 he complained about excessive mileage claims submitted by some MPs.

David Burrowes (Con, Enfield Southgate)
An outer London MP who could have claimed more than £23,000 in second home allowances, but chose not to. Instead he called for its abolition for outer London MPs.

Paul Burstow (Lib Dem, Sutton & Cheam)

Outer London Lib Dem chief whip who chose not to claim the second home allowance he was entitled to.

Vince Cable (Lib Dem, Twickenham)
The Liberal Democrat Treasury spokesman chooses not to claim the second home allowance for his outer London constituency, instead commuting by train to Westminster.

Ed Davey (Lib Dem, Kingston & Surbiton)
One of seven Lib Dem MPs representing outer London who chose not to claim second home allowance.

Iain Duncan Smith (Con, Chingford & Woodford Green)
The former Conservative leader stopped claiming additional costs allowance in 2007. Prior to this his ACA claims totalled £2,949, making him one of the lowest claiming MPs.

Philip Dunne (Con, Ludlow)
Philip Dunne, one of the co-founders of Ottaker's bookshops, has claimed nothing at all under the additional costs allowance since he was elected in 2005.

David Evennett (Con, Bexleyheath & Crayford)
The former schoolmaster and insurance broker chose not to claim second home allowance for his outer London constituency.

Lynne Featherstone (Lib Dem, Hornsey & Wood Green)
Along with other Lib Dem outer London MPs, Lynne Featherstone chose not to claim any additional cost allowances, and instead commuted from her constituency home.

Neil Gerrard (Lab, Walthamstow)
Oxford-educated MP who chose not to claim second home allowance.

Stephen Hammond (Con, Wimbledon)
Stephen Hammond has never claimed additional cost allowances since he became an MP in 2005.

David Howarth (Lib Dem, Cambridge)
Despite living sixty miles from Parliament, David Howarth has not made any second home allowance claims, and insists on commuting from his constituency home every night.

Nick Hurd (Con, Ruislip-Northwood)
Although Nick Hurd has a second property in his constituency, he does not claim an allowance for it. He says that as he does not live there, he feels he should not charge the taxpayer for it.

Susan Kramer (Lib Dem, Richmond Park)
Susan Kramer did not claim the additional cost allowance she was entitled to, and was one of the MPs who championed the abolition of the second home allowance for all MPs living in Greater London.

Siobhain McDonagh (Lab, Mitcham & Morden)
Does not claim any money under the second homes allowance, and writes on her website 'I do not claim anything at all for my mortgage, property maintenance, furniture or food. I pay all these myself'.

John McDonnell (Lab, Hayes & Harlington)
As MP for a constituency on the edge of London, John
McDonnell could claim for a second home but chooses not to.

Anne Milton (Con, Guildford)
Although her constituency residence in Surrey is more than
thirty miles from Westminster, Anne Milton does not claim
money under the second homes allowance.

Stephen Pound (Lab, Ealing North)
As an outer London MP, he could have claimed for the
second home allowance but chose not to.

John Randall (Con, Uxbridge)
John Randall is another outer London MP who was entitled to a second home allowance but decided not to claim
or buy a second property.

Geoffrey Robinson (Lab, Coventry North West)
Millionaire Geoffrey Robinson has more than one property
but does not charge the taxpayer for their upkeep.

Martin Salter (Lab, Reading West)
The MP refuses to have a second home in London despite
living fifty miles from Westminster.

Lee Scott (Con, Ilford North)
Outer London MP who has claimed nothing on his second
home allowance even though he is entitled to do so.

Virendra Kumar Sharma (Lab, Ealing Southall)
A former bus conductor, this MP chose not to claim any

second home allowances, even though he was entitled to
do so.

Sarah Teather (Lib Dem, Brent East)
Since she was elected in 2003, Sarah Teather has claimed
nothing for second home allowances, and nothing for
travel expenses.

Stephen Timms (Lab, East Ham)
As an outer London MP, Stephen Timms was entitled to
claim a second home allowance but chose not to.

Malcolm Wicks (Lab, Croydon North)
Another outer London MP who decided not to claim for
the £23,000 he was entitled to in second homes allowance,
instead commuting from his constituency home.

Rob Wilson (Con, Reading East)
With a constituency home forty-five miles from
Westminster, Rob Wilson opted to commute to London
every day rather than claim for a second home. He says 'I've
always preferred to commute so that I can take my children
to school in the morning'.

The Claims MPs were told to repay

Name	Constituency	Party	Repayment	Appeal?	Reduction on appeal
Bernard Jenkin	North Essex	Con	£63,250.00	Yes	£27,000
Barbara Follett	Stevenage	Lab	£42,458.21	No	
Peter Lilley	Hitchin and Harpenden	Con	£41,057.36	Yes	£41,057.36
Julie Kirkbride	Bromsgrove	Con	£31,827.26	Yes	£2,584.26
Andrew MacKay	Bracknell	Con	£31,193.00	Yes	£0
David Heathcoat-Amory	Wells	Con	£29,691.93	No	
John Gummer	Suffolk Coastal	Con	£29,398.46	No	
Liam Fox	Woodspring	Con	£24,878.27	No	
Douglas Hogg	Sleaford and North Hykeham	Con	£20,639.42	Yes	£0
Alun Michael	Cardiff South and Penarth	Lab	£19,169.56	No	
Ann Cryer	Keighley	Lab	£18,241.70	Yes	£16,646.45
Jeremy Browne	Taunton	Lib	£17,894.24	Yes	£17,894.24
Jonathan Djanogly	Huntingdon	Con	£17,364.76	No	
William Cash	Stone	Con	£15,269.33	Yes	£14,840
Michael Spicer	West Worcestershire	Con	£15,109.37	Yes	£0
James Arbuthnot	North East Hampshire	Con	£13,470.33	No	
Peter Viggers	Gosport	Con	£13,464.30	Yes	£218.50
David Clelland	Tyne Bridge	Lab	£13,401.36	Yes	£13,101.36
Wayne David	Caerphilly	Lab	£12,959.69	No	
Gordon Brown	Kirkcaldy and Cowdenbeath	Lab	£12,888.03	No	
Mike Hall	Weaver Vale	Lab	£12,639.28	Yes	£0
Tony Baldry	Banbury	Con	£12,197.36	No	
Paul Clark	Gillingham	Lab	£11,915.30	No	
Alan Meale	Mansfield	Lab	£11,859.47	No	
Sir Alan Haselhurst	Saffron Walden	Con	£11,679.81	No	
Alan Milburn	Darlington	Lab	£11,600.50	No	
Anthony Steen	Totnes	Con	£11,211.75	Yes	£0
Austin Mitchell	Great Grimsby	Lab	£10,627.07	No	
Rosie Winterton	Doncaster Central	Lab	£9,972.35	No	
Fabian Hamilton	Leeds North East	Lab	£9,734.74	Yes	£3,186.59
Colin Challen	Morley and Rothwell	Lab	£9,158.00	Yes	£8,795.00
John Baron	Billericay	Con	£8,821.10	Yes	£0
Eric Joyce	Falkirk	Lab	£8,602.56	No	

Name	Constituency	Party	Repayment	Appeal?	Reduction on appeal
Michael Howard	Folkestone and Hythe	Con	£7,039.00	Yes	£0
Mark Hendrick	Preston	Lab	£6,885.70	No	
Neil Turner	Wigan	Lab	£6,786.08	No	
Edward Leigh	Gainsborough	Con	£6,725.94	Yes	£3,613.94
Gillian Merron	Lincoln	Lab	£6,305.17	No	
Michael Ancram	Devizes	Con	£6,282.43	Yes	£0
Andrew Murrison	Westbury	Con	£5,525.64	No	
Charlotte Atkins	Staffordshire Moorlands	Lab	£5,434.06	No	
James Hood	Lanark and Hamilton East	Lab	£5,413.49	No	
Philip Willis	Harrogate & Knaresborough	Lib	£5,363.74	No	
Edward O'Hara	Knowsley South	Lab	£5,244.23	No	
Owen Paterson	North Shropshire	Con	£5,229.15	No	
Michael Connarty	Linlithgow and East Falkirk	Lab	£5,181.56	No	
Andrew Lansley	South Cambridgeshire	Con	£5,162.68	No	
David Willetts	Havant	Con	£5,133.32	No	
Joan Ryan	Enfield North	Lab	£5,121.74	No	
Michael Lord	Central Suffolk and North Ipswich	Con	£5,074.48	No	
Marsha Singh	Bradford West	Lab	£5,026.84	No	
Frank Field	Birkenhead	Lab	£4,587.99	Yes	£428.55
Bob Russell	Colchester	Lib	£4,539.45	No	
Gerald Kaufman	Manchester Gorton	Lab	£4,533.69	Yes	£0
Alan Simpson	Nottingham South	Lab	£4,515.89	No	
Ann Clwyd	Cynon Valley	Lab	£4,472.42	Yes	£2,360.62
William McCrea	South Antrim	DUP	£4,450.95	No	
Chris Bryant	Rhondda	Lab	£4,439.28	No	
Des Turner	Brighton Kemptown	Lab	£4,407.66	No	
Phil Hope	Corby	Lab	£4,365.65	No	
Andrew George	St Ives	Lib	£4,348.25	No	
Don Foster	Bath	Lib	£4,275.74	No	
Stephen Hesford	Wirral West	Lab	£4,256.91	No	
Christine Russell	City of Chester	Lab	£4,127.53	No	
Mark Prisk	Hertford & Stortford	Con	£4,125.08	No	
Nia Griffith	Llanelli	Lab	£4,099.77	No	
Margaret Moran	Luton South	Lab	£4,059.86	No	
Patrick McLoughlin	West Derbyshire	Con	£4,058.54	No	
Nigel Griffiths	Edinburgh South	Lab	£4,005.84	No	

Name	Constituency	Party	Repayment	Appeal?	Reduction on appeal
Robert Wareing	Liverpool West Derby	Ind	£3,892.00	Yes	£215.86
Paul Goodman	Wycombe	Con	£3,881.07	Yes	£3,881.07
Robert Blizzard	Waveney	Lab	£3,872.79	No	
Edward McGrady	South Down	SDLP	£3,854.00	No	
Gregory Campbell	East Londonderry	DUP	£3,673.38	No	
Colin Breed	South East Cornwall	Lib	£3,639.49	No	
Derek Wyatt	Sittingbourne & Sheppey	Lab	£3,611.50	Yes	£0
Phil Woolas	Oldham East & Saddleworth	Lab	£3,530.86	Yes	£2,644.70
Jim Knight	South Dorset	Lab	£3,451.67	No	
Ben Chapman	Wirral South	Lab	£3,387.91	No	
Patrick Mercer	Newark	Con	£3,372.57	No	
Graham Allen	Nottingham North	Lab	£3,341.74	No	
Andrew Gwynne	Denton and Reddish	Lab	£3,327.56	No	
Simon Burns	Chelmsford West	Con	£3,305.76	No	
Richard Shepherd	Aldridge-Brownhills	Con	£3,191.88	Yes	£0
Clare Short	Birmingham Ladywood	Ind	£3,187.94	No	
George Galloway	Bethnal Green and Bow	Res	£3,187.28	No	
Richard Younger-Ross	Teignbridge	Lib	£3,181.09	No	
Crispin Blunt	Reigate	Con	£3,077.42	No	
Gary Streeter	South West Devon	Con	£3,074.38	No	
Rosemary McKenna	Cumbernauld, Kilsyth and Kirkintilloch East	Lab	£3,008.93	No	
Martin McGuinness	Mid Ulster	SF	£3,000.00	No	
Linda Gilroy	Plymouth Sutton	Lab	£2,979.33	Yes	£1,842.45
John W Robertson	Glasgow North West	Lab	£2,975.00	No	
James Plaskitt	Warwick & Leamington	Lab	£2,958.09	No	
Anne Moffat	East Lothian	Lab	£2,873.53	No	
Andy Burnham	Leigh	Lab	£2,841.19	No	
Mark Oaten	Winchester	Lib	£2,826.94	No	
Gerry Sutcliffe	Bradford South	Lab	£2,786.14	No	
David Cairns	Inverclyde	Lab	£2,782.30	No	
Bill Rammell	Harlow	Lab	£2,782.24	No	
John Reid	Airdrie & Shotts	Lab	£2,731.88	No	
Tony Cunningham	Workington	Lab	£2,718.02	No	

Name	Constituency	Party	Repayment	Appeal?	Reduction on appeal
Mike Hancock	Portsmouth South	Lib	£2,674.26	No	
Andrew Mitchell	Sutton Coldfield	Con	£2,673.33	No	
Bill Olner	Nuneaton	Lab	£2,660.43	No	
Paul Flynn	Newport West	Lab	£2,625.61	No	
David Jones	Clwyd West	Con	£2,624.00	No	
Gordon Prentice	Pendle	Lab	£2,620.95	No	
Sandra Osborne	Ayr, Carrick and Cumnock	Lab	£2,612.12	No	
David Hamilton	Midlothian	Lab	£2,595.51	No	
William Rennie	Dunfermline & West Fife	Lib	£2,573.10	No	
Jane Kennedy	Liverpool Wavertree	Lab	£2,569.83	No	
Mark Tami	Alyn & Deeside	Lab	£2,557.69	No	
Margaret Beckett	Derby South	Lab	£2,539.75	No	
Ian Liddell-Grainger	Bridgwater	Con	£2,496.23	Yes	£2,146.23
Richard Ottaway	Croydon South	Con	£2,484.47	No	
Paul Murphy	Torfaen	Lab	£2,480.72	No	
Roger Gale	North Thanet	Con	£2,452.47	Yes	£2,452.47
Ivan Lewis	Bury South	Lab	£2,449.15	No	
Alison Seabeck	Plymouth Devonport	Lab	£2,406.65	Yes	£0
Caroline Spelman	Meriden	Con	£2,401.51	No	
John Butterfill	Bournemouth West	Con	£2,364.13	No	
John Healey	Wentworth	Lab	£2,354.35	No	
Stephen Hepburn	Jarrow	Lab	£2,321.44	No	
Greg Knight	Yorkshire East	Con	£2,259.99	No	
Roger Godsiff	Birmingham Sparkbrook and Small Heath	Lab	£2,224.30	No	
Tony Lloyd	Manchester Central	Lab	£2,210.00	No	
Parmjit Dhanda	Gloucester	Lab	£2,208.28	No	
Linda Riordan	Halifax	Lab	£2,171.81	No	
Peter Luff	Mid Worcestershire	Con	£2,170.34	No	
Douglas Carswell	Harwich	Con	£2,159.00	No	
Damian Green	Ashford	Con	£2,102.14	No	
Bob Spink	Castle Point	Ind	£2,051.38	No	
Patrick Cormack	South Staffordshire	Con	£2,022.00	Yes	£0
David Davies	Monmouth	Con	£2,021.39	No	
Huw Irranca-Davies	Ogmore	Lab	£2,008.19	No	
Michael Fallon	Sevenoaks	Con	£2,000.00	No	
Iris Robinson	Strangford	DUP	£1,974.89	No	
Joan Walley	Stoke-on-Trent North	Lab	£1,967.11	No	

Name	Constituency	Party	Repayment	Appeal?	Reduction on appeal
Kali Mountford	Colne Valley	Lab	£1,965.79	Yes	£0
Natascha Engel	North East Derbyshire	Lab	£1,934.25	No	
Ronnie Campbell	Blyth Valley	Lab	£1,892.79	No	
Cheryl Gillan	Chesham and Amersham	Con	£1,884.23	No	
Jeffrey Donaldson	Lagan Valley	DUP	£1,858.73	No	
Denis Murphy	Wansbeck	Lab	£1,841.84	No	
Alan Beith	Berwick-upon-Tweed	Lib	£1,841.23	Yes	£1,841.23
James Gray	North Wiltshire	Con	£1,742.91	Yes	£1,418.07
Dan Norris	Wansdyke	Lab	£1,730.19	Yes	£0
Alan Whitehead	Southampton Test	Lab	£1,723.28	No	
Ruth Kelly	Bolton West	Lab	£1,707.34	No	
David Curry	Skipton and Ripon	Con	£1,676.48	No	
Frank Cook	Stockton North	Lab	£1,652.71	Yes	£633.41
Stephen Crabb	Preseli Pembrokeshire	Con	£1,639.30	No	
Andrew Tyrie	Chichester	Con	£1,638.99	No	
Peter Wishart	Perth & North Perthshire	SNP	£1,632.50	No	
Annette Brooke	Mid Dorset & Poole North	Lib	£1,538.78	No	
Stephen Dorrell	Charnwood	Con	£1,530.16	No	
Christine McCafferty	Calder Valley	Lab	£1,529.81	Yes	£0
Robert Ainsworth	Coventry North East	Lab	£1,526.50	No	
Keith Vaz	Leicester East	Lab	£1,514.00	No	
Denis MacShane	Rotherham	Lab	£1,507.73	Yes	£0
Menzies Campbell	North East Fife	Lib	£1,490.66	No	
David Simpson	Upper Bann	DUP	£1,482.98	No	
Shaun Woodward	St Helens South	Lab	£1,470.15	No	
Jacqui Smith	Redditch	Lab	£1,469.87	No	
Angela E Smith	Basildon	Lab	£1,428.81	No	
Michael Jack	Fylde	Con	£1,427.74	No	
Louise Ellman	Liverpool Riverside	Lab	£1,410.15	No	
Michael Wood	Batley & Spen	Lab	£1,399.83	No	
Anne Main	St Albans	Con	£1,388.59	No	
Ann Coffey	Stockport	Lab	£1,381.08	No	
Yvette Cooper	Pontefract and Castleford	Lab	£1,363.21	No	
Ed Balls	Normanton	Lab	£1,363.17	No	

Name	Constituency	Party	Repayment	Appeal?	Reduction on appeal
Alan Duncan	Rutland and Melton	Con	£1,356.67	No	
Paul Beresford	Mole Valley	Con	£1,352.02	No	
Nicholas Soames	Mid Sussex	Con	£1,345.55	No	
Kenneth Clarke	Rushcliffe	Con	£1,345.00	No	
Shahid Malik	Dewsbury	Lab	£1,340.56	No	
Humfrey Malins	Woking	Con	£1,329.22	No	
Nadine V Dorries	Mid Bedfordshire	Con	£1,314.37	No	
David Mundell	Dumfriesshire, Clydesdale and Tweeddale	Con	£1,300.00	No	
Christopher Mullin	Sunderland South	Lab	£1,298.99	Yes	£899.00
Adam Holloway	Gravesham	Con	£1,283.73	No	
Vera Baird	Redcar	Lab	£1,279.23	Yes	£1,279.23
Kitty Ussher	Burnley	Lab	£1,271.65	Yes	£0
John Denham	Southampton Itchen	Lab	£1,265.51	No	
Ian Davidson	Glasgow South West	Lab	£1,241.39	Yes	£474.47
Roger Berry	Kingswood	Lab	£1,237.77	No	
Edward Garnier	Harborough	Con	£1,221.68	No	
Angus Robertson	Moray	SNP	£1,217.00	No	
Robert Flello	Stoke-on-Trent South	Lab	£1,200.00	Yes	£1,200.00
Elfyn Llwyd	Meirionnydd Nant Conwy	PC	£1,194.60	No	
Tom Levitt	High Peak	Lab	£1,189.95	No	
Ian Paisley	North Antrim	DUP	£1,181.94	No	
Timothy Paul Loughton	East Worthing and Shoreham	Con	£1,178.88	No	
Gerald Howarth	Aldershot	Con	£1,178.00	Yes	£0
Gareth R Thomas	Harrow West	Lab	£1,158.52	No	
Rob Marris	Wolverhampton South West	Lab	£1,153.98	No	
Christopher Huhne	Eastleigh	Lib	£1,152.05	No	
Geoffrey Hoon	Ashfield	Lab	£1,151.42	No	
Russell Brown	Dumfries and Galloway	Lab	£1,146.63	No	
Gordon Marsden	Blackpool South	Lab	£1,135.40	Yes	£1,135.40
Stephen Byers	North Tyneside	Lab	£1,125.00	No	
Philip Hollobone	Kettering	Con	£1,115.83	No	
Sian James	Swansea East	Lab	£1,105.64	No	
David Amess	Southend West	Con	£1,100.06	No	
Lorely Burt	Solihull	Lib	£1,087.50	No	

Name	Constituency	Party	Repayment	Appeal?	Reduction on appeal
Ben Wallace	Lancaster & Wyre	Con	£1,079.99	No	
Paul Goggins	Wythenshawe and Sale East	Lab	£1,075.93	No	
Julian Lewis	New Forest East	Con	£1,068.85	Yes	£0
Lembit Opik	Montgomeryshire	Lib	£1,064.42	Yes	£909.42
Jacqui Lait	Beckenham	Con	£1,041.59	Yes	£0
Michael Wills	North Swindon	Lab	£1,015.80	No	
Mary Creagh	Wakefield	Lab	£1,001.22	No	
Kenneth Purchase	Wolverhampton North East	Lab	£1,000.12	No	
Nick Herbert	Arundel and South Downs	Con	£988.95	No	
Albert Owen	Ynys Môn	Lab	£983.57	No	
John Bercow	Buckingham	Con	£978.51	No	
Kim Howells	Pontypridd	Lab	£953.11	No	
Anne McIntosh	Vale of York	Con	£948.00	No	
Ian Pearson	Dudley South	Lab	£941.46	No	
Tobias Ellwood	Bournemouth East	Con	£940.98	No	
Harry Cohen	Leyton and Wanstead	Lab	£933.38	No	
Mark Pritchard	The Wrekin	Con	£923.62	No	
Nick Clegg	Sheffield Hallam	Lib	£910.00	No	
Andy Reed	Loughborough	Lab	£891.48	No	
David Davis	Haltemprice and Howden	Con	£883.71	No	
Nigel Evans	Ribble Valley	Con	£858.33	No	
Nicholas Winterton	Macclesfield	Con	£850.81	No	
Claire Ward	Watford	Lab	£850.00	Yes	£850.00
Helen Jones	Warrington North	Lab	£840.05	No	
Julie Morgan	Cardiff North	Lab	£838.94	No	
Robert Walter	North Dorset	Con	£829.32	No	
Lynne Jones	Birmingham Selly Oak	Lab	£815.00	Yes	£0
David Miliband	South Shields	Lab	£808.34	No	
Iain Wright	Hartlepool	Lab	£805.97	No	
Andrew MacKinlay	Thurrock	Lab	£792.34	No	
Hugo Swire	East Devon	Con	£788.00	No	
Katy Clark	North Ayrshire and Arran	Lab	£782.89	No	
Nicolas Gibb	Bognor Regis and Littlehampton	Con	£780.83	No	
Nick Ainger	Carmarthen West and South Pembrokeshire	Lab	£777.70	No	

Name	Constituency	Party	Repayment	Appeal?	Reduction on appeal
Jeremy Wright	Rugby & Kenilworth	Con	£769.50	Yes	£769.50
Betty Williams	Conwy	Lab	£750.25	No	
Charles Clarke	Norwich South	Lab	£743.64	Yes	£743.64
Andrew Love	Edmonton	Lab	£736.70	No	
Dari Taylor	Stockton South	Lab	£719.06	No	
Graham Brady	Altrincham and Sale West	Con	£715.00	Yes	£0
Nicholas Brown	Newcastle upon Tyne East and Wallsend	Lab	£697.65	No	
Adrian Sanders	Torbay	Lib	£691.00	No	
John Smith	Vale of Glamorgan	Lab	£683.78	No	
Andrew Turner	Isle of Wight	Con	£681.60	No	
Quentin Davies	Grantham and Stamford	Lab	£658.00	No	
Gwyn Prosser	Dover	Lab	£650.00	No	
Celia Barlow	Hove	Lab	£635.00	No	
Malcolm Bruce	Gordon	Lib	£622.00	No	
Hywel Francis	Aberavon	Lab	£618.05	No	
Oliver Letwin	West Dorset	Con	£613.70	No	
William Hague	Richmond (Yorkshire)	Con	£601.14	No	
Jack Straw	Blackburn	Lab	£600.00	No	
Madeleine Moon	Bridgend	Lab	£599.25	No	
Jim Murphy	East Renfrewshire	Lab	£577.46	No	
Caroline Flint	Don Valley	Lab	£572.00	No	
John Hutton	Barrow and Furness	Lab	£568.09	No	
Barry Sheerman	Huddersfield	Lab	£557.21	No	
Alistair Darling	Edinburgh South West	Lab	£554.00	No	
Dennis Skinner	Bolsover	Lab	£550.76	No	
Dai Davies	Blaenau Gwent	Ind	£549.80	Yes	£439.80
John Thurso	Caithness, Sutherland and Easter Ross	Lib	£548.21	No	
Frank Roy	Motherwell & Wishaw	Lab	£545.79	Yes	£545.79
Ann Winterton	Congleton	Con	£544.42	No	
Khalid Mahmood	Birmingham Perry Barr	Lab	£544.21	No	
John Greenway	Ryedale	Con	£537.47	Yes	£0
Jon Cruddas	Dagenham	Lab	£535.36	No	
Robert Key	Salisbury	Con	£530.00	No	
Michael Jabez Foster	Hastings and Rye	Lab	£515.76	No	
Richard Spring	West Suffolk	Con	£510.00	No	
Brian Jenkins	Tamworth	Lab	£484.85	No	
James P Duddridge	Rochford and Southend East	Con	£480.98	No	

Name	Constituency	Party	Repayment	Appeal?	Reduction on appeal
Alistair Carmichael	Orkney and Shetland	Lib	£480.78	No	
Ed Vaizey	Wantage	Con	£463.42	Yes	£0
Richard Burden	Birmingham Northfield	Lab	£458.01	No	
Sally Keeble	Northampton North	Lab	£451.45	No	
Ashok Kumar	Middlesbrough South and East Cleveland	Lab	£450.00	No	
Gisela Stuart	Birmingham Edgbaston	Lab	£447.86	No	
Michael Meacher	Oldham West and Royton	Lab	£447.62	No	
Michael John Foster	Worcester	Lab	£438.71	Yes	£0
William Etherington	Sunderland North	Lab	£434.71	No	
Mark Hoban	Fareham	Con	£408.94	No	
James Sheridan	Paisley & Renfrewshire North	Lab	£400.00	No	
Eric Pickles	Brentwood & Ongar	Con	£388.00	No	
Jessica Morden	Newport East	Lab	£380.55	No	
Stewart Hosie	Dundee East	SNP	£379.45	No	
Christopher Chope	Christchurch	Con	£357.86	Yes	£357.86
Alan Keen	Feltham and Heston	Lab	£345.00	No	
Ann Keen	Brentford and Isleworth	Lab	£345.00	No	
Keith Simpson	Mid Norfolk	Con	£330.61	No	
Peter Kilfoyle	Liverpool Walton	Lab	£324.16	No	
Andrew Miller	Ellesmere Port and Neston	Lab	£316.00	Yes	£126.74
Martyn Jones	Clwyd South	Lab	£310.36	Yes	£310.36
David Crausby	Bolton North East	Lab	£307.10	No	
Stewart Jackson	Peterborough	Con	£304.10	No	
John Whittingdale	Maldon & Chelmsford East	Con	£301.58	No	
Terence Rooney	Bradford North	Lab	£297.02	No	
Danny Alexander	Inverness, Nairn, Badenoch and Strathspey	Lib	£290.82	No	
George Osborne	Tatton	Con	£284.26	No	
Bob Neill	Bromley and Chislehurst	Con	£283.50	No	
James McGovern	Dundee West	Lab	£266.54	No	
Patrick Hall	Bedford	Lab	£266.10	Yes	£266.10
Julian Brazier	Canterbury	Con	£248.49	No	
Mohammad Sarwar	Glasgow Central	Lab	£245.95	No	

Name	Constituency	Party	Repayment	Appeal?	Reduction on appeal
Jim Cunningham	Coventry South	Lab	£240.59	No	
David Cameron	Witney	Con	£237.07	No	
Tim Farron	Westmorland and Lonsdale	Lib	£235.00	No	
Phillip Davies	Shipley	Con	£232.64	Yes	£232.64
Robert Marshall-Andrews	Medway	Lab	£231.00	No	
Ann Widdecombe	Maidstone & The Weald	Con	£230.00	Yes	£0
Hazel Blears	Salford	Lab	£225.00	No	
Philip Wilson	Sedgefield	Lab	£224.92	No	
Charles Hendry	Wealden	Con	£223.26	No	
Christopher Fraser	South West Norfolk	Con	£193.55	No	
Claire Curtis-Thomas	Crosby	Lab	£191.12	No	
Mike Gapes	Ilford South	Lab	£186.89	Yes	£186.49
George Mudie	Leeds East	Lab	£182.51	No	
John Cummings	Easington	Lab	£180.00	No	
Ian Taylor	Esher & Walton	Con	£178.00	No	
Barry Gardiner	Brent North	Lab	£174.17	No	
Shailesh Vara	North West Cambridgeshire	Con	£174.00	No	
Kevin Brennan	Cardiff West	Lab	£171.40	No	
Julia Goldsworthy	Falmouth and Camborne	Lib	£171.32	No	
Clive Betts	Sheffield Attercliffe	Lab	£169.14	No	
Gregory Pope	Hyndburn	Lab	£166.79	No	
Paul Holmes	Chesterfield	Lib	£150.00	No	
Graham Stringer	Manchester Blackley	Lab	£146.67	No	
Chris Grayling	Epsom and Ewell	Con	£136.59	No	
Lyn Carol Brown	West Ham	Lab	£134.01	No	
Sarah McCarthy-Fry	Portsmouth North	Lab	£134.01	No	
Lynda Waltho	Stourbridge	Lab	£134.01	No	
Angus MacNeil	Na h-Eileanan An Iar	SNP	£133.00	No	
Graham Stuart	Beverley & Holderness	Con	£128.02	No	
Paul Farrelly	Newcastle-under-Lyme	Lab	£123.93	No	
Stephen O'Brien	Eddisbury	Con	£115.00	No	
John Redwood	Wokingham	Con	£112.00	Yes	£0
Liam Byrne	Birmingham Hodge Hill	Lab	£111.84	No	
George Young	North West Hampshire	Con	£104.48	No	

Index